Günter Paulus Schiemenz
Every Tongue Should Confess
that Jesus Christ is Lord

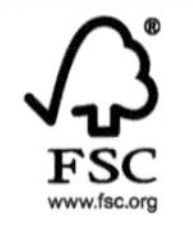

Günter Paulus Schiemenz

Every Tongue
Should Confess that
Jesus Christ is Lord

BoD Press
Norderstedt, 2018

Bibliografische Information der Deutschen Nationalbibliothek:
Die Deutsche Nationalbibliothek verzeichnet diese Publikation in
der Deutschen Nationalbibliografie; detaillierte bibliografische
Daten sind im Internet über http://dnb.d-nb.de abrufbar.

ISBN 97837502806007

Preface

The Christians accepted the Hebrew Bible as part of their Holy Scriptures, but they read it from their own viewpoint. The Hebrew Bible deals abundantly with JHWH, ὁ κύριος in the Septuagint, consistently *the Lord* in English Bibles, and the central dogma of Christianity is that Jesus Christ is *the Lord*, hence JHWH (the concept of the *Triune God* notwithstanding). As a matter of course, all mankind is exhorted to profess this dogma, and it was no question that only those who did qualified for admission to Paradise and Eternal Life at the end of days.

In the wall paintings of Orthodox churches, two compositions served to express this dogma. In the cupola of a naos, Jesus Christ the Pantokrator usually holds a book on which is written what he is speaking, and his portrait is surrounded by an inscription band citing psalm verses. To express the central dogma, it sufficed to choose as the words of Jesus Christ Dt *32, 39*, *See, see that I am, and there is no god except me*. The link with *all mankind*, πάντες λαοί in Ps *148*, 11, πᾶσα πνοή in Ps *150*, 6, was established by choosing verses of the *laud psalms* for the circular inscription band; illustration of the *laud psalms* thus became a suitable mean to express that *Jesus Christ is the Lord* and that *all mankind* is urged to profess this. In Psalm 148, the entire creation is exhorted to *praise the Lord*, with a special emphasis on *mankind*. Psalm 150 specifies that the praise is performed by music and dance, and ends with the summary *Let all breath praise the Lord!* In between, Psalm 149 assures the

Faithful that all oppression by infidels will come to an end.

At the end of days, *all mankind* is summoned to be judged. Many *nations, peoples and languages* did not yet comply, but they are given a chance of a favourable sentence provided that they, too, acknowledge that *Jesus Christ is the Lord*. Thus, the *Last Judgment* was another mean to convey the message.

This aspect is discussed in the chapter "The Peoples in the Slavonic *Last Judgment*. Matthew, Chapter 25, Daniel's Vision and Saint Peter's Speech at Pentecost". Already on earth and eventually in Eternal Life, all Faithful including the recent converts praise *the Lord* by joining the Hosts of Heaven in singing hymns in his honour. The nature of these hymns is explored in the chapter "The Role of the Inscription Bands in Wall Paintings of the *Laud Psalms*". The universal character of the exhortation is expressed in the final verse of the *laud psalms*. What *all breath, omnis spiritus* in the Vulgate, means, is the topic of the third chapter, "»Omnis spiritus laudet dominum«. Psalm *150*, 6 and the Realm of Spirits in the Illustration of the *Laud Psalms*". The common message of the *Last Judgment* and the *laud psalms* is best expressed by the hymn which the *kings of the earth and all peoples* of Psalm *148*, 11 are singing in the Bessarion monastery in Western Thessaly: *Every tongue should confess that Jesus Christ is Lord*. This quotation from St. Paul's letter to the Philippians, then, provides an appropriate title for all three chapters.

Kiel, July 2018   Günter Paulus Schiemenz

Contents

The Peoples in the Slavonic
Last Judgment
Matthew, Chapter 25, Daniel's Vision and
Saint Peter's Speech at Pentecost

Contents

Introduction
Nations, peoples, tribes, languages
All Saints in the *Hermeneia*
A *Last Judgment* icon in the Kremlin of Moscow
The *Last Judgment* in the Monastery Voroneţ
Who will be admitted to Paradise?
The peoples / nations and Moses
The texts on the book of the judge and the book on the
throne of the *Hetoimasia*
Russian *Last Judgment* icons with the snake of sin
Result
Illustrations

Introduction

In 1970, MILTOS GARIDIS published a paper entitled
*La représentation des «nations» dans la peinture
post-byzantine.*[1] Ten years later, ANDRÉ GRABAR
resumed the topic, but restricted his study to the *Last
Judgment: La représentation des «peuples» dans les
images du Jugement Dernier en Europe Orientale.*[2]
Both authors made baffling observations. In many

paintings of the *Last Judgment*, there are groups of people standing at either side of the *hetoimasia* below the Judge and his assessors, the apostles. GARIDIS as well as GRABAR took it for granted that those standing *on the right hand* of the Judge (on the left side, as seen by the beholder)[3] represent the *Blessed* and those *on the left hand* of the Judge, the *Damned*, according to Mt *25*, 34 and 41, respectively. On some Russian icons of the *Last Judgment*, however, there are *on the left hand* of the Judge not only Jews, but, together with alien peoples, also the Russians,[4] and on one icon, they are even called *the Orthodox Russians*.[5] Both authors admitted to be unable to propose a satisfactory explanation. Such conclusion always indicates that the key for proper understanding has not yet been found.

Nations, Peoples, Tribes, Languages

At the end of days, all humans are summoned to be judged – *all*, irrespective of their kinship, what language they speak, what creed they confess and to what people or nation they belong. In Slavic *Last Judgment* paintings, they have been arranged in groups called **ЛИКИ**. GARIDIS called these **ЛИКИ** *nations*. GRABAR preferred to call them *peuples*.[6] GARIDIS' and GRABAR's surprise to find the **ЛИК** of the *Orthodox Russians on the left hand* of the Judge indicates that religious affiliation was believed to be decisive for the defintion of what a *nation / peuple* is. This, however, is a hypothesis which deserves reconsideration.

In the popular French translation of the Bible by LEMAISTRE DE SACY,[7] *peuples* is the common term for λαοί, but not infrequently, it is also used for ἔθνη, whose standard translation, on the other hand, is *nations*. The *New English Translation of the Septuagint* (*NETS*) discriminates between ἔθνη = *nations* and λαοί = *peoples*.[8] Hence, an assessment of what the words ἔθνος and λαός in the pertinent passages of the Bible mean, is desirable.

The *Last Judgment* composition is not a snapshot of one particular situation, but a panorama in which consecutive events are depicted with many details. In the *Hermeneia*,[9] they are subdivided into two separate compositions, the *Second Coming*[10] and the *Last Judgment*.[11] The *Hermeneia* is considered to be a collection of prescriptions of rather different age,[12] but the two-part composition in the monastery Dečani (1347/48)[13] permits to ascribe the arrangement in two scenes to an early age. In most icons and wall paintings, however, the sequence of events is depicted in only one composition, for which the title of the first part, ἡ δευτέρα παρουσία, is common,[14] even when the aspect of the Judgment prevails. Both scenes, as described in the *Hermeneia*, agree in many details with the Judgment compositions discussed by GARIDIS and GRABAR so that they can serve as guidelines for understanding these wall paintings and icons.

Iconographically, the *Last Judgment* composition[15] is much indebted to the Revelation of St. John (*e. g.*, the angels rolling up the sky, with the black sun and the moon red as blood, Apc 6, 12, 14, the book of life,

Apc *20*, 12, the sea which returns the dead, Apc *20*, 13). The Revelation, in its turn, depends strongly on the visions of OT prophets, especially Daniel.[16] The arrangement of the humans in groups has prototypes in the Revelation and already in the Book of Daniel, and it is here that ἔθνη and λαοί play a role.

In Apc *5*, 9, the φῦλαί, γλῶσσαι, λαοί and ἔθνη are an expression for the *whole of mankind*, classified according to the major criteria of distinction. φυλή and γλῶσσα indicate a stress on kinship and a common language, respectively, but there may be a high degree of overlap, while in *nations / peoples*, these factors may be less important. In the context of the *Last Judgment*, religion may be a decisive factor, but the role it plays in these four categories is not obvious.

Only the order has been changed in Apc *7*, 9, *11*, 9, *13*, 7 and *14*, 6. In Apc *10*, 11, the φῦλαί have been replaced by their leaders for whom the title βασιλεῖς has been chosen;[17] in Apc *17*, 15, the word ὄχλοι[18] has been used instead of φῦλαί. In Theodotion's version[19] of Dan *7*, 13-14, the *Ancient of Days* delegates *the dominion and the honor and the kingship* to the *Son of Man*, and *all peoples, tribes and languages shall be subject [to] him*.[20] In the LXX version, πάντες οἱ λαοί, φῦλαί καὶ γλῶσσαι have been condensed to πάντα τὰ ἔθνη τῆς γῆς.

Daniel's vision of the transcendental realm has its prototypes in the contemporary terrestrial world. The great king Nabouchodonosor, ruler of a vast empire inhabited by a multitude of tribes / peoples / nations speaking different languages and confessing different creeds, issued a decree that his λαοί, φῦλαί, γλῶσσαι,[21] hence all of his subjects should worship a golden effigy,[22] and all the *peoples, tribes, languages* complied.[23] After the miracle of the fiery furnace, the decree is reversed in favour of the god of Israel;[24] wishing peace, Nabouchodonosor writes a letter to *all peoples, tribes and languages who live throughout the earth.*[25] Later, Daniel reminds King Belsazar that his father Nabouchodonosor had been the overlord of πάντες οἱ λαοί, φῦλαί, γλῶσσαι.[26] After Daniel's miraculous rescue from the lions' den, the great king Dareios wrote a similar letter to all inhabitants of his empire: πᾶσι τοῖς λαοῖς, φυλαῖς, γλώσσαις τοῖς οἰκοῦσιν ἐν πάσῃ τῇ γῇ Εἰρήνη ὑμῖν...;[27] in the LXX version (again with ἔθνη instead of λαοί), the *nations and countries and languages who inhabited his whole earth*[28] are expressly defined as πάντες οἱ ἀνθρώποι οἱ ὄντες ἐν τῇ βασιλείᾳ μου:[29] *everybody* – regardless which criterion of discrimination might be applied. Consequently, in all these cases, the different connotations of ἔθνος, λαός, φυλή, γλῶσσα *etc*. do not matter, and the word ἔθνος in Daniel (LXX) wherever Theodotion writes λαός, indicates a high degree of synonymy.

Similarly. the **ЛИКИ** of the *Last Judgment* can be assumed to represent the whole of mankind, but here, the criteria of discrimination do matter. The conventional opinion is that in this part of the composition the situation *after* the sentence has been pronounced, is depicted: Those to whom admission to Paradise has been granted, stand *on the right hand* of the judge, while those standing *on the left hand* have been sentenced to eternal damnation. An obvious alternative is that the scene depicts the situation *during* the process of judgment. All those who because of their godly life deserve eternal life in Paradise have already passed the judgment and stand – arranged in groups, called χοροί in Greek, **ЛИКИ** in Slavonic– *on the right hand* of the judge: the forefathers, the OT patriarchs, the prophets, the just kings, the apostles, the fathers of the Church, the *hosioi* (Slavonic Преподобніи, *venerable, i. e.* devout monks),[30] male and female martyrs and ascetics – all those who in the *Hermeneia* are subsumed under the category of *All Saints*, οἱ ἅγιοι πάντες.[31] All those whose fate is still pending stand *on the left hand* awaiting to be summoned to appear before the judge. They, too, are arranged in groups – several kinds of unbelievers (non-Christians as well as heretical Christians), but the true faith is not sufficient for admission to Paradise: The *Last Judgment* composition revels in the depiction of the punishment of those who infringed the rules of social life.[32] In this interpretation, the *Orthodox Russians* would occupy the adequate position.

As the correlation between the *Last Judgment* **ЛИКИ** and the *nations / peoples* is not straightforward, a closer inspection of these words may be useful. For the NT, all facets of the words ἔθνος, λαός, φυλή, ὄχλος and γλῶσσα have been scrutinized much more thoroughly than required for proper comprehension of the Orthodox *Last Judgment* composition while the OT was only cursorily dealt with.[33] Inasmuch as it was, the Masoretic Text (MT) was used. This is of little value for a composition which is based on the

Greek Bible or its Slavonic translation. Modern translations of the LXX suffer from the drawback that the Christian view on the OT is ignored; they cannot, therefore, contribute to the question what these words meant much later for those who conceived the *Last Judgment* compositions.

In the OT, ἔθνος and λαός correspond largely to Hebrew *goj*[34] and *ʿam*,[35] respectively. However, there is much mutual contamination: Hatch and Redpath list 13 cases of *goj* > λαός, while ἔθνος correlates in even 121 cases (*ca.* 11% of all LXX ἔθνη) with Masoretic *ʿam*.[36] This is indicative of a high semantic overlap which is even more pronounced when ἔθνος and λαός are the translations of *leʾom*:[37] Its LXX equuivalent is λαός almost as often as ἔθνος (12 *vs.* 15 cases). In 5 cases, *leʾom* has been translated by ἄρχων,[38] once by βασιλεύς,[39] hence the people replaced by their leader, indicating a tribal organization which is corroborated by an albeit singular case of *leʾom* > φυλή.[40]

Among the OT quotations the *Last Judgment* is indebted to, are some psalms and verses in the Book of Isaias. It is therefore of interest that in both OT books an abundance of *parallelismi membrorum* make use of the λαοί and ἔθνη[41] and thus testify to their close semantic similarity. A striking case is Ps *67 (68)*, 30, ... *the gathering of the bulls is among the heifers of the peoples (τῶν λαῶν)... Scatter nations (ἔθνη) that want wars,*[42] both *ʿam* in the MT but differentiated in the LXX.

In view of the universal call to judgment the phrasing πάντα τὰ ἔθνη / πάντες λαοί deserves consideration. In the psalms, πάντα τὰ ἔθνη is more frequent than πάντες λαοί. But this is an artifact of the LXX: While ἔθνος < *goj* predominates, ἔθνος in πάντα τὰ ἔθνη in Ps *46 (47)*, 1 and Ps *48 (49)*, 1 represents 'am whose standard translation is λαός. On the other hand, in Ps *148*, 11, βασιλεῖς τῆς γῆς καὶ πάντες λαοί, λαός is the translation of *le'om* which appears as ἔθνος in Ps *56 (57)*, 9[10], *64 (65)*, 8 and *107 (108)*, 4. In the *parallelismus membrorum* of Ps *116 (117)*, 1, αἰνεῖτε τὸν κύριον, πάντα τὰ ἔθνη, αἰνεσάτωσαν αὐτὸν, πάντες οἱ λαοί, ἔθνος represents its standard counterpart, *goj*, but λαός stands for *'uma.* This florilegium as well as the *parallelismi membrorum* of Ps *104 (105)*, 44, goj / ἔθνος *vs. le'om* / λαός, and of Ps *107 (108)*, 4, 'am / λαός *vs. le'om* / ἔθνος, demonstrate strikingly the high degree of synonymy of all these words. In Ps *148*, 11, the association of the λαοί with their leaders suggests again that at least *le'om* implies some tribal organization.

It emerges that originally, there has been no significant semantic difference between ἔθνος and λαός.. However, in Christian times, this seems to have changed. When the Greek Bible was translated into Slavonicc, for λαός the rather general and inconspicuous word ЛЮДЪ was chosen. On the other hand, ἔθνος has consistently been translated as ІАЗЫКЪ, the Slavonic word for Greek γλῶσσα, *language*. The choice of this word in the oldest Serbian psalters (at Sinai[43] and in Munich[44]) testifies that this usage is old and general in Church Slavonic.[45] Only when γλῶσσα and ἔθνος occurred side by side, a distinction became necessary. When the descendants of the sons of Noah were enumerated ἐν ταῖς φυλαῖς αὐτῶν, κατὰ γλὼσσας αὐτῶν, ἐν ταῖς χώραις αὐτῶν καὶ ἐν τοῖς ἔθνεσιν αὐτῶν,[46] γλῶσσα was rendered as **ꙗзыкъ**,[47] but for ἔθνος, **народъ** was chosen, the word which in Apc *17*, 15 was used for Greek ὄχλος. In Gen *10*, 5, the phrase ἕκαστος κατὰ γλῶσσαν (*language*) ἐν ταῖς φῦλαῖς αὐτῶν καὶ ἐν τοῖς ἔθνεσιν (*nations*) αὐτῶν is preceded by τῶν ἔθνῶν ἐν τῇ γῇ αὐτῶν. The second ἔθνη have been rendered as **народѣхъ**, the first as **ꙗзыксꙗвъ** which next to **по ꙗзыкоγ** = κατὰ γλῶσσαν makes sense only when ἔθνος means *people speaking the same language*. In the Revelation, one **ꙗзыкъ** has been retained and the other one replaced by a word meaning *tribe*,[48] either **племенъ**[49] or **колѣно**.[50]

These cases indicate a high degree of semantic overlap between all these words with an emphasis on *language* at least for ἔθνος. For the question to what extent these words had a religious connotation, neither the Greek Bible nor its Slavonic translation provide an answer. For Luther and the authors of the King James Bible (whose OT is a translation of the MT) and consequently in all vernacular Bibles based on them, *gojim* of the OT and ἔθνη in the NT meant *gentiles*: all peoples except God's *Chosen People*. In the context of the *Last Judgment* paintings, the ἔθνη then would be all peoples except those confessing the true faith, *i. e.* the Orthodox Christians, hence all those who face damnation. However, because of the quasi-synonymy of λαός (in singular the standard word for God's *Chosen People*) and ἔθνος in the LXX, such generalization is not applicable in the Orthodox realm.

For the Greeks living under Ottoman rule, some insight may be expected from the *Karamanlica* Bible, *i. e.* the Bible translated into Turkish and printed in Greek script for use of the turkophone Greek Christians. A *Karamanlica* Bible printed in Stambul in 1869,[51] though targeting Orthodox Christians, is not a translation of the Greek Bible. The canon of the OT books, the numbering of the psalms and the order of the prophets are according to the MT. There is conclusive evidence that this Bible is a translation of the King James Bible. In the Greek Bible, the tetragrammaton JHWH has been rendered as κύριος, similar in most other translations (Vulgate *dominus*, King James Bible *the Lord*, French *Le Seigneur*, German *der Herr,* Karamanlica Ραππ *(Rabb)*) though in the King James Bible with notable exceptions: *Jehovah* for the name of *the Lord* (Ex 6, 3, Ps *82 (83)*, 18, Is *12*, 2 and Is *26*, 4) and as part of place names *(Jehovah-jireh*, Gen. *22*, 14; *Jehovah-nissi*, Ex *17*, 15; *Jehovah-shalom*, Judges *6*, 24) which have been *translated* in other Bibles (LXX: Gen *22*, 14 κύριος ὤφθη, Ex *17*, 15 κύριος καταφυγή μου, Judges *6*, 24 εἰρήνη κυρίου). In respect of this idiosyncrasy, the *Karamanlica* Bible correlates perfectly with the King James Bible, with literal transcription of the place names: Ἰεοβὰ ἰρὲ, Ἰεοβὰνισσὶ, Ἰεοβὰ σαλὼμ.

The Turkish words for *ʿam* (LXX: λαός, less frequently ἔθνος) and for *goj* (LXX: ἔθνος, less frequently λαός) are (in modern orthography) *kavm* and *taïfe*, respectively. *kavm* is a general word for *people, taïfe* the word for *a group or class of humans, an ethnic entity.*[52] LXX φυλή corresponds with *kabile, tribe,*[53] ὄχλος with *kalabalık, crowd.*[54] There is a strict

1:1 correlation between γλῶσσα and *dil, language,*[55] which is never used for *goj* / ἔθνος. Another Turkish word meaning *people* is *halk;*[56] This has only seldom been used, mainly for *ʿam* (LXX ἔθνος: Esther *1*, 5, Prov *14*, 28, Ez *26*, 7; LXX λαός: Prov *24*, 24 (*30*, 39)). None of these words has any religious connotation.

In Prov *11*, 26, *halk* stands for *le'om*. Elsewhere, Hebrew *le'om*, in the LXX ἔθνος as well as λαός, less frequently ἄρχων and βασιλεύς, is consistently rendered as *ümmet*. In principle, *ümmet* does qualify for a religious meaning. In Ottoman Turkey, *peoples* were not defined according to language, but according to their religion, either as *ümmetler* or as *milletler*. *ümmet* was comprehensive, while *millet* was the word for all peoples not confessing the true faith, hence all non-Muslims.[57] *ümmet* is an Arabic loanword; in the Ḳur'ān, *umma* usually refers to communities sharing a common religion (as *ümmet* in Turkish), whereas later it almost always means the Muslim community as a whole.[58] *Mutatis mutandis*, for the Orthodox Christians it might mean *their* community as a whole, and in the turkophone Christian Bible, *ümmet* might have such meaning.

ümmet, then, (and hence *le'om*) is the only word which – at least in Ottoman time – may in some way refer to religion. But it is unlikely that it did. *le'om* and all its LXX equivalents and hence *ümmet* are largely confined to poetry. 67% of all λαοί (< *le'om*) and 40% of all ἔθνη (< *le'om*) occur in the psalms, another 33% of the ἔθνη (< *le'om*) in Isaiah. 60% of all *le'om* ~ *ümmet* (ἔθνος and λαός) are part of a *parallelismus membrorum* in which the counterpart has no religious connotation.[59] *ümmet*, then, may owe its choice to the fact that the translator wished to maintain the variety of Hebrew words meaning *people*.

In addition to *ümmet < le'om*, *ümmetler* are found in Gen *25*, 16, Ps *116* (*117*), 1 and in the Book of Daniel (Dan *3*, 4, 7, 29 (Greek Bible: 96); *4*, 1 (Greek Bible: *3*, 98); *5*, 19; *6*, 25; *7*, 14); their Greek / NETS / King James equivalents are ἔθνη / nations / nations (Gen *25*, 16), λαοί / peoples / people (Ps *116* (*117*), 1), and φῦλαί / peoples / nations (Dan). In all these cases, the MT word is *'uma*. Via Arabic *umma*, both words correspond with each other. Obviously, the translator consulted the Hebrew original and chose *ümmet* because of the etymology.

In none of these cases, *'uma* has any religious connotation.[60] In Gen *25*, 16, it is used for the nomadic tribes of the *Sons of Ismael*. In Ps *116* (*117*), 1, it is part of a *parallelismus membrorum* with *goj* (LXX / NETS / King James / *Karamanlica*: ἔθνη / *nations* / *nations* / *taïfeler*). The phrase *peoples, tribes and languages* of Daniel means *everybody*, and religion does not matter (*vide supra*). Its Turkish equivalent *ümmet* will be synonymous. That *'uma* has retained its meaning *tribe* in the *Karamanlica* Bible is shown by Num *25*, 15 where the word is used for a tribe of the Madianites: As an exception, the Hebrew word, ἔθνος / *nation* / *people* in LXX, NETS and King James, respectively, has been translated as *kabile*, a *nomadic tribe*.

In conclusion, the Bible provides no evidence that in the *Last Judgment* organization of *all mankind* in groups religion played a significant role.

All Saints in the Hermeneia

In the *Hermeneia*, *All Saints* occur already in the *Second Coming*. Like the nine τάγματα of the *Hosts of Heaven*,[61] they are organized in nine χοροί which clearly do not represent the *Blessed* of Mt *25*, 34: They appear on clouds; their job is to properly acclaim the Lord on his *adventus*.[62] They participate again in the *Last Judgment*: *the twelve apostles seated on twelve thrones, and with them all the saints standing on his right in three ranks*.[63] The first *chorus* shows that they do not line up to be judged: The apostles function as the assessors of the Judge.[64] In analogy with the organization of the nine τάγματα of the *Hosts of Heaven* in three τάξεῖς, *All Saints* stand in three lines; a subdivision of the *chorus* of the female saints into martyrs and ascetics restores the original number of nine *choruses*. The apostles sit at both sides of the Judge, *on his right hand* as well as *on his left hand*; likewise the intercessors stand at either side of the throne: The Mother of God is highest in rank and therefore occupies the place of honour *on the right hand* while the place *on the left hand* is assigned to the less dignified Saint John Prodromos. How scrupulously the ceremonies of the Imperial court were followed, is shown by a late Bulgarian icon of the *deesis* type in which Saint John stands *on the right hand*: His counterpart is Saint Parakevi[65] who is of lower rank. In Dečani, the *choruses* of *All Saints* approach the Judge enthroned between the Mother of God and Saint John from both sides.[66] Mt *20*, 21 shows that the place *on the left hand* is not indicative of damnation.

Like the *Hosts of Heaven*, *All Saints* in clouds are part of the entourage of the Universal Ruler. In some Greek *Last Judgments*, entitled ἡ δευτέρα παρουσία, they are distinct from the δίκαιοι whom the Lord is welcoming with the words of Mt *25*, 34. *E. g.*, in Roussanou (Meteora) the dialogue of Mt *25*, 34-45 has been extensively illustrated.[67] Adjacent to the χοροί of *All Saints* in clouds, the δίκαιοι are depicted as one group in distinctly different iconography; on the other hand, they face a mirror image group representing the *Cursed*. Both groups are shown engaged in the conversation with the Lord which, as a matter of course, is *preceding* the sentence whose execution has here and elsewhere[68] been illustrated according to Mt *13*, 41-42, 49-50, angels pushing the *Damned* into the fire. In the Russian icons discussed by GARIDIS and GRABAR, the same choruses of *All Saints* are depicted; here, too, they cannot represent the **ПРАВЕДНИЦЫ** of Mt *25*, 34: If they did, the common believers would not have been depicted at all, and the place of the Orthodox Russians would be *on the left hand* of the Judge among the heretics and heterodox, deprived of all hope for admission to Paradise: an entirely pessimistic prospect.

A Last Judgment Icon in the Kremlin of Moscow

A *Last Judgment* Icon in the Uspenskij cathedral in the Kremlin of Moscow (fig. on p. 52)[69] is believed to be the oldest icon of this topic.[70] Not yet as complicated as some later icons, it is exclusively devoted to the *Last Judgment* and its consequences. While in the aforementioned Greek *Last Judgment* compositions the emphasis is on the Second Coming and the *Judgement* plays only a subordinate role, the icon ignores everything which, according to the *Hermeneia*, belongs to the *Second Coming*, as the angel rolling up the sky, the *choruses* of *All Saints* in clouds, the raising of the dead from the earth and the sea and the angel blowing his trumpet. In the lower part of the icon, Paradise and Hell are depicted. The upper part consists of two horizontal zones below the slightly curved band of the sky across the whole width of the icon, studded with stars and held at either end by an angel. The centre of the upper zone is occupied by the *deesis*. Christ is sitting on a rainbow within a dark glory. He has raised his right arm; the palm is turned outwards. The left arm is turned down, and the back of the hand is shown – these are the gestures of acceptance and rejection as depicted, *e. g.*, in the Kahriye Cami (*vide infra*),[71] in Barlaam (Meteora),[72] in the Phaneromeni monastery (Salamis, 1735);[73] in Russia in the wall paintings of the Uspenskij cathedral in Vladimir (1408)[74] – to be sure, very appropriate in the *Last Judgment*, but not necessarily referring specificly to Mt *25*, 34, 41. The Mother of God and Saint John Prodromos are followed by numerous standing angels; all of them have raised their arms and look towards the Judge. Below the enthroned Judge, there is the *hetoimasia*, flanked on either side by six apostles as the assessors of the court. All angels and apostles are nimbed. In the centre of the lower zone, Adam and Eve are kneeling. Behind them, numerous people are approaching. Those on the left side are organized in six groups. To the right, the first group is separated from a crowd of people behind them. All of them wear rich, long garments and stand in calm attitude.

As elsewhere, the stream of fire[75] originates at Christ's feet. At first, it is narrow. It winds down behind the *hetoimasia*, then turns right and twines itself round the people *on the left hand of the Lord* who are thus characterized as *the Damned*. It finally broadens to form the lake of fire in the lower part of the icon. The garments of the *Damned* are not much diversified. Some of the men standing in the first picture plane wear red-and-white headgears. In view of the red fezes surrounded by white turbans worn by Turks in the *Last Judgment* of Voroneţ,[76] they may be regarded as indicating Muslim people, but similar headgears occur also among the *Just*. In the rear, some pointed, white hats resemble the headgears worn elsewhere by Oriental people and may, therefore, symbolize alien people. However, they are not significantly distinct from other *Damned*; the small differences in details within an altogether rather homogeneous crowd may simply express that *all Damned* are meant: Jews as well as alien peoples – all those who are *rejected*, hence including the sinners within the new *Chosen People*. It does not matter what ꙗзыкь an unbeliever or sinner belongs to: **ВСИ ІАЗЫЦЫ** are subject to the *Last Judgment*.

Opposite the *Damned*, six groups stand *on the right hand of the Lord*. The first group behind Adam consists of bishops in white garments; two of them wear white headgears resembling the Russian *klobuk*. They are followed by monks. In the rear, three men of the first group wear red-and-white caps resembling Moses' headgear in Voroneţ (*vide infra*).[77] The last group in the rear consists of women. All these groups can be viewed as six of the nine *choruses* of *All Saints*, the men with red-and-white caps as the prophets, the monks as the Преподобніи.

However, such assignment remains tentative. Unlike the apostles, these people are not nimbed. Red-and-white caps are not a prerogative of prophets. They are also worn by Saints Floros and Lauros;[78] as part of the *Persian costume*, they are met with the three Magi riding to Bethlehem and presenting their gifts,[79] with Daniel and with the three Hebrews in the fiery furnace.[80] Furthermore, they occur also among the *Damned* (*vide supra*). Indeed, GRABAR traced these groups back to a secular source, *viz*. the receptions given in the imperial palace in Constantinople where the dignitaries appeared in groups of equal title or rank.[81] The Russian society was similarly organized as bishops, monks, princes *etc*. It is, therefore, possible to regard the six groups as that part of the Orthodox Christians who can hope for a favourable sentence. However, the *klobuk*-like headgears of two bishops do not permit a decision in favour of GRABAR's proposal, because the Russian Church has canonized some of her metropolitans.[82]

Thus, two interpretations are at hand. If the groups *on the right hand of the Lord* are the *choruses* of *All Saints*, the faithful viewer would see the dichotomy of the prototypes of a pious life and the damned sinners, Alternatively, though, this zone may show the situation after the sentence: The groups *on the right hand* could represent the *Blessed,* those *on the left hand* the *Cursed*. In this case, members of the new *Chosen People* may appear on either side, depending on the length of their list of transgressions. However, in the Meteora monasteries and in Mardaki (Messenia, 1635), the presence of the δίκαιοι *on the right hand* is corroborated by pertinent inscriptions; in the icon it is not. Likewise, the fate of the *Damned*, elsewhere shown as an illustration of Mt *13*, 41-42, 49-50,;[83] is absent in the Kremlin icon. Such reserve in showing the consequences of a sinful life is paralleled in the bottom zone of the icon: Black devils hold two black circular disks which presumably represent *outer darkness*. Elsewhere, the detailed depiction of the chambers of torture is much more terrifying.[84]

The Last Judgment in the Monastery Voroneţ

In the *Last Judgment* compositions of the Moldovian monasteries, the alien peoples occupy a conspicuous position *on the left hand of the Lord*. The large *Last Judgment* at the western facade of the church of Saint George of the monastery Voroneţ (1547) consists of five horizontal zones.[85] In the top zone, angels roll up the sky.[86] In the centre, angels hold the doors of heaven which frame a medallion of *the Lord* wearing a double square nimbus (*nimbus of eternity*[87]). A similar medallion above the scene of judgment is met already a century earlier on the famous Novgorodian *Last Judgment* icon in the Tretyakov Gallery (fig. on p. 53).[88] In Voroneţ, *the Lord* is called ВЕ[Т]ХИ [ДЕ]НЬМИ, *the Ancient of Days* (fig. on p. 54).

Mt *24*, 27-31 describes the (second) παρουσία τοῦ υἱοῦ τοῦ ἀνθρώπου: πᾶσαι αἱ φυλαὶ τῆς γῆς *shall see the Son of man coming in the clouds of heaven with power and great glory* (μετὰ δυνάμεως καὶ δόξης πολλῆς). Mt *25*, 31-32: *When the Son of man shall come in his glory, and all the holy angels with him, then shall he sit upon the throne of his glory. And before him shall be gathered all nations* (πάντα τὰ ἔθνη).[89] Saint Matthew's account has its prototype *in* the vision of the prophet Daniel: *and lo, as it were a son of man coming with the clouds of heaven.*[90] Here it is the παλαιὸς (τῶν) ἡμερῶν, the *Ancient of Days*, who delegates to the υἱὸς ἀνθρώπου all power so that *all peoples, tribes, languages* (Dan (Θ) *7*, 14: πάντες οἱ λαοί, φῦλαί καὶ γλώσσαί; Dan (LXX) *7*, 13: πάντα τὰ ἔθνη τῆς γῆς) *shall be subject to him* (*vide supra*). The medallion of the ВЕТХИ ДЕНЬМИ, then, is evidence that Daniel's vision is incorporated in the *Last Judgment*.

The παλαιὸς (τῶν) ἡμερῶν is not restricted to the vision of Daniel; the way how he is portrayed depends on the context. In the so-called *NT trinity icons*, the first and the second person of the Trinity are distinguished by their nimbi: *God Father* has the double square nimbus,[91] *the Son* the circular nimbus with a cross, into which the words ὁ ὤν [92] are frequently inscribed. Both nimbi correlate with the epithets: The *Father* is designated either *Lord Sabaoth*[93] or (*e. g.* in two NT trinity icons in the museum of the Orthodox Patriarchate in Belgrade) the *Ancient of Days*,[94] the *Son* IC XC. In Voroneț, then, **ВЄТХИ ДЄНЬМИ** has to be regarded as a synonym of **ГОСПОДЬ САВАѠѲЪ**,[95] the first person of the Trinity.

However, the inscription **ВЄ[Т]ХИ [ДЄ]НЬМИ** is accompanied by the letters IC XC. The apparent discrepancy expresses the twofold meaning of the *Amcient of Days*: *He conveys the eternal oneness of Christ with the Father, ...the incarnate and mortal son is, at the same time, the eternal and pre-existent Father... The Ancient of Days... functioned as a visualization of Christ's coeternity with the preexistent Father.*[96] Depending on the context, the traits of the first or of the second person of the Trinity prevail. In a medallion in the zenith of the vault above the altar of the church of Nereditsa (1199), the *Ancient of Days* is flawlessly depicted as Christ: He is accompanied by the letters IC XC and wears a nimbus with an inscribed cross studded with jewels.[97] Similar pictures are met in the chapel of Saint Blasios near Brindidi (1197) and in the miniature of Saint Matthew in the gospel of the Bulgarian tsar Ivan Aleksandar (ruled 1331-1371) where Christ *alias* the *Ancient of Days* wears a nimbus with inscribed cross though without the letters ὁ ὤν.[98] In the trilogy Παλαιὸς τῶν ἡμερῶν, Παντοκράτωρ, Ἐμμανουήλ (or Μεγάλης βουλῦς ἄγγελος) he is one of the three hypostases of Christ and is, correspondingly, characterized by the nimbus with inscribed cross and the legend IC XC.[99] In the composition of the Heavenly ladder of Jakob (Gen *28*, 12-15) in the church Sv. Sofija at Ohrid, *the Lord* at the upper end of the ladder is designated O ΠΑΛΕΟ$_C$ Η... The head of the half-figure is surrounded by a nimbus with inscribed cross (without ὁ ὤν).[100] In the iconographically very similar scene of the ladder of Joannes o Klimakos, it is Christ as the *Pantokrator* who at the top of the ladder receives the virtuous monks.[101] Therefore, the absence of the epithet IC XC notwithstanding, *the Lord* in the Ohrid painting is best interpreted as Christ, the *Preexistent Logos*.[102] Whenever, on the other hand, the *Ancient of Days* represents *God Father* (as in the NT trinity icons in Belgrade), he is depicted in the iconography of the *Lord Sabaoth*, *viz*. with the double square nimbus and without the letters IC XC.

However, iconographic and epigraphic contaminations are not infrequent. On the icon of the Annunciation of Ustjug in the Tretyakov Gallery,[103] a segment of heaven on top of the icon contains *the Lord*. The legend, as recorded by A. W. CARR, *Jesus Christ thrice Holy Ancient of Days*,[104] combines Christ with the Lord Sabaoth (Is. *6*, 3) as well as with the *Ancient of Days* (Dan *7*, 9, 13, 22). At the eastern wall of the narthex of the Patriarchate at Peć, there is a bust of the [в]єтхи д[є]нми[105] with a nimbus which combines both types: A transparent square nimbus is placed upon a golden circular nimbus into which no cross is inscribed. The square rests on its bottom corner which is concealed by the neck. The other corners bear the letters **O Ѡ N**. The bust is framed by the letters IC XC. An inscription on both sides of the shoulders quotes the seraphic hymn of Is. *6*, 3 in its liturgical version,[106] *Holy, holy, holy, Lord Sabaoth; heaven and earth are full of Thy glory*. In the liturgy, the hymn continues with the acclamation of Jesus at the Entry to Jerusalem, Mt *21*, 9. This way, the *Lord Sabaoth* and the Lord Jesus Christ are equated. Only a few metres apart, the three busts of the *Ancient of Days*, the *Pantokrator* and the *Angel of the Great Council* are lined up in the zenith of the western vault of the church of the apostles, the **ВЬСЕДРЪЖИТЕЛЬ** with the nimbus with inscribed cross and ὁ ὤν, the **ВѢТХИ Д[Е]НЬМИ** as in the narthex with the epithet IC XC,[107] hence the three hypostases of Christ. In Melé (Messenia, 1676), the three hypostases are similarly depicted; the association with the *Pantokrator* and the *Angel of the Great Council* as well as the nimbus with inscribed cross and the epithet IC XC identify the third medallion as a representation of Christ, and yet,

the inscription is CABAѠΘ rather than the *Ancient of Days*. The nimbi notwithstanding, each of these busts is inscribed in a large double square[108] expressing the *eternal oneness of Christ with the Father*; again, the epithets Παλαιὸς τῶν ἡμερῶν and Σαβαώθ turn out to be synonymous.

In the NT trinity icons mentioned above, a small iconographic difference is noteworthy: Represented as the *Ancient of Days*, *God Father* has light grey hair and beard indicative of his age; hair and beard of the *Lord Sabaoth* are light brown. At Melé, the meaning of the *Ancient of Days* is intimated by the bluish-light grey hair and beard of the *Lord Sabaoth*.

Another representation of the three hypostases of Christ exists in the vaults of three window recesses of the 'church of the princes' at Curtea de Argeş, the juvenile Christ again as Μεγάλης βουλῦς ἄγγελος, the *Ancient* without legend, but iconographically the *Lord Sabaoth*, i. *e.* with light brown hair and beard and with the double square nimbus. All three medallions are in front of a double square aura. In a Serbian 14th century miniature illustrating Ps. *76*, 2-3,[109] the Pantokrator has been omitted and the Ancient of Days (with grey rather than light-brown hair) united with the Emmanuel (both with the letters IC XC) in a single medallion[110] representing the combined visions of Isaias and Ezechiel.[111]

While at Melé and Curtea de Argeş elements of the first person of the Trinity have invaded representations of Christ, the illustration of the Revelation in the narthex of the catholicon of the monastery Xeropotamou (Mount Athos, 18th cent.) shows the inverse process. In four flat cupolas, scenes of the chapters 5, 11-14 encircle identical medallions of *the Lord*. He is designated twice as Ο ΠΑΛΕΟC ΤѠΝ ΗΜΕΡѠΝ, once Ο ΠΑΤΗΡ and once Ο CΑΒΑѠΘ. The three epithets were obviously viewed as synonyms; πατήρ leaves no doubt that the first person of the Trinity is meant. Nevertheless, the nimbi with inscribed cross and ὁ ὤν refer to Christ. In Voroneţ, then, the *Ancient of Days*, synonymous with the *Lord Sabaoth*, represents *God Father* in spite of the epithet

IC XC. His inclusion into the composition of the *Last Judgment* points to a joint illustration of Dan *7, 9-27* and Mt *24, 27-31*: *A court sat in judgment, and books were opened*[112] (Dan 7, 10); *until the Ancient of Days came and he gave the judgment* (Dan 7, 22). The *Ancient of Days* delegates the ἐξουσία καὶ τιμὴ βασιλική to the υἱὸς ἀνθρώπου (Dan 7, 14) who is enthroned below him.

The second zone illustrates the tribunal. Christ resides on a rainbow within a round glory; below his feet, there are the winged fiery wheels.[113] Both arms are slightly turned downwards; while the gesture of acceptance of his right hand is indistinct, the gesture of rejection of the left hand is similar to that in Kahriye Cami (*vide infra*), in Barlaam, on the icon in Moscow and in the Uspenskij cathedral in Vladimir. Behind Christ, his angelic bodyguard is positioned; from both sides, the Mother of God and Saint John Prodromos approach him in the gesture of supplication. On either side, the apostles are sitting;[114] a crowd of angels stand behind them.

The centre of the third zone is occupied by the throne of the *hetoimasia*, flanked by Adam and Eve. From the left, four *choruses*, each called **ЛИК**, of *All Saints* are approaching in calm attitude, from right to left the prophets,[115] the hierarchs, the martyrs and finally the Преподобніи – with the words of Daniel's vision *and the Saints of the Most High will receive the kingdom and possess it forever and ever* (Dan (Θ) 7, 18). In these *choruses*, nobody is nimbed. Behind the Преподобніи, Saint Paul holds a scroll (fig. on p.

55).[116] The text on it is a slightly abridged quotation of 1Thess *4, 16*,[117] *For the Lord himself shall descend from heaven with a shout, with the voice of the archangel, and with the trump of God; and the dead in Christ shall rise first* – first *the dead in Christ*: these are the groups of *All Saints*, οἱ Ἅγιοι Πάντες (*Hermeneia*), ἅγιοι Ὑψίστου (Dan *7, 18*) who stand next to Saint Paul.

From the right, Moses and the alien peoples approach.[118] Each of these groups is designated **ЛИК**. Interpreted as the illustration of Dan *7, 14*, they are πάντα τὰ ἔθνη τῆς γῆς (LXX), or, in Theodotion's version, πάντες οἱ λαοί, φῦλαί καὶ γλῶσσαι: first those the Orthodox Christians were familiar with: Hebrews, Turks, Tatars and Armenians, followed by those who came from afar: the black-a-moors.[119] In Daniel's vision, none of them is threatened with eternal damnation.

In the fourth zone, the left part (*on the right hand of the Lord*) is occupied by a large crowd of standing people, first men, then many women.[120] All of them are nimbed; in the rear, several rows of nimbi symbolize an indefinitely large crowd. First stand two men in bishops' garments; their heads conform with Saint Basileios and Saint John Chrsysostom.[121] Towards the centre, a smaller group stands apart; here the desert ascetics Makarios and Paulos of Thebes can be reckognized, as well as Saint Spyridon who wears his typical beehive cap.[122] In the centre of this zone, the scale of justice and the angels and the devils fighting for the souls are depicted.[123] Here, the records of sins are weighed against the records of good deeds.

This cannot possibly apply to the groups of *All Saints*; on the other hand, it expresses the chance that, by the help of the angels, a sinner may be granted admission to Paradise even when the scrolls of his good deeds weigh less than those of his misdeeds. As a matter of course, the benevolent intervention of the angels presupposes that the sinner confesses the true faith. It is here that the Orthodox Christian sinners (hence the *Orthodox Russians* of the aforementioned icon) find their consolation.

Further to the right the stream of fire which emanated from below Christ's feet and passed the third zone between Eve and Moses, runs down; at the right end, the terrestrial raising of the dead is accommodated.[124] Below it, in the bottom zone, it is supplemented by the maritime raising of the dead.[125] From right to left, this is followed by the much broader stream of fire, the admission of the Elect to Paradise[126] and Paradise.[127]

At the top of the third zone, Mt *25*, 34 and 41 are inscribed, to the left of the centre verse 34, to the right of the narrow stream of fire, verse 41 until ДІАВОЛȢ. Legends of the χοροί of *All Saints* and of the groups *on the left hand of the Lord* would be expected above their heads, but on either side, this space was not made use of. Verse 34 begins above the heads of the two prophets in front (presumably Aaron and Moses),[128] continues above the empty space between them and Adam and then from above Adam to the left perimeter of the *hetoimasia*. Mt *25*, 41 extends from the stream of fire to Moses' nimbus. Beyond Moses' head, the quotation terminates with the words [ȢГОТО]ВАННОЄ ДІАВОЛȢ[129] above the outstretched arm of one of the first Hebrews. The space above the heads of the alien peoples is left to their names.[130]

In the *Hermeneia*, the verses Mt *25*, 34 and 41 are not quoted in the *Last Judgment*; in the *Second Coming*, they are part of the picture of the Lord arriving on clouds.[131] The statements accompany a gesture of benediction. The phrasing εὐλογῶν ταῖς ἀρχάντοις χερσὶν αὐτοῦ implies that it is performed with *both* hands, and yet, the verses are written on an Εὐαγγέλιον ἀνοικτὸν ἐπὶ τοῦ στήθους αὐτοῦ. The prescription thus deviates from the standard iconography of the enthroned Christ who has raised his right arm in the gesture of speaking and holds the book in his left hand.[132] In the joint composition in the Kahriye Cami, the scene has been depicted more dramatically: In the upper part, the *Second Coming* is shown. The choruses of *All Saints* arrive in clouds from afar.[133] Christ, below the title ἡ δευτέρα παρουσία, expresses his address by the gestures of both hands, right and left *acceptance* and *rejection*, respectively, so that his left hand was not free to hold a book and his statement had to be written elsewhere: The fingers of both hands point to the inscriptions of Mt *25*, 34, 41.[134] Beside the inscription of Mt *25*, 41, the fate of the *Damned* is anticipated, but they are depicted as an unstructured crowd already half-immersed in the fiery stream and not organized in nations or peoples. The same arrangement occurs in the Panagia ton Chalkeon (Thessaloniki),[135] and, again below the title ἡ δευτέρα παρουσία, in Barlaam.[136] Here, the words of Mt *25*, 41 have been written between the fiery wheels (the *thronoi*) and the feet of Saint John Prodromos, hence much closer to Christ's feet than to the *Damned,* corresponding with Mt *25,* 34 written between the fiery wheels and the feet of the Mother of God rather than next to the first *chorus* of *All Saints*, the hierarchs, approaching from the left within a cloud. In the *Last Judgment* of Voroneţ, this iconography has been used for the judge pronouncing the sentence; but again, the inscriptions of Mt *25*, 34 and 41 belong to the image of Jesus Christ rather than to the groups to be judged.

In Voroneţ, the *Blessed* of Mt *25,* 34 would be expected below the *choruses* of *All Saints*. Indeed, in the fourth zone is a large, unstructured crowd of nimbed persons.[137] They are quite different from the four *choruses* and cannot, therefore, represent the five *choruses* of *All Saints* who had not been depicted in the third zone. On the other hand, Saint Peter admitting the Elect to Paradise is illustrated separately in the bottom zone. Hence, no alternative to their interpretation as the *Blessed* of Mt *25,* 34 is at hand. The *Damned* and the souls carried into damnation by devils have been depicted in the same zone as the *Blessed,* hence at an apt position.[138] If the *choruses* of *All Saints* in the third zone do not illustrate Mt *25,* 34, then there is no incentive to affiliate the inscription of Mt *25,* 41 with the groups *on the left hand of the Lord.*

Who will be admitted to Paradise?

The search for the meaning of *nations* / *peoples*, including the *Orthodox Russians*, may profit from an investigation who has the chance to be granted salvation. Paradise is not a citadel for which only the *choruses* of *All Saints* acquired a right of residence by exceptional merits. In Voroneţ and elsewhere, Saint Peter unlocks the gate of Paradise for a large crowd, indicating that the demands of the Judge can be met. The damnation of Mt *8*, 12 is preceded by the promise *And I say unto you that many shall come from the east and the west, and shall sit down with Abraham, and Isaac, and Jacob in the kingdom of heaven.* The Son of man *shall send his angels with a great sound of a trumpet, and they shall gather together his elect from the four winds, from one end of heaven to the other* (Mt *24*, 31).

The movements of the stars (including sun and moon) and the course of the sun through the signs of the zodiac serve to measure time which comes to an end at the Last Day. In the *Second Coming / Last Judgment*, the beginning of eternity is illustrated by the βίβλιον studded with the celestial bodies and the signs of the zodiac[139] rolled up by angels.[140] The motif is provided by the Revelation (Apc *6*, 4) which in its turn has borrowed it from Isaia (Is *34*, 4): *Heaven shall roll up like a scroll, and all the stars shall fall like leaves from a vine and as leaves fall from a fig tree.* In the Revelation, it is augmented by *the sun* which *became black as sackcloth of hair, and the moon* which *became as blood* (Apc. *6*, 12). This phenomenon has first been described by the prophet Joel (Joel *2*, 31[141]). In the *Second Coming* chapter of the *Hermeneia*, the description is supplemented by pictures of the prophets Isaia and Joel (as well as Daniel) who hold scrolls with quotations referring to the *Last Judgment.* Saint Peter (who later leads the Elect into Paradise) began his speech at Pentecost with a literal quotation of Joel's prophesy (Joel *2*, 31-32): *The sun shall be turned into darkness, and the moon into blood, before the great and notable day of the Lord come. And it shall come to pass that whosoever shall call on the name of the Lord shall be saved* (Acts *2*, 20-21). The speech was preceded by the miracle of Pentecost which had enabled all peoples, each one in its own language, to hear the message of Jesus Christ. Joel continued: *I will also gather πάντα τὰ ἔθνη and bring them down to the valley of Iosaphat [= to the place of judgment[142]] (Joel 3, 2) … Let all the ἔθνη rouse themselves and come to the valley of Iosaphat, for there I will sit to pass judgment on πάντα τὰ ἔθνη* (Joel *3*,12).

Saint Paul, too, takes up Joel's promise (Ro *10*, 9-13): *That if you shall confess with your mouth the Lord Jesus, and shall believe in your heart that God has raised him from the dead, you shall be saved. For with heart man believes unto righteousness, and with the mouth confession is made unto salvation. For the Scripture says whosoever believes on him shall not be ashamed. For there is no difference between the Jew and the Greek: for the same Lord over all is rich unto all that call upun him. For whosoever shall call upon the name of the Lord shall be saved* (= Joel *2*, 32).

The Peoples / Nations and Moses

It is only on some Russian and Ukrainian icons and in the *Last Judgment* compositions of the Moldovian monasteries that those *on the left hand of the Lord* are conspicuously arranged in groups and labeled by inscriptions as the Jews and several alien peoples. All of them have in common that these groups are led by a man who looks back to them, points with his right arm to Christ and holds a scroll in his left hand. On the scroll is written what he is speaking.[143] On the icons, he is not identified. In 1969 GARIDIS tentatively identified him as Saint John the Theologian (again 1985 on two Russian *Last Judgment* icons, though in the monasteries Humor (Moldovia, 1535) and Phaneromeni (Salamis, 1735) as Aaron, on a *Last Judgment* icon in the Louvre (Paris, 17th cent.) and in the monastery Hurezu (Wallachia, c. 1700) as Moses).[144] GRABAR once left it open whether he is Moses or Saint John;[145] elsewhere he opted for John.[146] In the Moldovian monasteries, inscriptions ensure that he is throughout Moses. He is found in this iconography even where there are no alien peoples. The description of the *Last Judgment* in the *Hermeneia* ignores alien peoples, but enumerates all kinds of *social sinners*[147] who, as a matter of course, are mainly those among *the own people*, hence among Orthodox Christians. *Before all are the impious and ungrateful* γραμματεῖς *and Pharisees, and the rest of the Jews; these wail loudly, some tearing their beards and others their garments, looking at Christ and all the saints, and at the prophet Moses who shows them Christ with his hand...* GODEH. SCHÄFER,[148] A. PAPADOPOULO-KÉRA-MEUS[149] and PAUL HETHERINGTON[150] believed that the text on Moses' scroll, προφήτην ἀναστήσει κύριος ὁ θεός ἐκ τῶν ἀδελφῶν ἡμῶν ὡς ἐμε. αὐτοῦ ἀκούσεσθε κατὰ πάντα, is a quotation of Dt *18*, 15, προφήτην ἐκ τῶν ἀδελφῶν σου ὡς ἐμε ἀναστήσει κύριος ὁ θεός σου σοί, αὐτοῦ ἀκούσεσθε;[151] in fact, it is the variant which Saint Peter quoted when he addressed the Jews (Acts *3*, 22): [Μωϋσῆς εἶπεν ὅτι] προφήτην ὑμῖν ἀναστήσει κύριος ὁ θεός ἐκ τῶν ἀδελφῶν ὑμῶν ὡς ἐμε. αὐτοῦ ἀκούσεσθε κατὰ πάντα [ὅσα ἄν λαλήσῃ πρὸς ὑμᾶς].

In the churches of Saint Nicholas at Proastio (1750) and Kastanea (late 18th cent.), both on Mani, the text is restricted to the beginning.[152] In the churches of Sts Peter and Paul at Levkothea (1778) and of St. Nicholas at Tsepelovo (1786), both in Epirus and presumably by the same painters, words from Mt *11*, 10 = Lk *7*, 27 are followed by a longer, though still abridged quotation:[153] οὗτος ἐστιν περὶ οὐ (Mt *11*, 10 = Lk *7*, 27) ἐγω εἶπον [rather than Μωϋσῆς εἶπεν] ὑμεν ὅτι προφήτην ἀναστήσει ΚΣ ὁ ΘΣ ἐκ τῶν ἀδελφῶν ὑμῶν ὡς ἐμε,[154] *I said* [instead of *Moses said*] *'The Lord God will raise up a prophet from among your brothers as he raised me'.* Like elsewhere, the limited space on the scroll prevented to write the full message;[155] the reader would add what follows: *And it shall come to pass that every soul which will not hear that prophet shall be destroyed from among the people.* ἐκ τοῦ λαοῦ – in this context the Israelites. In both Epirotic churches an angel standing near Moses pushes the Jews (Levkothea: ΙΑΙΒΡΕΗ) with his trident into the stream of fire:[156] Mt *13*, 41-42, 49-50, but here also Acts *3*, 23.

Mt *11*, 10 / Lk. *7*, 27 and Dt *18*, 15 / Acts *3*, 22 served as the prototypes of the text on Moses' scroll in the *Last Judgement*s of the Moldovian monasteries, but here, Saint Peter's speech becomes a reprimand (Suceviţa: *This is the Messiah whom I prophesied to* *you, but you did not believe him* (similar in Voroneţ and Moldoviţa).[157] ADOLPHE N. DIDRON found an even harsher version on a scroll in the Phaneromeni monastery on Salamis: οὗτος ἐστίν ὄν ὑμεῖς ἐσταυρώσατε, *Voilà celui que vous avez crucifié*;[158] similar reproofs are encountered in the Snetogorsky monastery at Pskov (1313)[159] and on an Ukrainian *Last Judgment* icon.[160] It is the abridged version of another sentence in Saint Peter's speech at Pentecost: *Therefore let all the house of Israel know assuredly that God has made that same Jesus, whom you have crucified, both Lord and Christ* (Acts 2,36). Peter, repeating an exhortation which before him Saint John Prodromos and the Lord himself had made (Mt *3, 2* ; *4, 17*), added *Repent, and be baptized every one of you in the name of Jesus Christ, for the remission of sins* (Acts *2, 38*). His addressees were the *men of Israel* (Acts *2, 22*), but even for them, the reproof was not a verdict of damnation, and the way to Christ and hence to salvation was open even to the alien peoples: *For the promise is unto you, and to your children, and to all that are afar off, as many as the Lord our God shall call* (Acts *2, 39*).

ἐκ τοῦ λαοῦ, from the Jews, but οὐ γάρ ἐστιν διαστολὴ Ἰουδαίου τε καὶ Ἕλληνος, *there is no difference between the Jew and the Greek* (Ro *10, 12*) – between the members of God's *Chosen People* and the gentiles. *The Greek* is the collective term for all peoples who experienced the miracle of Pentecost (Acts *2, 9-11*). In the *Last Judgment* compositions of the Moldovian monasteries and in the icons discussed by GARIDIS and GRABAR they have been replaced by those peoples the new *Chosen People* was acquainted with – the Turks, Tatars, Saracenes, black-a-moors, heretical Christians (Armenians and *Latins*, hence Catholics, in the Russian paintings also the Poles, Lithuanians, Swedes and Germans): *All* of them are urged to confess the Lord Jesus Christ with heart and mouth and thus to obtain salvation. *All* – including the members of the new *Chosen People*, in the narrower sense the Orthodox Russians, with the addition *repent* for those sinners who would have deserved the fire of hell and *outer darkness* because of their social misdeeds.

In the Moldovian monasteries, the Armenians and the *Latins* appear as separate peoples. For the region between the Ottoman empire with its system of *millets* and the Christian (though not Orthodox) kingdom of Hungary one has to consider a religious segregation. However, the various Muslim peoples, too, are separately enumerated. On the Russian icons, the Poles and the Lithuanians are not united as Catholics, nor are the Swedes and the Protestant Germans as Lutherans. The Russian translation ВСИ ꙖЗЫЦЫ for πάντα τὰ ἔθνη reveals a classification by language. Like the Muslim Tatars, all of them were enemies of the *Orthodox Russians* so that for them, a distinction between *Just* and sinners was pointless. In some *Last Judgment* compositions, they are surrounded by a long rope drawn by devils towards the realm of damnation[161] – just as elsewhere the Jews are,[162] who had missed the chance which Moses *alias* Peter had offered.

The Texts on the Book of the Judge and the Book on the Throne of the Hetoimasia

For an adequate appreciation of the *Last Judgment*, the texts on the book held by the Judge are revealing: the words he is speaking. In the *Second Coming* chapter of the *Hermeneia*, the description of Christ's book on which Mt *25*, 34, 41 is written precedes the raising of the dead, and as a matter of course, Christ's *Second Coming* precedes the *Judgment*. Hence, at this time, the quotations can neither refer to the *choruses* of *All Saints* who *walk towards him* nor to the sinners whose fate has not yet been decided. On the book held by Christ on *Last Judgment* icons and wall paintings, the text is frequently illegible. Some information, however, may be drawn from related material. Jesus Christ enthroned of the *Last Judgment* compositions is the central part of the *deesis*. Therefore, all *deesis* representations may be informative. The *deesis* is one of the standard themes of icon painting. In addition, an icon of IC XC the Pantokrator is often the centre of a series of icons which on an iconostasis form an *extended deesis*. For many Pantokrator icons it is not possible to decide whether they once belonged to this category; therefore such icons shall be inspected, too.

A survey of an extensive material (mainly icons, some wall paintings)[163] had the following result: The benediction of Mt *25*, 34 (-35) is rare on Greek objects, but one of the most popular quotations on Slavic (Russian, Serbian, Bulgarian) icons, whereas the damnation, Mt *25*, 41, does not occur at all. On the Slavic icons, the invitation *Come unto me all* [*you*] *that labour and are heavy laden, and I will give you rest* (Mt *11*, 28(-29)) is even more frequent than Mt *25*, 34; it is also common on Greek icons where, however, it is surpassed by John *8*, 12, *I am the light of the world*, a quotation not so frequently met on Slavic icons. A Cypriot icon of Christ shows a combination of John *8*, 12 and Mt *11*, 28,[164] a Pantokrator icon from Nesebar (1607) with Greek inscriptions[165] a series of Jesus' sayings: *I am the light of the world* (John *8*, 12). *He that believes in me, though he were dead, yet shall he live, and whatsoever lives and believes in me shall never die* (John *11*, 25-26), *he shall never see death* (John *8*, 51); *while you have light, believe in the light, that you may be the children of light* (John *12,* 36): altogether a promise similar to what Saint Peter told his audience at Pentecost and resembling Moses' exhortation, at the same time the antithesis of *outer darkness* (Mt *8*, 12), the punishment of the sinners.[166] The exhortation *Judge not according to the appearance, but judge righteous judgment* (John *7*, 24) is quite frequent in the Slavic realm;[167] several times it is supplemented by *For with what judgment you judge, you shall be judged, and with what measure you mete, it shall be measured to you again* (Mt *7*, 2).[168] These texts express the same aspect as the title Ἰησοῦς Χριστός ὁ δίκαιος κριτής assigned to Christ in the *Hermeneia*.[169] Other quotations met less frequently are the commandment to love each other of John *15*, 17,[170] and the invitations of John *10*, 9 (*I am the door...*),[171] John *14*, 6 (*I am the way, and the truth, and the life...*)[172] and John *15*, 1 (*I am the true vine*).[173] In some *deesis* compositions, John Prodromos seconds the Lord with the text on his scroll *Repent, for the kingdom of heaven is at hand*

(Mt *3*, 2),[174] another statement of Jesus himself (Mt *4*, 17) and at Pentecost repeated by Saint Peter (Acts *2*, 38) (*vide supra*).

All of these texts characterize the Kyrios of the *Last Judgment* as the benevolent though admonishing, but never as the condemning judge. Where he is not holding a book, his hands sometimes express acceptance and rejection, but more frequently, both arms are outstretched in a gesture of invitation: Mt *11*, 28; the marks of the nails emphasize his role as the Saviour. A friendly attitude of the Judge is also indicated in the *Last Judgment* in the church Panagia Phorbiotissa Asinou (1332/33) in Cyprus. The narthex consists of a central part surmounted by a dome to which two apses have been annexed at the northern and the southern ends by means of two narrow vaults.[175] In the conch of the northern apse, the personifications of land and sea are depicted. On the right side of the zone below, there is Paradise with the Mother of God, the good thief and the three OT patriarchs.[176] Approaching from the left, Peter is unlocking the door of Paradise. He is followed by the Elect, who are welcomed by an inscription band framing the conch. Its text is the benediction of Mt *25*, 34-35.[177] Though elsewhere the chambers of torture are depicted, the counterpart of Mt *25*, 41 has been ignored. The conch of the southern apse has not been devoted to the *Last Judgment*.[178]

In the description of the *Hermeneia*, the *hetoimasia*[179] is part of the *Last Judgment* (though not of the *Second Coming*). On the throne, there lies a book, in the paintings frequently closed,[180] in the *Hermeneia* open and showing the text of Apc *20*, 12, 15[181] and thereby identified as the *book of life*. In compliance with the biblical text, verse 12 which deals only with the judgment but not with the sentence, is written on the left, the *verso* page while verse 15, according to which the sinners are committed to the fire of damnation, is left to the right, the *recto* page. In Tsepelovo (where there are neither Jews nor alien peoples), the differentiation is sharper: the *verso* page contains Mt *25*, 34, the *recto* page verse 41. The book is placed on a low table flanked by two angels.[182] A horizontal red line separates this composition from the lower zone in which the enthroned rulers of the four kingdoms (somehow indebted to though not really illustrating Dan *7*, 17), the stream of fire, Moses pointing to Christ and an angel pushing the *Damned* into the fire (Mt *13*, 41-42, 49-50) are depicted. The dividing line clearly shows that the Mt 25 quotations do not refer to this zone. As in Kahriye Cami, the Panagia ton Chalkeon, Barlaam and Voroneţ they serve to point out the general meaning of the *Last Judgment* and are not the legends of particular pictures. The angels at either side of the book hold scrolls. Only the text on the right scroll is still legible; somewhat abridged, it is the *sanctus*[183] which in liturgy is sung during the Eucharist[184] and consists of Is *6*, 3 and Mt *21*, 9,[185] the acclamation of Jesus in his Entry to Jerusalem (*vide supra*). It is obviously suitable for a dignified reception of the Lord in his *Second Coming* (the Rumanian *Erminia* has it as the acclamation of the Hosts of Heaven in the *Second Coming*[186]). The book is not so much the *Book of Justice* whose contents is decisive for salvation and damnation than the book held by Christ in the *Second Coming*; it serves the preparation of the trial. Again in Tsepelovo, the Mt 25 quotations are no legends of the groups of the *Blessed* and the *Cursed*.

Russian Last Judgment Icons with the Snake of Sin

The discussion of GARIDIS and GRABAR focussed on the often reproduced Novgorodian *Last Judgment* icon in the Tretyakov Gallery (henceforth: *TG*) (fig. on p. 53),[187] an icon in Stockholm (henceforth: *St*)[188] and on an icon formerly in the Hann collection (henceforth: *Hann*).[189] All of them are of North Russian origin; a related icon exists in St. Petersburg (henceforth: *SPb*).[190] All these icons are highly complicated compositions consisting of a multitude of scenes part of which defied straightforward explanations and gave rise to speculative interpretations. The present discussion is restricted to the zone in which allegedly Mt *25*, 34, 41 is depicted. The fiery stream emanating from below Christ's feet (Dan *7*, 10) has been replaced by the snake of sin (with the toll booths[191]) which comes out of hell, winds upwards and bites Adam's heel.[192] The 20 or so toll booths represent the different sins; after the physical death, the souls must pass them in their ascent to the abode of the *Blessed*. Depending on the weight and the nature of their deeds recorded in the *Book of Justice*, after the raising of the dead and the reunification with their bodies, some of them will find themselves *on the right hand of the Lord*, but many *on the left hand*. Even for them, however, this is no reason for *wailing and gnashing of teeth*: If they repent and acknowledge that Jesus Christ is the Lord, they can hope for a benevolent sentence. This applies to the Orthodox Russians as well as to the aliens.

These icons share with the Moldovian monasteries that crowds of people, more or less divided into groups, are standing at either side of the judge. The groups are identified by inscriptions which however are seldom legible. Those *on the left hand* are always preceded by Moses who, again, holds a scroll, regrettably with an illegible text. In *TG*, such groups approach the *hetoimasia* from either side. The *hetoimasia* is flanked by two angels, so that Moses is standing close to the right angel.[193] The text on this angel's scroll is claimed to be Mt *25*, 34. As usual, PRISCILLA HUNT identified the groups *on the right hand* as the *Blessed* and those *on the left hand* as the *Cursed*.[194] She assigned the benediction to the latter and drew far-reaching conclusions. In her interpretation, Moses points to the scroll of this angel and thus promises salvation to the sinners. These, according to the author, do not rank too much behind the *Just* on their common way to salvation.[195] For Moses' own scroll, HUNT postulated his *traditional words of excoriation*,[196] but his left arm and the scroll turned downwards is believed to indicate that its text is visibly devalued in favour of the gesture of the right hand.

For a variety of reasons, HUNT's considerations cannot be correct. Scrolls *always* render what the respective person is speaking; the text on Moses' scroll is not known. Moses does not point towards the scroll of the right angel, but, near its first letters, towards the Lord Jesus Christ. In *Hann* and *St*, Moses' position, far away from the *hetoimasia* and the right angel, excludes any relation between his gesture and the angel's scroll.[197] In *SPb* (as in Moldoviţa) Moses holds his scroll in his *right* hand; it is flying towards Christ whereas the scroll of the right angel is below the outstretched right arm of Moses. In *TG*, the texts of the scrolls of both angels (as well as of Moses) remain absolutely illegible even upon strong magnification,[198] so that the reading as Mt *25*, 34 cannot be accepted as an unbiased decipherment. If it were correct, the text on the scroll of the left angel would be left to the curse of verse 41 which then would apply to the *choruses on the right hand* – an obvious impossibility. In conclusion, Moses' function is the same as in the Moldovian monasteries: to promise a benevolent sentence to all those unbelievers and malefactors who are willing to confess that Jesus is the Lord. – HUNT reckognized that Moses is depicted again as the leader of those *on the right hand*. Here he is the first in the *chorus* of the prophets (as prescribed in the *Hermeneia* for the composition of *All Saints*[199]) so that no further discussion is needed.

By means of the snake of sins and its toll booths, these icons address an admonition to the religious though sinful viewers who may see themselves represented in *St* in the groups of the Orthodox Russians. A similar thought is expressed in the heavenly ladder of Joannes o Klimakos[200] which is depicted in the bottom zone of *Hann*. To the right of it, and below the fire of hell, the compartments are shown in which the individual misdeeds are punished; in *St* and *SPb*, they fill the entire bottom zone, hence even below Paradise.[201] Thus, the pedagogical function of the *Last Judgment* composition is emphasized in these icons. On the other hand, the entry of the Elect into Paradise has been illustrated much less conspicuously than in Voroneţ. The representation of the *choruses* of *All Saints* is similar in the icons and the wall paintings. Quotations of Mt *25*, 34, 41 have occasionally been postulated for these icons, but have nowhere been corroborated.

Result

In conclusion, the groups discussed by GARIDIS and GRABAR are not illustrations of Mt *25*, 34, 41. Some indication for proper apprehension is given by the *Hermeneia*. The upper part of the *Last Judgment* composition, as painted in the Moldovian monasteries, and the first part of the *Last Judgment* chapter of the *Hermeneia* are devoted to the situation preceding the trial, not to that after the proclamation of the sentence: *Christ sitting on a high and radiant throne* [in the Moldovian monasteries: on a rainbow] *robed in white and brighter than the sun; he is guarded by all the mighty angels with great fear and terror* [in the monasteries in the calm attitude of the bodyguard] ... *on either side of him are the Virgin and the Forerunner* [whose intercession for mankind is meaningful only *before* the sentence] ... *the twelve apostles seated on twelve thrones,* [for Jesus had told them] *When the Son of man is seated on his throne in heavenly splendour, you my followers will have thrones of your own, where you will sit as judges of the twelve tribes of Israel* (Mt *19*, 28), *and with them all the saints standing on his right in three ranks.*[202] The *hetoimasia*, too, is part of the *preparation* of the

Judgment[203] (in Dečani this is expressly stated by the title[204]).

All Saints are the *Just* of the OT and all those who testified during their lives that Jesus is the Son of God; their nine *choruses* are enumerated in the *Hermeneia* and named by legends in the *Last Judgment* compositions. In the Moldovian monasteries, they are faced by all those who so far have been unbelievers and whom Moses admonishes to acknowledge that Jesus is the Lord, so that they, too, may qualify for salvation. Not all of them will comply – in particular, the Jews and, among them, especially the doctors of the law and Pharisees are obstinate. On some icons, the latter, reckognizable by their white headgear,[205] are the first in the group of the Jews; they face the fire of hell and *outer darkness* which are depicted below. The damnation of King Herodes is anticipated: In the Moldovian monastery Moldoviţa (1537), a black devil has grasped his beard to draw him into hell. In this monastery, the full text of Mt *25*, 41 is quoted, ...ꙋГОТОВАННОЄ ДЇ [Moses' head] ДВОЛꙋІАГГЄЛ[ѠМЪЄ]Г[Ѡ], and yet, like the truncated version in Voroneţ, it does not extend above the Jews, but ends above Moses' left hand and above the fingers of a Jew who has stretched out his hand. The space to the right of Moses' head and above the hand of a Jew standing in the background has already been used for the legend ЛИК үЄВРЄСКь. In Suceviţa (1601), Mt *25*, 41 is again fully quoted, but here the final words extend until the end of the group of the Jews and may, therefore, apply to all of them. The alien peoples lined up behind the Jews, however, are not threatened by the verdict of Mt *25*, 41 in any of these monasteries. In two Bulgarian churches painted *circa* 1840, even the fate of the Jews is still undecided: In the baptismal church of the monastery Bačkovo, the Jews are encircled by a rope, by which a devil attempts to draw them into the stream of fire. But in front of them, Moses is standing. With his right hand, he points to Christ. What he is speaking is written in Greek on his scroll: Acts *3*, 22.[206] In Trojanski Manastir, the Pharisees (ФАРИСЕИ) show their teeth as an expression of the *wailing and grinding of teeth*. The first of them tears his long beard; a black devil grasps the last one. However, again Moses is standing in front of them. His long scroll flutters above all of them and even above the devil: Again Acts *3*, 22, not Mt *25*, 41.[207] Moses and his scroll are meaningful only if the success of the devilish efforts has not yet been decided. The *Last Judgment* in the porch of the katholikon of the Rila monastery (1842-1844) is different only in so far, that Moses does not hold a scroll and stretches out his left hand towards the Jews in a gesture of invitation.

All those Orthodox Christians who did not too severely transgress the Christian commandments, may hope for a benevolent sentence; after the remission of their sins, they qualify for a nimbus. In the bottom zone of the *Last Judgment* in Voroneţ, Peter leads *All Saints* of the third zone – now with nimbi – and the *Blessed* of the fourth zone jointly into Paradise. Peter and Paul approach the gate hand in hand; they are followed by four other apostles and then by Moses,[208] Solomon, Aaron and David, behind them, only indicated by nimbi, the countless number of other Elect.[209] In the Uspenskij cathedral of Vladimir, behind and above Peter, Saint Paul is standing whose right hand points to Paradise while he looks back and holds his left arm above the heads of the Elect.[210] He holds a scroll fluttering to the right; the text on it is part of a sticheron sung at the eve before the feast of Sts Peter and Paul (June 29th):[211] St. Paul who had been granted a short glimpse into Paradise during his lifetime[212] and, as a matter of course, is one of the first to be admitted, shouts to the *Blessed*: *Come with me, and we shall not lack the blessings* [of Paradise].[213] At Asinou, the welcome of the Elect is expressed by the inscription band with the benediction of Mt *25*, 34-35 which surrounds the entry into Paradise.[214]

Viewed in the light of Peter's speech at Pentecost, the contradictions seen by GARIDIS and GRABAR become meaningless. The essence of the miracle of Pentecost is the knowledge that other ἔθνη exist besides God's *Chosen People* (originally the Israelites, then the (Orthodox) Christians). It is certainly possible to deduce the incorporation of the alien peoples into the *Last Judgment* composition from the political situation in the 15th century and later. But for an apprehension of the phenomenon, this is an unnecessary hypothesis.

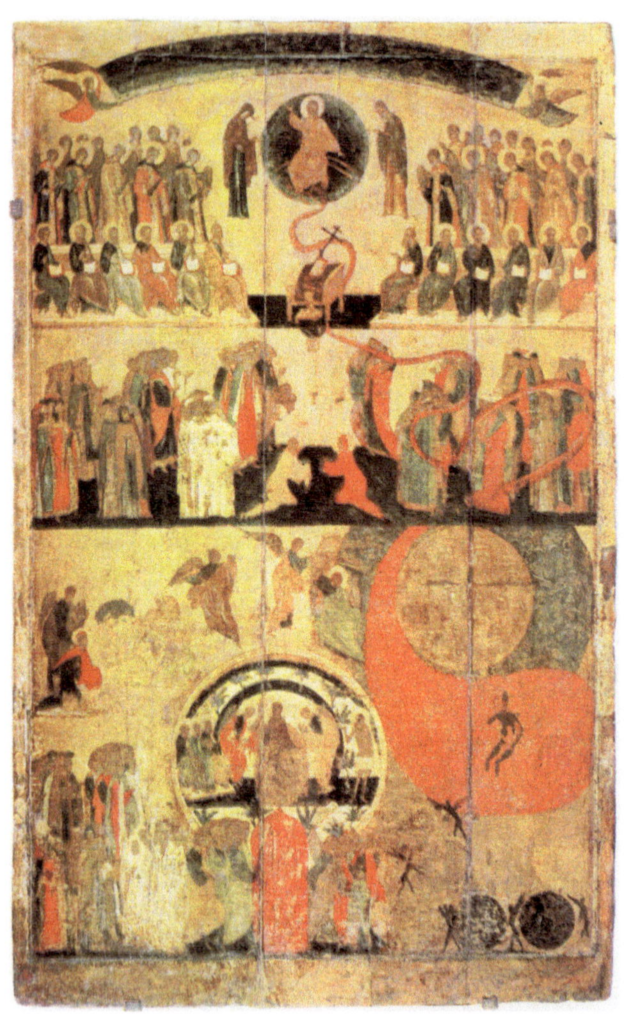

The *Last Judgment* icon in the Uspenskij cathedral in the Kremlin of Moscow

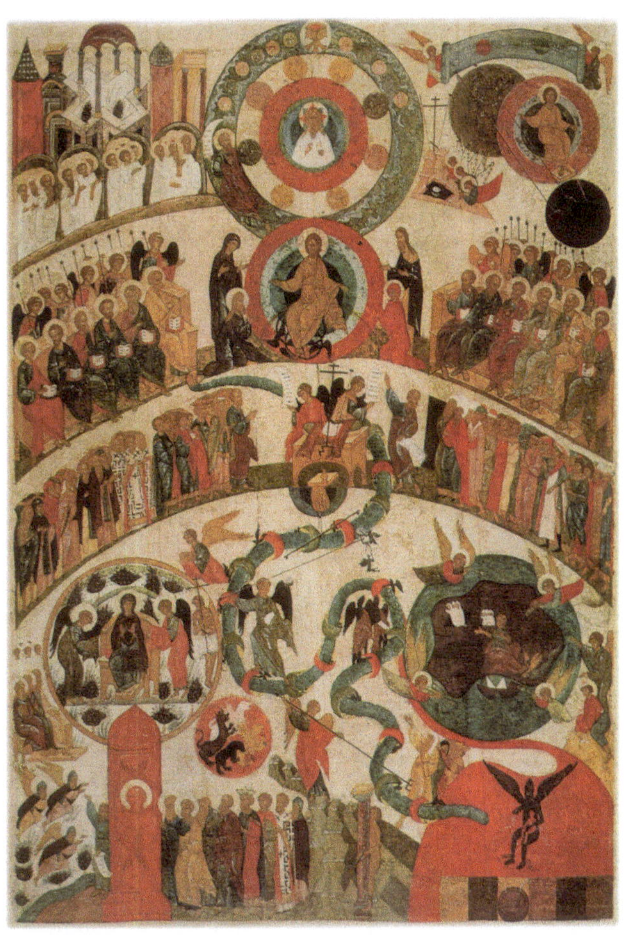

The Novgorodian *Last Judgment* icon in the Tretya-kov Gallery

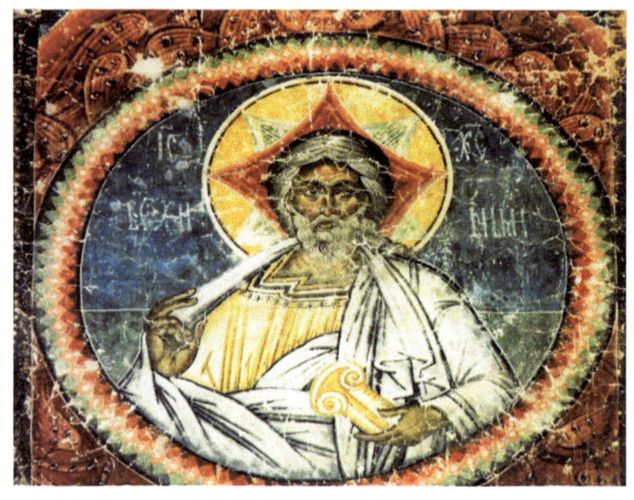

Monastery Voroneţ, *Last Judgment*: The *Ancient of Days*

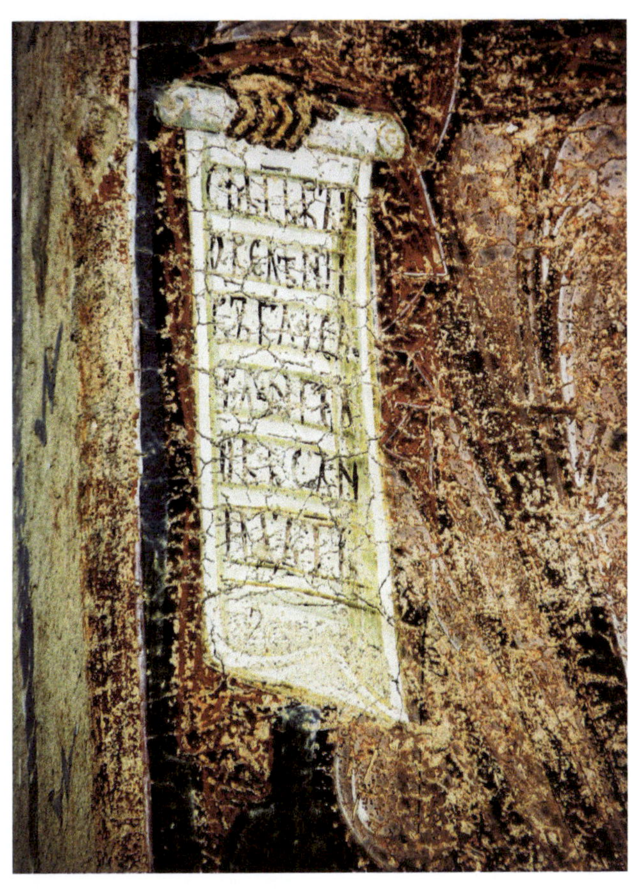

Monastery Voroneţ, *Last Judgment*: The scroll of St. Paul

The Role of the Inscription Bands in Wall Paintings of the *Laud Psalms*

Contents

Introduction
The praise of the Lord by the celestial creation
The inscription band
The praise of the Lord by the terrestrial creation
The hymn of mankind
The praise of the Lord by the hosts of heaven
Inscription bands with Ps 150, 6
Inscription bands with Ps 64, 2a
Inscription bands with Ps 150, 6 and Ps 64, 2a
The inscription band: Legend of the illustrations or text of a hymn?
Kyrios Jesus Christos

Introduction

Since an early date, manuscripts of the book of psalms have profusely been decorated with miniatures. This is not paralleled in wall painting. Much later, only the last three psalms, Ps 148-150 (the *laud psalms*) became part of the canon of Orthodox church decoration. In Tsar Stefan Dušan's Serbian empire, some churches contain paintings of Ps 148 and 149[1] while in Greek churches of the 16th century and occasionally even later, only Ps 148 received attention.[2] In this psalm, the entire creation is exhorted to praise the Lord while Ps 149 deals mainly with the liberation of the *Faithful* from oppression. Ps 150 is in principle dispensable, because it is merely a continuation of the last part of Ps 148, the praise of the Lord by mankind, specified as a praise by music, a topic which is addressed already in Ps *149*, 3. In fact, when, as a latecomer, Ps 150 was added, illustration was largely restricted to the verses 3-5, the praise of the Lord by dance and music performed with all kinds of instruments. The beginning of Ps 150, verses 1-2, has only very rarely been illustrated,[3] and the final verse, Ps 150, 6, only exceptionally.[4] While in the Munich Serbian psalter (14th cent.), this verse has been highlighted by a large, independent miniature,[5] in wall painting it is occasionally dealt with together with the preceding verses[6] and recognizable only by the accompanying inscription, πᾶσα πνοὴ αἰνεσάτω τὸν κύριον.

And yet, in the scholarly literature dealing with wall paintings of the *laud psalms*, Ps *150*, 6 assumes a prominent place. In the Old Testament context and viewed as the summary of Ps 150, it exhorts only mankind to praise the Lord.[7] Neither the angels (who, as ἀσώματοι, lack a body and, consequently, a lung for breathing[8]) nor the celestial bodies, the natural phenomena, mountains, hills and trees of Ps *148*, 2-9 qualify for πᾶσα πνοή, *All breath*. Nevertheless, Ps *150*, 6 has been viewed as a summary of the whole of the *laud psalms*; the beginning, πᾶσα πνοή, became the title of the illustrations of these psalms.[9]

Ps *150*, 6 owes this special role to the circular inscriptions which are frequently inserted in the illustration of the verses Ps *148*, 1-6, the praise of the Lord by the celestial part of the creation. They are written on circular bands between the figurative scenes and consist of the verses of the first part of Ps 148. They never exceed verse 6, but frequently contain alien verses: They often begin with Ps *150*, 6 while Ps *64*, 2a, σοὶ πρέπει ὕμνος, ὁ θεός,, may be inserted, occasionally even twice. These alien elements and their doubling have often been taken as evidence that the inscriptions represent hymns.[10] Ps *150*, 6 and *64*, 2a, are sung together with Ps *148*, 1 on Sundays and some religious holidays in the morning service, the ὄρθρος, and from this use and the doubling of Ps *64*, 2a, typical for hymns, it has been concluded that the *laud psalms* compositions represent *painted liturgy*.[11] However, various discrepancies between the inscriptions and the figurative paintings call for a reinvestigation of their interrelationship.

The Praise of the Lord by the Celestial Creation

The favourite location of the *laud psalms* paintings were narthex cupolas. Their shape conditions a circular composition for which the naos cupola could serve as a model. Here, the Pantokrator, as a rule depicted as a bust, looks down.[12] He has raised his right hand in the gesture of speaking. In his left hand, he holds a book;[13] when it is opened, the words of his speech are shown. He is surrounded by the hosts of heaven, the four evangelists and an inscription band which displays appropriate psalm verses (most frequently Ps *32*, 13-15[14]).

This composition was well suited to illustrate Ps *148, 1-2, Praise the Lord from the heavens; praise him in the highest heights! Praise him, all his angels; praise him, all his hosts!*, and served indeed that purpose with insignificant iconographic modification. In most cases (though not always[15]), the bust was replaced by the full figure of the enthroned Pantokrator (as in the *Last Judgment*[16]) who usually (again: not always[17]) holds a scroll rather than a book. The text on it, hence, what he is speaking, varies greatly, but is never taken from the *laud psalms*. Thus, the illustration of Ps *148*, 1-2 is not at all self-explanatory and therefore is in need of a legend. For this, the circular inscription could be used which was placed either around the central *Kyrios*[18] (Ps *148*, 1) or further outside around the ring of the angels (Ps *148*, 2). The influence of the naos cupola is most obvious at Makryalexi (Epirus, *ca.* 1610) where the scroll of the Ps *148*, 1 *Kyrios* shows Ps *32*, 13, ἐξ οὐρανοῦ ἐπέβλεψεν ὁ κύριος.[19] In the *laud psalms* illustrations, the texts of the naos cupolas were first replaced by verses taken exclusively from Ps 148, though frequently not restricted to the verses 1-2. Later, Ps *64*, 2a was added, and in many cases, Ps *150*, 6 was used as the initial verse. Obviously, such inscription bands were not simply legends of the Ps *148*, 1-2 illustration.

The ἄγγελοι and δυνάμεις of Ps *148*, 2 were usually organized in the nine τάγματα of Pseudo-Dionysios Areopagites.[20] In their praise of the Lord, rhey are followed by the celestial bodies (verse 3): the sun, the moon and the stars: πάντα τὰ ἄστρα: *all* stars, the planets as well as the fixed stars. In two early *laud psalms* cycles, at Lesnovo (1349) and in the Megali

Panagia, Samos (1596), the planets were characterized by their mythological names and depicted as the corresponding figures.[21] In the Bessarion monastery Dousiko (1557/58) and the katholikon of the monastery Dochiariou, Mount Athos (*Dochiariou I*, 1568),[22] they are particularly large stars characterized by their phenomenological names.[23] In Dousiko, Dochiariou and the monastery Roussanou (Meteora, 1560), the great number of fixed stars is represented by smaller stars.[24] Already at Lesnovo and in the Megali Panagia, they are organized in the signs of the zodiac and depicted as the respective symbols which have been placed, together with the symbols of the planets, beside the circular composition of Ps *148*, 1-2 without strict order.[25]

The passage of the sun through the signs of the zodiac is the reliable indicator of the course of the year; as such, it provided an excellent mean to illustrate Ps *148*, 6, *He* [= the Lord] *established them* [= the celestial bodies] *forever and forever and ever; an ordinance he issued, and it will not pass away.* Known since antiquity,[26] the circular arrangement expressed the course of time without beginning and end.[27] Therefore, the cyclic zodiac with the sun, often studded with stars, soon became the standard illustration of both Ps *148*, 3 and 6; it surrounds the praise of the Lord by the angels. Like the course of the sun, the phases of the moon reliably demonstrate God's order. Therefore, the moon, mentioned in Ps *148*, 3, could easily be integrated into the joint illustration of the verses 3 and 6.

Ps *148, 4, Praise him, you heavens of heavens, and you water above the heavens*, has been depicted at Lesnovo as a round cloud outside the central picture of Ps *148*, 1-2.[28] Later, the verse was symbolized by a circular cloud which forms the outermost of the rings surrounding the Ps *148*, 1-2 illustration. The *water above the heavens* is intimated by a wavy hatching which is occasionally explained by the respective quotation (Bombokou (1703-1722): τὸ ὕδωρ τὸ ὑπεράνω τῶν οὐρανῶν). In the Koukouzelissa chapel of the Great Lavra (Mount Athos, 1715), the sequence of the zodiac and the circular cloud is inverted. Again, the cloud is authenticated as the illustration of Ps *148*, 4 by the legend κ(αὶ) τὸ ὕδωρ.[29] The cyclic zodiac lacks the sun, the moon and stars; hence it illustrates exclusively Ps *148*, 6 so that the correct order of the psalm verses is preserved.

In this way, the praise of the Lord by the celestial creation developed into a large circular composition which was separarated from the terrestrial sphere, in most cases by the circular cloud. The celestial bodies, though mentioned already in Ps *148*, 3, could alternatively be assigned to the terrestrial sphere because of their physical perceptibility; hence, there was a choice to incorporate them either into the band of the zodiac or into the real sky above all those who *praise the Lord from the earth* (Ps *148*, 7) (e. g., in the Koukouzelissa chapel[30]).

Already at Lenovo, the initial part of the composition is situated in a barrel vault, with a cyclic picture of Ps *148*, 1-2 in the zenith.[31] In the psalm text, there is a border between the celestial and the terrestrial sphere

(Ps *148*, 1-6 and Ps *148*, 7-14, respectively); at Lesnovo, the border is between the transcendental and the real world. *The Lord*, enthroned upon seraphim, is surrounded by many angels in circular arrangement (Ps *148*, 1-2). The celestial bodies are depicted outside this round picture together with the *water above the heavens* and the natural phenomena of Ps *148*, 8 in non-circular arrangement at the lower parts of the vault.[32] In later paintings in barrel vaults, a similar round picture in the zenith illustrates the whole of Ps *148*, 1-6. Occasionally, the *laud psalms* were depicted on a (vertical or curved) wall. Even there, the conventional round picture was chosen for Ps *148*, 1-6.[33]

The Inscription Band

Placed around the central picture of the Lord and the angels, the inscription band had a little radius and hence a small capacity which was sufficient to accommodate Ps *148*, 1-2 and even verse 3. Space for longer inscriptions could be procured by placing the band further outside or by adding a second band. In the earliest Greek *laud psalms* compositions, Dousiko, Roussanou and Dochiariou I, the circular inscription surrounds the enthroned *Kyrios* and quotes Ps *148*, 1a-2b.[34] The inscriptions are to be read *from within*. Later, in the monastery Karakallou (Mount Athos, 1750) and in the Pateron monastery near Zitsa (Epirus, 1617), the band contains the same text which, however, is to be read *from outside* and hence counter-clockwise.[35] In the Pateron monastery, the quotation leaves a void which is filled by an ornament – an indication that no longer text was intended. On the other hand, in the Koukouzelissa chapel, already the verses Ps *148*, 1a,b, 2a required the entire space.[36] In all these cases, the quotations comply perfectly with a role as legends of the picture and contain nothing which might indicate another function.

Elsewhere, the inscription band is still situated between the circular picture of the *Kyrios* and the circle of the angels, but contains a longer quotation from Ps 148. At Tsepelovo (Epirus, 1786), the complete verses Ps *148*, 1a,b, 2a,b, 3a,b fill the band completely (the ring of the angels is surrounded by the zodiac with the sun, the moon and stars). Likewise, in Hagios Nikolaos Vathias (not conclusively dated), presumably Ps *148*, 1-3 is quoted (the inscription begins with αἰνεῖτε and ends with τὸ φῶς). Sometimes, the final verse is incomplete. At Mcxeta (proposed date 1784[37]) Ps *148*, 1a,b, 2b,a (sic!), 3a,b is quoted until πάντα τὰ ἄστρα; in the Phaneromeni monastery on Salamis (1735; Ps *148*, 1a,b, 2a,b, 3), the entire half-verse Ps *148*, 3b is missing (verse *148*, 3a is justified by the zodiac with the sun and the moon outside the ring of the angels). In the church of Sts Peter and Paul at Levkothea (Epirus, 1778), an inscription band between the Ps *148*, 1-*Kyrios* and the ring of the angels contains the verses Ps *148*, 1a,b, 2a,b, followed by αἰνεῖτε αὐτὸν + illegible letters (Ps *148*, 3a?), and finally again αἰνεῖτε αὐτὸν (beginning of Ps *148*, 3b?), indicating that the quotation should continue. (Ps *148*, 3 is *illustrated* by a circular band studded with the sun, the moon and many stars between the angels and the circular cloud.) In the church of Hagios Dimitrios at Katarrakti Oktonias (Euboea, 1636), a carefully written inscription fills the band completely; it consists of the full text of Ps 148 from verse 1a until the beginning of verse 5a, but ends abruptly within a word: (αἰνεσάτωσ[αν τὸ ὄνομα κυρίου]).

Such quotations indicate that the complete text of the celestial praise of the Lord, Ps *148*, 1-6, was intended. This is corroborated by compositions in which the text has been accommodated on two concentric bands. In the church of the Panagitsa at Ligourio (18th cent.), the inner circle contains Ps *148*, 1a,b, 2a,b, the outer circle Ps *148*, 4a,b, 5a,b,c, 6a,b, though lack of space forced to omit the last word of verse 2b, αὐτοῦ, and the last three words of verse 6b. Nearby, in the church of Hagios Merkourios (18th cent.), the inscriptions are no longer fully legible, in the inner ring Ps *148*, [1a,b, 2a,] 2b, 3b, in the outer circle … Ps *148*, 5c, 6a,b. At Zerbitsa (Laconia, early 18th cent.), the inner circle contains Ps *148*, 1a,b, 2a,[b?], the outer circle Ps *148*, 3a-6a. In Timios Ioannes Prodromos at Melé (Messenia, 1676), Ps *148*, 1a,b, 2a,b is again quoted in the inner ring. In the outer ring, the verses Ps *148*, 3a,b, 4a,b, 5[a,]b,c and 6a,b did not fill the available space; verse 6b is followed by another αἰνεῖτε τὸν κύριον (in the orthography κυρηων) which still did not suffice to fill the void. The final words may either be a repetition of the beginning, or the beginning of Ps *148*, 7a was used as a filler though the adequate place of verse 7a is not here but in the praise of the Lord by the terrestrial creation.

In the Panagitsa of Ligourio, Ps *148*, 3 was skipped. Elsewhere the text of the outer band is always the immediate continuation of the quotation on the inner band. Hence, both represent a single inscription. Each part is located close to the pertinent illustration and thus qualifies as a legend. In detail, a stringent correlation is impossible, because the circular arrangement and the sequence of the psalm verses are not strictly compatible. *E. g.*, two of the angelic τάγματα, the ἄγγελοι and the δυνάμεις, occur in Ps *148*, 2. A perfect legend should have the two words near the corresponding τάγματα. This is nowhere the case. On the other hand, neither the illustration of Ps *148*, 1-6 nor any of these inscription bands contain details alien to the psalm text and thus indicative of foreign influences. In the Koukouzelissa chapel, Ps *148*, 2b, αἰνεῖτε αὐτὸν πᾶσαι αἱ δυνάμεις αὐτοῦ, has been omitted, at Mcxeta, the end of Ps *148*, 3b, καὶ τὸ φῶς. In both cases, another disposition would have permitted full quotation. Obviously, this was not intended.

The omissions concern only redundant phrasing: If Ps *148*, 2 exhorts the entire host of heaven to praise the Lord, ἄγγελοι and δυνάμεις are virtually synonymous, and τὸ φῶς of Ps *148*, 3b is only an abstract version of πάντα τὰ ἄστρα which has nowhere been separately illustrated. For legends, then, Ps *148*, 2b and the end of verse 3b were indeed dispensable. Likewise, the verses Ps *148*, 5-6 were difficult to illustrate due to their abstract character. While for verse 6 the combination with verse 3 by means of the zodiac solved the problem, verse 5 was never illustrated. And yet, both occur in some of the circular inscriptions, indicating that the praise of the Lord by the celestial sphere was meant as a unified whole, adequately described by the complete text of Ps *148*, 1-6.

Only in compositions without inscription bands quotations from these verses serve the purpose of specific legends. At Lesnovo, Ps *148*, 1 is written (in Slavonic language) above the round picture of the *Kyrios* amid the angels.[38] Its function is vague and possibly multiple – the title of the entire composition or the legend of the round picture. At Bombokou, Ps *148*, 2a, αἰνεῖτε αὐτὸν πάντες οἱ ἄγγελοι αὐτοῦ, is written above the heads of the angels, Ps *148*, 4b within the circular cloud. In the cathedral of St. John at Nicosia (18th cent.), the words of Ps *148*, 1 appear under the feet of the *Kyrios*,[39] again more probably as the title of the composition than the remnants of a circular inscription. In the Koukouzelissa chapel, the inscription κ(αὶ) τὸ ὕδωρ is not part of the circular inscription around the central *Kyrios*, but is written on a blue circular band inserted between the angels and the zodiac and is the legend which explains that this band is the circular cloud of Ps *148*, 4.[40]

The Praise of the Lord by the Terrestrial Creation

Outside the circular composition of Ps *148,* 1-6 with the more or less complete text of these verses in one or two inscription bands, the terrestrial creation praises the Lord, in cupolas of sufficient size as another circle outside the cloud of Ps *148*, 4. This arrangement demonstrates that the *Kyrios* in the centre is likewise the object of the devotion of the terrestrial creation. The focus on the centre was attenuated when the *laud psalms* were painted elsewhere, *e. g.* in a barrel vault. Here, the round composition of Ps *148*, 1-

6 (only Ps *148*, 1-2 at Lesnovo) occupies the zenith. Already its shape segregates the celestial from the terrestrial praise of the Lord which is depicted in the lower parts of the vault, arranged in horizontal friezes, to be *read* from left to right. Incorporation of the tympana at the ends of the barrel vault permitted to retain the circular arrangement (Arbanasi (Bulgaria), 1681,[41] Bombokou, Hagios Nikolaos Vathias, Hosios Meletios (Kithairon range of mountains; not conclusively dated),[42] Monodendri (Epirus, 1619), Kelepha (Mani, 18th cent.); in Makryalexi beneath the cupola). The central round picture covers part of the upper frieze.[43] The illustration of Ps *148*, 7-14 is not comprehensive: Verses which lack a concrete content are seldom illustrated. The pertinent verses are written above the respective scenes or even within. In the upper frieze, both the scenes and the inscriptions are adapted to the curvature of the round composition in the centre. Unlike the text of Ps *148*, 1-6, the inscriptions are not within bands. The function of legends for the pictures is much more obvious than for the inscription bands.

As Ps *148*, 7a is already implied in the central round picture, the illustration begins with the chant of the dragons and the depths [of the sea]. The psalm text, however, includes verse 7a so that the inscription and the picture do not perfectly correspond. In Dousiko and Roussanou, the scenes are accompanied by the full text of Ps *148*, 7-14 except those parts which have not been illustrated: verses 11b, 13b,c, 14a,c. When the space above the picture was insufficient, the pertinent text was divided into two or three lines. Thus, the text corresponds exactly with the illustration; it clearly serves the purpose of a legend. It does not, on the other hand, meet the criteria of a liturgical chant which consists of the unabridged text. In both churches, the δράκοντες and πᾶσαι ἄβυσσοι are depicted separately though in a single scene; later, dragons raise their heads out of dark caves. Elsewhere, the ἄβυσσοι are represented by a pool of water with fishes; a mermaid symbolizes the unknown depths of the sea.[44] Both the abode of the dragons and the ἄβυσσοι belong to the lowest parts of the earth; this is accounted for by painting them at the bottom of the frieze, still accompanied by the words of Ps *148*, 7b. This position outside the continuous inscription at the upper rim shows again that the whole of the quotations is meant as a legend rather than a recital of the psalm.

In a number of cases, the terrestrial part of the *laud psalms* is not illustrated verse by verse, but as a unified composition.[45] The sword-bearers of Ps *149*, 6 act as jailers who conduct the captive kings of Ps *149*, 8 to the judges of Ps *148*, 11 (Zoodochos Piyi Zarnatas (1787), Proastio (1750), Kampos (1760), Panagia Chelmou (18th cent.), all on Mani). The musicians of Ps *149*, 3 and Ps *150*, 3-5 play their instruments jointly, and the people of Ps *148*, 11-12 join the ὅσιοι of Ps *148*, 14b and *149*, 1 in their procession to the church of Ps *149*, 1, or they are even equated with them (Kozani, 1730).[46] In these cases, isolated psalm quotations have been written beside the respective persons, obviously as legends.

The composition in Hagios Panteleimon Silitzani Kissavou near Anatoli (1640/41)[47] is revealing because of deviations from he canonical order. The circular illustration begins with brownish red mountains below the text of Ps *148*, 9a,b + τὰ θηρία (the beginning of verse 10, in the orthography ΤΑ ΘΕΙΡΙΑ, ΕΙ as ligature), written in three lines. The quotation is continued in a single line (with two small exceptions) arranged around the circular cloud of Ps *148*, 4b and to be read continuously from left to right: First Ps *148*, 8a, then 7a,b (its beginning αἰνεῖτε τὸν κύριον omitted), the word ΔΡΑΚΟΝΤΕC above Κ(αὶ) ΠΑCΕ ΑΒΙCΙ. Beside the dragons looking out of their caves, people proceed to the church of Ps *149*, 1b. A cross on its roof is beneath the sun in the centre of the zodiac, and the sun is above the head of the *Kyrios*. Thus, the church is the centre of the composition; from either side, it is approached by humans. In the inscription, Ps *148*, 7b is followed by verse 11a, of verse 11b only ΑΡΧωΝΤΕC, then verse 14b and beyond the church the second part of Ps *149*, 1b, *148*, 12a,b (μετὰ νεωτέρων omitted), Ps *150*, 3a,b, 4a, 4b (αἰνεῖτε αὐτὸν not repeated), 5a; *149*, 6b (in two lines), 8a. *All the cattle, creeping things and winged birds* of Ps *148*, 10 as well as the nobles of Ps *149*, 8b are not mentioned in the inscription though snakes and birds and the fettered nobles are depicted. At the lower rim, the anthropomorphic stormy wind is blowing out of his cave; the inscription, Ps *148*, 8b, is situated outside the continuous text below the snow precipitating from a cloud.

The quotations, then, do not include the *judges of the earth* and the νεωτέροι of Ps *148*, 11b and 12b, the verses Ps *148*, 13a-c, 14a,c and parts of the 149th and the 150th psalm. The position of Ps *148*, 12a and the beginning of verse 12b between Ps *149*, 1b and the 150th psalm indicate that the παρθένοι are equated with the maidens dancing the *choros* of Ps *150*, 4a, accompanied by the wind players and the drummers of Ps *150*, 3a.

It emerges that it had not been intended to scrupulously illustrate the *laud psalms* but to use these psalms to depict a procession of all *Faithful* and even the wicked rulers towards the church and further to the Lord Jesus Christ. The canonical order did not matter. The text correlates perfectly with the illustration; it serves hence as legends and is not suitable for a hymn.

Legends of pictures and recitals of psalms can be discriminated when the inscription and the sequence of the scenes run in opposite direction. This happens when groups of persons approach a common goal from both sides: in the church of Hagios Georgios at Redina (1715) the central picture of the Lord,[48] elsewhere the church of Ps *149*, 1b.[49] At Redina, only the 148th psalm is illustrated – not in a cupola, but on a wall. The central round picture of the Lord amid the angels is the standard illustration of Ps *148*, 1-2, but at the same time, it serves to illustrate verse 7a (verse 7a,b is *written* somewhat lower at the left side of the round picture above the heads and tails of a tetracephalic dragon coming out of a dark cave). To praise the Lord, the groups of Ps *148*, 11a and 12a,b approach from either side, in compliance with the psalm text those of verse 11a ahead of those of verse 12: from the left, the kings and peoples (Ps *148*, 11a), below them the νεανίσκοι (beginning of verse 12a), from the right, the παρθένοι (end of verse 12a), followed by the πρεσβύτεροι (beginning of verse 12b), below them the *young men* (μετὰ νεωτέρων, end of verse 12b), followed by a group of men, identified by nimbi and the text of Ps *148*, 14b,c as the ὅσιοι. For the groups of the verses 12 and 14, the inscriptions, to be read from left to right, correlate with the illustration. However, to properly illustrate verse 11a, it was necessary to put the kings to the right of their peoples. The pertinent quotations no longer render the coherent text and can be understood only as legends.

The cathedral of St. John at Nicosia provides a similar case. Two friezes in the lower part of the huge composition are devoted to the praise of the Lord by mankind. In the middle of the upper frieze, two groups of four kings each face each other.[50] The words βασιλεῖς τῆς γῆς (beginning of Ps *148*, 11a) are written above the first two kings. The left group of kings is followed first by the *rulers* (beginning of Ps *148*, 11b), then by the lads (beginning of Ps *148*, 12a) and finally by the virgins (end of Ps *148*, 12a),[51] the right group of kings by the judges (end of Ps *148*, 11b), the presbyters (beginning of Ps *148*, 12b) and finally the *young men.* (end of Ps *148*, 12b).[52] All of them are identified by short inscriptions. πάντες λαοί are neither illustrated nor quoted, and of verse 11b only two key words have been retained, but the spurious abbreviation κ(αὶ) in κ(αὶ) παρθένοι indicates that the whole psalm text is meant. However, the inscriptions make up the canonical (though strongly abbreviated) text only on the right side, [βασιλεῖς] τῆς γῆς [καὶ πάντες] κριταὶ [γῆς] πρεσβύτεροι μετὰ νεωτέρων. To the left, continuous reading is precluded by the inverted direction; it is obvious that the inscriptions, κ(αὶ) παρθένοι νεανίσκοι ἄρχοντες βασιλεῖς, serve exclusively as legends. The lower frieze is devoted to the 149th and the 150th psalm.[53] From both sides, groups of people approach a church; the appropriate psalm verses are written above their heads. Again, only on the right side they yield a coherent text, αἰνεῖται αὐτων ἐν ἤχῳ σάλπιγγος ἐν ψαλτηρίῳ καὶ κιθάρᾳ ἐν χορῷ ἐν χορδαῖς ἐν τυμπάνῳ, Ps *150*, 3-4 though abbreviated and slightly irregular (the word ὀργάνῳ has been written in lower case letters beside the instrument). On the left, the text of each verse of Ps 149 is to be read from left to right, but the verses correlate with the illustrations which are arranged from right to left: beside the church Ps *149*, 1b, then verse 6b, followed by verse 8a,b and finally τοὺς ἐνδόξους [αὐτῶν ἐν χειρο]πέδαις σιδηραῖς. There is an analogous arrangement at Melissourgoi (Epirus, 1846).[54]

The Hymn of Mankind

Mankind praises the Lord by dance and music (Ps *149*, 3, *150*, 3-5). The musicians do not only play for the dancers, but also accompany singers. This could be expressed well in the illustration of Ps *148*, 11a, the praise of the Lord by all peoples and their kings. In Dousiko, two groups, representing *the kings of the earth* and *all peoples*, stand above the head of the *Kyrios*, hence in an outstanding position. They face each other and have their hands raised. What they sing is written in 13 lines placed between them:[55] the verses 8-11 of the *Hymn of Christ* in St. Paul's letter to the Philippians, Phil *2*, 6-11. They are an excellent choice: *He humbled himself, becoming obedient to the point of death, even to death on a cross. That is why God has highly exalted him and graciously bestowed on him the name above all other names, in order that in honour of Jesus' name every knee shall bow – all beings in heaven, on earth and in the world below –, and every tongue shall acknowledge that Jesus Christ is Lord, [to the glory of God the Father].* The name *Jesus Christ* of the canonical text is not mentioned, but as the abbreviation IC XC, it is written beside the head of the *Kyrios* of the central round picture (Ps *148*, 1).[56]

In later *laud psalms* compositions, the first king of the βασιλεῖς τῆς γῆς acts as the choirmaster. As such, he holds a scroll on which the beginning of the hymn is written which he and his companions sing: Ps *148*, 1a in three Epirotic churches of the early 17th century (Makryalexi, Monodendri, Vanista (1617)), Ps *148*, 1a,b and the first word of verse 2 in the katholikon of the Philanthropinon monastery on the island of Lake Pamvotis,[57] Ps *150*, 6 in the church of the Koimesis of the Mother of God at Stavropiyi (Mani, 1786). In the Panagia Chelmou[58] and at Tsepelovo, the beginning of Ps *148*, 1 has been added, indicating how the hymn is going on. At Mcxeta, Ps *103*, 24 [59] demonstrates that other psalms could serve the same purpose. Sometimes, the first king has the features of King David; as such, he holds a scroll with Ps *150*, 6 at Levkothea.[60]

In different context, the text on David's scroll cannot generally or not unambiguously be interpreted as the beginning of the chant of the *Faithful*. In the monastery of Timios Ioannes near Serres (1630), the text may have a twofold meaning. Christ looks out of a semicircular heaven on the people of Ps *150*, 4a.[61] Below, the nimbed kings David and Solomon stand between four men without instruments, obviously singers, five musicians (two of them playing a lute, one a kithara, one beating a drum and one blowing a wind instrument) and seven female dancers. Solomon, too, plays a kithara. David holds in his right hand a scroll which rises towards Christ; it bears the text of Ps *150*, 6. He has raised his left hand in a gesture demanding attention. The scene may describe the moment when David gives the sign to start singing, and the words on the scroll are his final exhortation: All those who use their breath for singing or to blow their wind instruments (and of course, the other musicians and the dancers, too) are requested to start praising the Lord. The location of the scroll in the centre of the composition and its upright direction may, on the other hand, express that a chant beginning with these words is being sung which rises towards the Lord.[62]

At Timios Ioannes, Melé, too, the meaning is ambiguous: King David, nimbed, stands in front of the swordbearers of Ps *149*, 6b and looks at them. His right index finger points at his scroll.[63] The text on it is no more clearly legible, but compatible with Ps *150*, 6. Either the king tells the soldiers what they shall sing, or his gesture and the text mean the words he is speaking to them. In both churches, the text on the scroll cannot be a legend, because it does not refer to what is illustrated, *viz.* Ps *150*, 4a and Ps *149*, 6b, respectively.

In the church of the Birth of Christ at Arbanasi, David is standing behind a group of people. He has raised his hand and exhorts the *Faithful* to praise the Lord *with trumpet sound* (Ps *150*, 3).[64] He is the king *speaking to* the people, not *singing with* the people. At the same time, the text meets the criteria of a legend. At Seltsou (Epirus), only the latter meaning is feasible. The text of Ps *149*, 8a is written above the captive kings as a legend. To the left, the ὅσιοι of verse 5 look at the Lord. Behind them, King David holds a long scroll with the text of Ps *149*, 5a,b.

In Hagios Panteleimon near Anatoli, there is no direct relation between David and the musicians: The king stands below the frieze with the praise of mankind in one of the squinches of the cupola.[65] Iconographically, he is a copy of David the prophet in the tambour of the cupola of the naos.[66] His function as a prophet is emphasized by the full legend Ο ΠΡΟΦVΤΗS ΔΑΒΙΔ instead of the common abbreviation.[67] He points and looks at the *Kyrios* of the central picture. His scroll flutters into the same direction; the text on it, Ps *148*, 1a, 2a, corresponds with his gesture.[68]

In most cases, the iconographic and epigraphic details indicate that the text on David's scroll is the beginning of the hymn which he and his retinue are singing. In the Episkopi at Palaiochora (Aigina, 1610), in the chapel of Hagia Paraskevi in the monastery of the Koimesis near Sophiko (nomos Korinth, 1617) and in the cathedral of St. John at Nicosia,[69] David does not *speak* to the musicians and singers of Ps *149*, 3/*150*, 3-5, but acts as their choirmaster, with the scroll in his hand. At Nicosia, the organ of Ps *150*, 4b, standing directly beside the scroll,[70] indicates that the singing is accompanied by instrumental music. At Bombokou, the text of Ps *149*, 2b serves as a legend for a picture of David and instrumentalists. The king does not hold a scroll but plays a harp to accompany his own singing. In he chapel of the Birth of St. John the Baptist of the monastery Vilitza (Epirus, 1737), Ps *150*, 1 is the legend of a scene preceding the singing of the chant of praise: King David holds a long scroll in his left hand. The text on it, again Ps *150*, 6, is the beginning of the hymn to be sung by his nimbed followers. David holds a stylos in his right hand, indicating that he is still in the course of writing, and there is still much free space on the scroll. In the visual image, writing stands for speaking; thus David is just reciting a text which begins with Ps *150*, 6. This must be the words the *Faithful* are going to sing. Ps *150*, 6 taken as David's exhortation addressed to the choir would be complete in itself and not admit an addition.

Some 18th cent. churches on the Mani peninsula contain a medallion of King David – a bust or a half figure – holding a scroll on which *laud psalms* verses are written,[71] in the churches of the Koimesis of the Mother of God at Stavropiyi, of the Metamorphosis of the Lord above Kotrona (18th cent.)[72] and of Hagios Basileios at Kelepha Ps *150*, 6. On the eastern tympanon of the aisle of Hagios Basileios, it is situated between two groups of people. According to the legend, ὕμνος πᾶσι τοῖς ὁσίοις αὐτοῦ, this is an illustration of Ps *148*, 14b. Ps *150*, 6, then, is the beginning of the hymn David and the *Faithful* are singing. On similar medallions in the church of Hagioi Theodoroi at Kampos[73] and nearby in the church of Zoodochos Piyi Zarnatas,[74] Ps *150*, 6 is followed by the next words of the hymn, Ps *148*, 1 and the first word of this verse, respectively. Ps *148*, 1 exhorts the celestial creation, not mankind, to praise the Lord. The addition, then, rules out that Ps *150*, 6 means David's address to his people. In the church of Hagios Nikolaos at Proastio, David has not been integrated into the *laud psalms* composition, but is depicted nearby; again, his scroll is inscribed with Ps *150*, 6.[75] No gesture indicates that the verse is meant as David's exhortation to do correspondingly.

At Makryalexi, David functions as the choirmaster of the lads and virgins of Ps *148*, 12a; the text on his scroll is Ps *64*, 2a.[76] In the Pateron monastery, the king stands near the inscription καὶ πάντες λάοι ἄρχοντες (Ps *148*, 11a,b)[77] and above the musicians (Ps *149*, 3?) beside an angel; again, he sings the verse Ps *64*, 2a. At Mcxeta, King David stands close to the female dancers and the musicians of Ps *150*, 3-5 and sings Ps *103*, 31.[78] At Melissourgoi, the first king of Ps *148*, 11a (as the leader of the people of Ps *148*, 11-12) and King David (as the leader of the people of Ps *150*, 1-5) face each other. David's scroll bears the same text as that of the Ps *148*, 11a king at Mcxeta: Ps *103*, 24.[79] At Sophiko, a long quotation of *laud psalms* verses above the heads of the people praising the Lord includes exceptionally Ps *150*, 6. Directly below, King David holds his scroll with the same text. If the latter represents the hymn, the text above it cannot. The doubling reveals that the long inscription functions as a legend.

It emerges that the *Faithful* (ὅσιοι, Ps *148*, 14b, *149*, 1, 5, 9) praise the Lord by singing hymns which could vary greatly: They could consist of verses of the *laud psalms* which could include verses of other psalms, or they could even lack any reference to the *laud psalms*.

The Praise of the Lord by the Hosts of Heaven

Ps 148 exhorts the *entire* creation to praise the Lord. The hosts of heaven have the duty to sing lauds to the Lord anyway. In two *laud psalms* compositions, they do so by singing the *sanctus* of the seraphim (Is *6*, 3: Ἅγιος ἅγιος ἅγιος κύριος σαβαώθ, πλήρης πᾶσα ἡ γῆ τῆς δόξης αὐτοῦ). In Hagios Georgios Armas (Euboea, 1637[80]), the seraphim hold rhipidia with the inscription ΑΓ[ι]ΟC [ἅγιος ἅγιος] Κ[υ]Ρ[i]ΟC C[α]Β[α]ωΘ ΠΛ[η]Ρ[η]C. The last words show that it is not the text of Apc. *4*, 8, ἅγιος ἅγιος ἅγιος κύριος ὁ θεὸς ὁ παντοκράτωρ, whose final word is frequently an epithet of the *Kyrios*. The letters on the rhipidia of the cherubim, ΑΓ[ι]ΟC ΑΓ[ι]ΟC ΑΓ[ι]ΟC Κ[υ]Ρ[ι]ΟC, do not permit to decide between the two quotations, but it would appear that both τάγματα as well as the other groups of the hosts of heaven praise the Lord with the same hymn. This, however, may not be a precise quotation of Is *6*, 3: In the late *laud psalms* composition in the porch of the katholikon of the monastery Iviron (Mount Athos, 1888), perhaps a rather faithful copy of the paintings of 1795 destroyed by fire, anthropomorphic angels hold a tablet with the text as used in liturgy, Ἅγιος ἅγιος ἅγιος κύριος σαβαώθ, πλήρης ὁ οὐρανός καὶ ἡ γῆ τῆς δόξης σου;[81] The liturgical origin is obvious. In the liturgy of the Eucharist this text is preceded by τὸν ἐπινίκιον ὕμνον ᾄδοντα βοῶντα κεκραγότα καὶ λέγοντα, the words which are used as epithets of the Evangelists who surround the *Kyrios* of Ps *148*, 1.[82] Nevertheless, in Iviron the paintings are an illustration of the *laud psalms* rather than a representation of liturgy.

The more obvious thing would be that in the composition of Ps *148*, 1-6, the angels praise the Lord in unison with mankind on earth. Their hymn could be accommodated in the inscription bands. Insertion of those verses on the scrolls of the kings which are typical for hymns would transform the legends – Ps *148*, 1-2 up to verse 6 – into chants of praise. Ps *150*, 6 and *64*, 2a would qualify while Ps 103 as well as the hymn of Phil *2*, 8-11 lack a point of contact and were therefore unsuitable.

Inscription Bands with Ps 150, 6

In many *laud psalms* compositions, mainly in 18th century churches on Mani and in late paintings on Mount Athos, the circular inscription bands consist of verses of Ps *148*, 1-6 preceded by Ps *150*, 6, πᾶσα πνοὴ αἰνεσάτω τὸν κύριον: At Cozia (Wallachia, *ca.* 1700)[83] and at Proastio Ps *150*, 6, *148*, 1a,b, 2a, at Dekoulou (Mani, 18th century) Ps *150*, 6, *148*, 1a,b, 2a,b + αἰνεῖτε αὐτὸν, in the Zoodochos Piyi Zarnatas

Ps *150*, 6, *148*, 1a-2b + αἰνεῖτε (*i. e.*, the beginning of verse 3), at Toskesi (Epirus, 1810) Ps *150*, 6, *148*, 1a-3a,[84] at Stavropiyi Ps *150*, 6, *148*, 1a-3b, followed by the beginning of verse 4, αἰνεῖτε αὐτὸν οἱ οὐραν[οὶ τῶν οὐρανῶν], in Hagia Sophia, Gournitsa (Mani, *ca.* 1700), Ps *150*, 6, *148*, [1a,b,] 2a,b, 3a,b, in Dochiariou II (19th cent.) Ps *150*, 6, *148*, 1a, 2a,b, 3a,b,[85] in Koutloumousiou (19th cent.) Ps *150*, 6, *148*, 1a, 2a, 3a,b, 4a,b,[86] at Kotrona Ps *150*, 6, *148*, 1a-5c (the end of verse 5c, καὶ ἐκτίσθησαν, omitted because of lack of space), at Myrsini (Laconia, 1746) Ps *150*, 6, *148*, 1a-5b, in Hagios Georgios Armas Ps *150*, 6, *148*, 1a-6b.[87] At Myrsini, the inscription band has been inserted at the periphery (*viz.*, between the zodiac (Ps *148*, 6) and the circular cloud (Ps *148*, 4)) and was thus sufficiently long to accommodate the long quotation. In Hagios Georgios Armas, the complete text of Ps *150*, 6 + *148*, 1-6 (verse 5c excepted) is distributed on two rings, Ps *150*, 6, *148*, 1a-3b between the central medallion and the angels, Ps *148*, 4a-6b between the angels and the zodiac, both as close as possible to the pertinent pictures.

Inscription Bands with Ps 64, 2a

Elsewhere the verses of the celestial praise of the Lord were augmented by Ps *64*, 2a, consistently in its variant τῷ θεῷ, occasionally twice. On the one hand, such repetitions are typical for liturgical hymns. On the other hand, the *laud psalms* quotations are sometimes insufficient to fill the bands completely. The unused space indicates that the texts are not *pars pro toto* of a longer quotation; in these cases Ps *64*, 2a might have been added as a filler.

In the Megali Panagia, Ps *148* and *149* have been illustrated though not Ps 150. The circular inscription is not entirely legible. It is to be read *from outside*. It seems to have filled the band completely and consists of Ps *148*, 1a,[b], *64*, 2a, *148*, 2[a],b, *64*, 2a. At Redina, too, Ps *64* 2a is quoted twice. The inscription is situated between the central medallion and the ring of the angels and is to be read *from within*: Ps *148*, 1a, *64*, 2a, *148*, 1a,b, *64*, 2a, followed by the beginning of Ps *148*, 2, αἰνεῖτε αὐτὸν. At Horezu (Wallachia, 1694), the connection between the inscription band and the angels has been weakened by the insertion of a circular rainbow[88] and the focus on the central *Kyrios* thus emphasized. The pertinent laud psalm verses, Ps *148*,1a, 2,a,b, were insufficient to fill the band so that a verse familiar from liturgical use was added as a filler.

At Barlaam (Meteora, 1566 or 1780/82), the inscription is restricted to Ps *148*, 2a,b and 64, 2a. The bottom part of the band, clock positions 7-6-5, was not used.[89] The inscription looks like a legend for the angels to which Ps *64*, 2a has been added as a filler. At Makryalexi, the words of Ps *148*, 1a,b, 2a,b, *64*, 2a have been written very broadly, and yet, there remained empty space at the end. Placed between the central medallion and the angels, the band fits well as a legend for which, however, Ps *64*, 2a is out of place. The verse may be explained as being copied from the scroll of King David;[90] however, the *laud psalms* in the Pateron monastery (executed by the same painters) do not provide a parallel (Ps *148*, 1a,b, 2a,b, the final word αὐτοῦ quite spread out, followed by ornaments as fillers). At Monodendri, again by the same painters, the band is in the same position and again to be read *from outside.*[91] Ps *64*, 2a has been inserted in the middle of the laud psalm quotation: Ps *148*, 1a,b, 2a,b, *64*, 2a, *148*, 3a,b, 4a. The unused end of the band was too short to be used for the initial word of verse 4b.

In the Episkopi at Palaiochora, at Sophiko and in Hagios Dimitrios at Klimatia (Epirus, not conclusively dated to the 16th cent.), the inscription has been distributed upon two rings. At Palaiochora,[92] both bands have to be read *from within.* The inner band is situated between the central medallion and the angels; it contains the same verses as in Makryalexi. Ps *148*, 1-2 would have sufficed to serve as a legend, but was too short to fill the band. The painter chose to add Ps *64*, 2a which, however, was too long. To squeeze it in completely, he had to resort to a narrower writing. The outer band quotes Ps *148*, 3a-6a, the immediate continuation of the laud psalm verses of the inner ring. As a rule, legends are written *above* the respective scene. The outer band has been inserted between the ring of the angels and the ring of the zodiac, the sun and the moon (Ps *148*, 3, 6) which in its turn is surrounded by the circular cloud (Ps *148*, 4). The inscription thus qualifies as a legend. The second part of verse 6a and the half verse 6b had to be omitted because of lack of space. The abrupt end could have been avoided, if Ps *148*, 3 had been quoted already in the inner ring rather than Ps *64*, 2a, but this position would have been inappropriate.

The tendency to place the text as close as possible to the respective scene, hence to permit to regard it as a legend, is also discernible at Sophiko. Here, both bands are to be read *from outside*, hence counter-clockwise. In the inner ring, Ps *148*, 1a,b, the appropriate legend for the central medallion, fills the clock positions 12 to 5. In the clock positions 4-3-2, Ps *64*, 2a is written in a very broad way; at the clock positions 1-12, the band is empty. By contrast, full use has been made of the space of the outer band which is situated between the angels and the zodiac; towards the end, the writing becomes narrower. The text is restricted to Ps *148*, 4a,b, 5a,b,c and the first half of verse 6a. The zodiac ring includes the sun and the moon (though no stars), but Ps *148*, 3 has not been quoted: Again, the painter did not make use of the possibility to accommodate the verse in the inner ring. In the terrestrial part, King David holds a scroll with Ps *150*, 6, the beginning of the hymn sung by mankind. The circular inscriptions provide no evidence that the celestial creation sings the same hymn.

At Klimatia, the *laud psalms* paintings have become very sooty; the two circular inscriptions are only partially legible. They have to be read *from within*. The inscription of the inner ring begins at clock position 12 and consists of Ps *148*, 1a,b, [Ps *64*, 2a], Ps *148*, 2a,b, Ps *64*, 2a. Ornaments were used as fillers and indicate that no longer inscription was intended. In the outer ring, the text consists of four parts with empty space in between; only Ps *148*, 3a and Ps *148*, 4a in the clock positions 11-12 and 5, respectively, are clearly legible. It emerges that again, the laud psalm verses served as legends. Verse 3 would have been inappropriate in the inner ring whose unused space was filled with an alien verse.

Inscription Bands with Ps 150, 6 and Ps 64, 2a

In some inscription bands Ps *150*, 6 as well as Ps *64*, 2a have been added to the celestial part of Ps 148. None of these verses has been illustrated so that the inscriptions can no longer be understood as legends. At Vilitza, King David and his retinue sing a hymn which begins with Ps *150*, 6. The bands permitted an extended quotation. Thus, the verses Ps *150*, 6, *148*, 1a,b, 2a,b, *64*, 2a may be the complete text of the hymn which the entire creation sings in praise of the Lord. The text is to be read *from within*; as an exception, it begins at the feet of the *Kyrios*. In the first quadrant (clock positions 6-9), the writing is rather narrow, thereafter much broader: On the one hand, full use should be made of the available space; on the other hand, the text is obviously complete.

In Hagios Panteleimon near Anatoli, the band contains the same verses, though Ps *64*, 2a is quoted twice: Ps *150*, 6, *148*, 1a,b, *64*, 2a, *148*, 2a,b, *64*, 2a. The repetition indicates a hymn. Unlike Vilitza, the inscription band and David's scroll are not related. The king is represented outside the frieze of *laud psalms* verses and does obviously not function as the choirmaster of the *Faithful* (*vide supra*). An abridged version is met in the Panagia Chelmou: Ps *150*, 6, *148*, 1a,b, *64*, 2a, followed by another ενειτε αυτων (sic!), written broadly to fill the space, presumably the beginning of Ps *148*, 2 which the painter preferred to break off here rather than after the word πάντες. Here, the inscription is compatible with the shorter quotation on the scroll of the first king of Ps *148*, 11a.[93]

In the cemetery chapel of the monastery Grigoriou (Mount Athos, 1739),[94] the verses Ps *150*, 6, *148*, 1a,b, *64*, 2a, *148*, 2a,b, *64*, 2a, *148*, 3,a,b are quoted. The inscription band is situated between the ring of the angels and the zodiac with the sun, the moon and stars, hence in the adequate position to function as a legend of the Ps *148*, 1-3 illustration. On the other hand, καὶ τὸ φῶς, the end of Ps *148*, 3b, has been omitted in favour of the repetition of Ps *64*, 2a. The repetition is obviously significant and indicates once more that this is the text of a hymn. In the katholikon of Grigoriou (1779), the circular band is again outside the ring of the angels.[95] Some letters following Ps *150,* 6 and Ps *148*, 1a,b are covered; the visible parts are compatible with CO so that the illegible part may be reconstructed as Ps *64*, 2a. It is followed by Ps *148*, 2a,b and Ps *64*, 2a. Ornaments fill the rest and indicate that the quotation is complete. Obviously, the band was not meant as a legend for the sun, the moon and the stars in the zodiacal ring.

In two 19th century *laud psalms* compositions, the inscription bands begin with the same verses, but are longer, at Melissourgoi Ps *150*, 6, *148*, 1a,b, *64*, 2a, *148*, 2a,b, 3a,b, 4a,b.[96] In Iviron,[97] the beginning is not clearly marked. If Ps *150*, 6 is taken as the final verse, the sequence is a selection of *laud psalms* verses in the canonical order from Ps *148*, 1a until Ps *150*, 6 though with Ps *64*, 2a being inserted. Alternatively, Ps

150, 6 may be the initial verse. The quotation, Ps *150*, 6, *148*, 1a,b, 2a,b, *64*, 2a, *150*, 4a,b, then resembles the preceding cases but is continued with verses of the praise by mankind. That mankind and the celestial creation praise the Lord in unison, is shown in the church of Hagios Achilleus at Pentalopho (1774) where, however, the composition is an eclecticism of the *laud psalms* and the illustration of the feast of *All Saints*.[98] The circular inscription is written outside the circular cloud and thus not in the celestial sphere, not on a band but above the people praising the Lord, and yet, it is not the pertinent legend: Ps *150*, 6, *148*, 1a,b, *64*, 2a, *148*, 1a,b, *64*, 2a, *148*, 2a, αἰνεῖτε αὐτὸν[99] (presumably representing the beginning of Ps *148*, 2b). Again, the repetitions indicate that it is a hymn, and this is corroborated by the fact that there is no inscription where there are no heads for singing. Instead, hail, snow and ice drop from a cloud (Ps *148*, 8).

At Arbanasi, the *laud psalms* composition contains two inscription bands.[100] The inner circle is arranged around the central medallion and reads Ps *150*, 6, *148*, 1a,b, *64*, 2a. In the surrounding ring, the angels, as an exception, have to be viewed *from within*; hence, they look towards the *Kyrios*. The outer inscription is thus situated above their heads, hence in the position typical for legends. However, it is to be read *from outside* and thus does not refer to the angels. On the other hand, it does not belong to the terrestrial sphere either, because from the latter, it is separated by the circular cloud. The text is the immediate continuation of the inner band: Ps *148*, 2a,b, *64*, 2a, *148*, 3a,b, 4a,b (the end τῶν οὐρανῶν omitted).

The Inscription Band: Legend of the Illustrations or Text of a Hymn?

Those inscription bands which are restricted to verses of Ps 148 quote only verses of the celestial praise of the Lord and thus may be regarded as legends of the illustrations (Dochiariou I, Dousiko, Karakallou, Katarrakti Oktonias, Koukouzelissa, Levkothea, Ligourio, Hagios Merkourios and Panagitsa, Mardaki (Messenia, 1635), Melé, Pateron monastery, Phaneromeni, Roussanou, Tsepelovo, Vathia, Zerbitsa). There is no evidence that they represent the texts of hymns.

In three churches in Epirus, Makryalexi, Monodendri and Vilitza, and in five churches in the Peloponnese, Kotrona, Panagia Chelmou, Proastio, Stavropiyi and Zoodochos Piyi, the circular inscription qualifies as an extended version of the texts on the scrolls of the first king of Ps *148*, 11a or of King David. At Makryalexi, the equivalency is underscored by the fact that in the circular inscription, Ps *148*, 1b-2b connects the two verses written on the scrolls of the two kings. It emerges that the inscription band renders the text of the hymn which the *entire* creation sings in praise of the Lord. At Makryalexi and at Monodendri, the hymn begins with Ps *148*, 1a, elsewhere with Ps *150,* 6. It is, then, not everywhere the same hymn. Of the hymn which begins with Ps *150*, 6, Kotrona has the most extended version; it ends with Ps *148*, 5c and thus does not exceed the celestial part of Ps 148. It does not contain Ps *64*, 2a. The texts at Stavropiyi and in Zoodochos Piyi are shorter, but have an open end and may therefore represent the same hymns.

Understood as *pars pro toto*, the inscription band at Proastio would likewise comply, but criteria are lacking. In the Panagia Chelmou, the incomplete end indicates a longer text, into which, however, Ps *64*, 2a is inserted. Ps *150*, 6 on David's scroll in the Episkopi of Palaiochora and at Sophiko as well as on the scroll of the first king of Ps *148*, 11a at Levkothea (= David) and Tsepelovo is not quoted in the respective circular inscriptions (those at Levkothea and Tsepelovo do not extend beyond Ps *148*, 3 and thus qualify as legends, as those in the Pateron monastery and at Mcxeta do; *vide supra*). At Palaiochora and at Sophiko, the insertion of Ps *64*, 2a exhibits the criteria of a filler; the verses of Ps 148 are in the fitting position to serve as a legend. Here as well as in the churches without an inscription band – Nicosia, Kampos, Philanthropinon monastery – the scroll of David or of the first king must symbolize the chant of mankind as well as of the angels. At Kampos, the extended role is indicated by the position of King David: He is not integrated into the praise of the Lord by mankind, but depicted in a medallion directly adjacent to the *Kyrios* of Ps *48*, 1,[101] obviously a borrowing from the circle of the prophets in the tambour of the naos cupola.[102] The text on his scroll is unusually long and thus can replace the inscription band. Its beginning, Ps *150*, 6, indicates that it means a hymn; its position close to the angels, but in the hand of a human permits to regard it as the common hymn sung by the entire creation.

If at Mcxeta the inscription band represents a legend, *viz*. of the illustration of Ps *148*, 1-3, the text on the scrolls of the kings could serve a different purpose: the singing even of a different hymn, here of Ps 103.

The 24th verse of this psalm is met again on King David's scroll at Melissourgoi[103] while the circular inscription, Ps *150, 6, 148,* 1a,b, *64,* 2a, *148,* 2a-4b, shows that the hosts of heaven sing an altogether different hymn. It must be taken into account that Ps *103,* 24 – according to Spitzing the most frequent quotation on David's scroll, regardless of the context[104] – has been understood as a prophecy on Christ[105] and is therefore common on the scroll of David as prophet in the tambour of the naos cupola, *e. g.* in churches which contain the *laud psalms* illustration: Lesnovo (cupola of the narthex, 1349), Vitsa (Epirus, 1618), Monodendri (Epirus, 1619), Hagios Chrysostomos at Skoutari (Laconia, 1750), in the katholikon of Hosiou Grigoriou as well as in the church of the Apostles at Kalamata.[106] At Melissourgoi, the quotation has presumably been adopted from the prototype of the Ps *148,* 1-6 composition, the program of the naos cupola. The circular inscription is the hymn sung by the creation.

On the other hand, the psalm verses above the scenes of the terrestrial praise of the Lord are not always pure legends. The *laud psalms* compositions in the church of the Metamorphosis at Milia (Mani, 18th cent.) and in Hagios Basileios at Kelepha have certainly been executed by the same painters. In both churches, these texts are arranged circularly around the circular cloud (though not on a band); therefore they can be read as a continuous inscription (*from outside*, hence counter-clockwise). Due to the great radius, much space is available; at Kelepha, full use has been made of it. As in most circular bands, a cross marks the beginning and the end. The inscription consists of Ps *148,* 1a, 2a,

3a,b, 4a,b, 7a,b, [8a,b, 9a[107]], 10a. Ps *148*, 11a, βασιλεῖς τῆς γῆς, has been written below the ring. Several verses already quoted in the circular inscription are repeated further down: καὶ πᾶσαι ἄβυσσοι adjacent to the 'sea', with the mermaid), accompanied by πῦρ χάλαζα χιών κρύσταλλος τὰ ὄρη καὶ πάντες οἱ βουνοί, ξύλα καρποφόρα. These quotations of Ps *148*, 7b, 8a, 9a,b clearly serve as legends. In the circular inscription, both parts of Ps 148 are treated as a unity. On the one hand, an exclusive function as legends is ruled out by the repetitions. On the other hand, Ps *150*, 6 and Ps *64*, 2a which would prove their character of hymns, are absent. At Milia, this is different. The circular inscription is not well preserved. Several short quotations leave unused space in between. Again, a cross above the head of the *Kyrios* marks the beginning and the end. The inscription begins with Ps *150*, 6 which is followed by Ps *148*, 1a, 2a,b, 4a,b, 10a, then by a vacant section. Beyond it, nothing is preserved. Ps *148*, 7, 9a,b, 11a, 12a and *150*, 4 (!) are not part of the circular inscription but typical legends. If Ps *150*, 6 at the beginning is taken as evidence that the circular inscription represents a hymn, then Ps *148*, 10a would prove that a hymn may include verses of the terretrial part of Ps 148. It is, however, noteworthy that in both churches, the praise of the Lord by mankind is not part of the circular inscription; the respective verses appear as legends.

In the related *laud psalms* composition at Kastanea (Mani, 18th cent.), verses of the terrestrial praise of the Lord are distributed all over the illustration, accompanying the respective scenes as legends.

Above the mountains and trees of Ps *148, 9*, a continuous inscription follows the curvature of the circular cloud, though not in a band. The verses Ps *148, 9a,b, 10a* qualify as legends, but they are preceded by Ps *150, 6* and Ps *148, 1a,b*. They are located above the head of the *Kyrios* (Ps *148, 1*) in the clock positions 10-11-12-1-2. The remaining two thirds of the circle remained vacant. Hence, the inscription, though curved, is not *circular*.

It is however questionable whether Ps *150, 6* is a safe criterion for a hymn. Repeatedly, the verse became independent. At Kleidonia (Epirus, 1617), it assumed the role of the title of the entire composition, just as Ps *148, 1* did at Lesnovo. In the monastery Philotheou (Mount Athos, 1752/65 or 1848), the ring of the angels is accompanied by πάντες οἱ ἄγγελοι αὐτοῦ (Ps *148, 2a*, in the clock positions 7-6-5) as a legend as well as by Ps *150, 6* (in the clock positions 1-12-11).[108] The katholikon of the monastery Xeropotamou (Mount Athos, 1783) features three rings outside the picture of the *Kyrios* which contain fragmentary inscriptions: Ps *150, 6* between the medallion and the angels, Ps *148, 4b* between the angels and the circular band of the stars, and Ps *148, 3b within* the band of the stars,[109] here certainly a legend. Ps *148, 4b* serves to identify the adjacent grey band as the circular cloud. The three quotations from Ps 148 do not yield a coherent text; by analogy, Ps *150, 6* has to be regarded as an independent quotation serving as the title of the entire composition. The *Kyrios* of the Ps *148, 1* illustration bears frequently the epithet *Pantokrator*; at Bombokou and at Kozani, this word has been replaced by πᾶσα πνοή.

Since the early days of research on the *laud psalms* illustrations, it has been postulated that these paintings and the accompanying texts are the visual version of particular liturgical hymns, *viz.* the chants sung at the end of the ὄρθρος service: either the complete text of Ps 148-150 is sung or, on Sundays and certain feast days, the three verses Ps *150, 6, 148, 1, 64,* 2a.[110] If indeed, the circular inscriptions first were legends which only in the course of time and after appropriate adjustment became hymns to praise the Lord, no strict conformity with these chants can be expected, and, in fact, there is none. The standard version is ruled out, because it consists of all three *laud psalms* while the circular inscriptions never exceed Ps *148,* 6. To be sure, Ps *150,* 6 is frequently quoted, but it is not compulsory, and its position is always at the beginning and not at the end. Frequently, Ps *64,* 2a is inserted which is not part of the common ὄρθρος chant. Furthermore, the pictorial scenes do not correspond with the weekdays chant in so far as the early paintings and some later ones are restricted to Ps 148 and 149 or even to Ps 148; in most compositions which include Ps 150, the final verse was ignored (*vide supra*).[111]

The Sunday version does not match either. Though never comprehensive, the illustration is always detailed. The final verse of the Sunday version is never illustrated, the beginning seldom. The inscription bands feature occasionally the sequence of the Sunday hymn, though never as a distinct unit, but either as the beginning of a longer text, or with insertions of other verses of the first part of Ps 148. At Arbanasi, the inner band contains comprehensively and exclusively the verses of the Sunday ὄρθρος chant.[112] However, the inner and the outer circular inscription constitute a unit so that, again, this cannot be taken as a quotation of the Sunday ὄρθρος hymn. The same sequence of verses is encountered in several other churches. In the Panagia Chelmou, at Melissourgoi, at Pentalopho as well as in the cemetery chapel and the katholikon of the monastery Grigoriou the continuation precludes to view it as the ὄρθρος chant, at Vilitza the insertion of Ps *148*, 2, in Iviron both verse *148*, 2 and the continuation. In Hagios Panteleimon near Anatoli, the carefully written circular inscription consists of two equal parts which are separated from each other by a kind of punctuation mark: at clock position 12, the beginning and end of the inscription, a cross with a dot in each angle, at clock position 6 two dots with a horizontal dash in between. The semicircle of the clock positions 12-1-2-3-4-5-6 accommodates the verses Ps *150*, 6, *148*, 1a,b, *64*, 2a, the other semicircle the verses Ps *148*, 2a,b, *64*, 2a. Both parts can be viewed as the legends of the illustrations at either side of the band to which Ps *64*, 2a has been added as a filler. On the other hand, the hiatus at clock position 6 affords some autonomy to the first part which is – perhaps accidentally – the text of the Sunday ὄρθρος hymn. However, read as a whole, the circular inscription does not represent one of the common hymns.

The other verses on the scrolls of King David and the first king of Ps *148*, 11a, too, experienced liturgical use. The psalms 64-69, and hence Ps *64*, 2a at the beginning, are sung in the Saturday Ἀκολουθία μεσονύκτικου. However, this cannot be the source of the quotation either, because in the midnight service, the canonical text, σοὶ πρέπει ὕμνος, ὁ θεός, ἐν Σειὼν, is sung[113] while the inscriptions consistently use the dative version, τῷ θεῷ, as is the case in the Sunday ὄρθρος service.[114] At Mcxeta, the verses Ps *103*, 24 on the scroll of the first king of Ps *148*, 11a and Ps *103*, 32 on David's scroll may symbolize that mankind sings the complete psalm 103.[115] This psalm is part of the Ἀκολουθία τοῦ ἑσπερινοῦ,[116] but no criteria suggest the evening service as the source. At least for verse 24, an alternative explanation is at hand (*vide supra*).

The conclusion, then, is that many circular inscriptions, in particular those in later paintings, do represent hymns by which the entire creation praises the Lord, but that these hymns cannot be equated with the chants sung at the end of the ὄρθρος or in other services, furthermore that these hymns are not the verbal equivalent of the illustrations, and finally that the *laud psalms* cycles are not the visual representation of distinct liturgical chants. The reason why out of 150 psalms only the final three have been selected for church wall painting, must be looked for elsewhere.

Kyrios Jesus Christos

The first verses of Ps 148 contain seven times the exhortation to praise the *Kyrios*. In verse 5a and again in the terrestrial part of the psalm (Ps *148*, 13a) it is the *name of the Kyrios* which shall be praised. In Dousiko and a few years later in Roussanou and in

Dochiariou I, it is clearly stated who this Old Testament *Kyrios* is: In later *laud psalms* compositions, the text of the circular inscription begins and ends almost invariably above the head of Christ (clock position 12); in these three churches, it starts at clock position 10½;[117] the Pantokrator points with his right hand[118] to the first word of Ps *148*, 1. The abbreviation KN for κύριον is located just beside the letters IC which, together with XC, frame the crossed nimbus of Christ. If the reader leaves at this point the circular inscription and turns right, the text acquires a new meaning: αἰνεῖτε τὸν κ(ύριο)ν IC XC ὁ Παντοκράτωρ. The verbal and the pictorial message become identical in Pauline exegesis:[119] *Kyrios Jesus Christos*. This is the essence of the acclamation which the *kings and all peoples* address to the *Kyrios* in Dousiko: *in honour of Jesus' name every knee shall bow – all beings in heaven, on earth and in the world below –, and every tongue shall acknowledge that Jesus Christ is Lord*, the end, *to the glory of God the Father*, omitted because of lack of space as on many scrolls.[120] In Karakallou, the composition is iconographically identical. The circular inscription is to be read *from outside*, hence counter-clockwise. It begins near the head of the *Kyrios* (with the letters IC XC beside the shoulders) so that his right hand points to the word K(ύριο)N.[121]

Ps *149*, 3a resumes the exhortation αἰνεσάτωσαν τὸ ὄνομα κυρίου of Ps *148*, 5a, 13a; Ps 150 begins with αἰνεῖτε τὸν θεὸν, the next four verses with αἰνεῖτε αὐτὸν. The final verse is a minute variation of the beginning, Ps *148*, 1, in which the words τὸν κύριον are picked up. This way, both Ps 149 and Ps 150, though not essential, were well suited to supplement the message of Ps 148.

Thus, the *laud psalms* composition is an exhortation to confess that Jesus Christ is the Lord. In the *Last Judgment*, Moses tries to induce the Jews and other unbelievers (including heretical Christians) to make the same confession.[122] He holds a scroll which contains the words he is speaking. In the Phaneromeni monastery, it is an abridged version of the speech which St. Peter addressed to the Jews with the same intention: *Therefore let all the house of Israel know assuredly that God has made that same Jesus, whom you have crucified, both Lord and Christ*, ὅτι καὶ κύριον αὐτὸν καὶ χριστὸν ἐποίησεν ὁ θεός (Acts *2*, 36).[123] Elsewhere the Lord himself speaks through Moses' mouth (Dt *32*, 39): ἴδετε ἴδετε ὅτι ἐγώ εἰμι καὶ οὐκ ἔστιν θεὸς πλὴν ἐμοῦ. ἐγώ ἀποκτεννω καὶ ζῆν ποιήσω. Strongly abbreviated, this is the most frequent text on the scroll of the *Kyrios* in the *laud psalms* cycles.

The *Hermeneia*[124] prescribes Dt *32*, 39 until πλὴν ἐμοῦ + Is *45*, 12 for the circular inscription around the Pantokrator of the naos cupola; in the monastery Philotheou, it has been relegated to the calotte of a side chapel. In the naos cupola, other psalm quotations are much more frequent, in particular Ps *32*, 13[125] which occurs at Makryalexi on the scroll of the Ps *148*, 1 *Kyrios* (*vide supra*). By analogy, Dt *32*, 39 on the scrolls may be ascribed to an adoption from the naos cupola. However, in Dousiko, Roussanou and Dochiariou I, the scroll text is different in so far as the first sentence is not followed by Is *45*, 12, but by the second part of Dt *32*, 39,[126] and in Roussanou and Dochiariou I, the word θεός is preceded by ἄλλος. The addition points to a contamination with Is *45*, 21, 22: ἐγώ [only in verse 22: εἰμι] ὁ θεός, καὶ οὐκ ἔστιν ἄλλος [only in verse 21: πλὴν ἐμοῦ]. This statement of the Lord is immediately followed by the prototype of the *Hymn of Christ* in Phil 2, Is *45*, 23, ὅτι ἐμοὶ κάμψει πᾶν γόνῦ καὶ ὁμεῖται πᾶσα γλώσσα τὸν θεόν, *to me, every knee shall bow and every tongue shall acknowledge God*. In different phrasing, this is what Moses tells the Jews and the unbelievers in the *Last Judgment*.

Much later, an abbreviated version of the second part of Dt *32*, 39 is met in the Phaneromeni monastery: ...ὅτι ἐγώ εἰμι ΘC. ἐγώ ἀποκτενω κ(αὶ). On the other hand, the scrolls in three churches situated in rather different regions depend more on Is *45*, 21-23: Anatoli ηδετε ιδετε οτι εγω ημει κ(αὶ) ουκ εστι αλως ΘC πλ(ὴν) εμου; Milia ιδεται ιδεται οτι εγω ημη ο θεος, και πλην εμου ουκ εστιν αλλος; Redina: ιδετε ιδετε οτι εγω ημι ο ΘC κ(αὶ) ουκ εστιν αλος; πλην εμου. At Vilitza, the introductory words ἴδετε ἴδετε ὅτι are followed by the precise text of Is *45*, 21.[127] In the majority of churches, the quotation has been reduced to the essentials: ἴδετε ἴδετε ὅτι ἐγώ [εἰμι ὁ] θεὸς (Androbevitsa (Mani, 1704), Ano Doloi (Mani, 1752), Grigoriou, cemetery chapel, Kastanea, Ligourio, Hagios Merkourios and Panagitsa, Mardaki, Mcxeta, Myrsini, Palaiochora, Panagia Chelmou, Proastio, Sophiko, Xeropotamou, Zerbitsa). In Karakallou, the meaning as in Phaneromeni is somewhat shifted by the addition of ὁ πιστός which goes back to Dt *32*, 4 (θεὸς πιστός καὶ … δίκαιος καὶ ὅσιος κύριος) as well as Is *45*, 21 (… θεός …δίκαιος καὶ σωτήρ).[128] At Dekoulou, it is left to the reader how to complete the quotation ἴδετε ἴδετε ὅτι ἐγώ. Exod *3*, 14, ἐγώ εἰμι ὁ ὤν,[129] cited in Hagios Georgios Armas, has the same meaning; in its abbreviated version ὁ ὤν in the nimbus of the *Kyrios* it is ubiquitous.

It has been known for a long time that the *laud psalms* illustrations are much indebted to the *Last Judgment*.[130] It appears that also their theological meaning is related. It may therefore not be accidental that both have often been painted close to each other, *e. g.* in a narthex,[131] the *Last Judgment* frequently on its eastern wall, the *laud psalms* in the vault (Mardaki,[132] Melé) or in a calotte (Barlaam, Roussanou, Hurezu, Cozia, the Colţea church),[133] so that those who entered and raised their heads, first viewed the *Last Judgment* and higher up the *laud psalms*. In the narthex of Hagios Nikolaos Vathias, the *laud psalms* are located in the longitutinal vault and the eastern tympanon, the *Last Judgment* on the western wall. In the church of Hagios Georgios at Nigrita (Thrace, 18th cent.), the entry from the narthex into the naos is framed by the *Last Judgment* and the *laud psalms* at the southern and the northern part of the eastern wall, respectively. In the narthex of the church of Sts Peter and Paul at Levkothea, the *Last Judgment* is below the terrestrial praise of the Lord of the *laud psalms*; its central part, the Pantokrator between angels and Adam and Eve kneeling at his feet, projects into the upper zone, separating the verses Ps *148*, 7-10 and 11. The enthroned judge is depicted right below the *Kyrios* of Ps *148*, 1.[134]

In small barrel-vaulted churches, the usual location of the *laud psalms* is the western part of the vault, that of the *Last Judgment* the western wall (*e. g.*, at Dekoulou, Kastanea, Katarrakti Oktonias and Kotrona). At Kelepha, the *laud psalms* occupy the barrel vault and both tympana of the aisle; on the western wall, below the illustration of Ps *148*, 7-10, the hosts of heaven (31 anthropomorphic angels) are depicted and in front of them the apostles John, Mark, Simon, Bartholomew and Philipp holding scrolls. In a number of churches (Dekoulou, Kastanea,[135] Kotrona, Proastio, probably also at Kampos), the *laud psalms* scenes in the barrel vault frame the *Crucifixion* on the western tympanon and the *Last Judgment* on the western wall. At Ano Doloi and in Hagios Dimitrios at Klimatia, the western wall including the tympanon has been used to accommodate both the *Crucifixion* and parts of the *laud psalms*, at Ano Doloi the birds of Ps *148*, 10, at Klimatia the groups of Ps *148*, 11-12, *149*, 3 / *150*, 3-5. Again, the *Hymn of Christ* provides the connection: In it, the glorification of the *Kyrios* according to Is *45*, 23 is preceded by the humiliation by his death on the cross (Phil *2*, 8: *he humbled himself by becoming obedient to the point of death, even to death on a cross*). This way, it has been visualized what in Dousiko the kings and peoples sing in praise of the Lord: Above the words of the promotion to *Kyrios* (Phil *2*, 9-11)[136] is written ὁ ΚΣ μέχρι θανάτου (St Paul: θανάτου δὲ σταυροῦ). In the *laud psalms* composition at Vilitza, the *Crucifixion* is indicated by the distinct marks of the wounds on the right hand and in both feet of the *Kyrios*.[137] At Sistrouni[138] and Toskesi (both in Epirus),[139] the raised arms of the enthroned *Kyrios* may express this meaning though no wound marks are visible (the fingers of both hands show the gesture of speaking; this does not rule out such interpretation, because according to Lk *24*, 39-40 Jesus, after his resurrection, shows his wound marks while speaking to the disciples[140]).

The *Last Judgment* is ambivalent: At his second *parousia*, Christ is either ὁ φοβερὸς κριτής, the *terrible judge*,[141] or *the benevolent judge*. It is the latter to whom Moses tries to lead the unbelievers and heretics so that they, too, may gain admission to Paradise.[142] Christ's invitation is expressed by an appropriate gesture of his hands,[143] *e. g.* in the *Last Judgment* at Levkothea, Horezu and Cozia[144] (always below the *laud psalms* composition) as well as in the Megali Panagia, a gesture which also occurs in *laud psalms* cycles (in Timios Ioannes near Serres in the illustration of Ps *150*, 4a[145]). In St. John's cathedral at Nicosia, the *Kyrios* of Ps *148*, 1 holds his right hand in the gesture of speaking, his left hand in the gesture of invitation.[146] At Horezu and Cozia, his right arm is slightly turned downward, the typical gesture of invitation, while the fingers indicate speaking, as a whole an expression of the verbal invitation of the Lord.

To sum up: In wall painting, the *laud psalms* have not been illustrated for their own sake – the visual version of two percent of the psalter –, nor are they the illustration of a particular liturgical hymn. They serve to communicate a distinct theological statement: Together with the *Crucifixion* and the *Last Judgment*, they shall convey the message *Kyrios Jesus Christos*, that *Jesus Christ is the Lord*. The *laud psalms* are only the means by which the message is transmitted; only the message is important, not the means.

Ps 148 would have sufficed to proclaim the message *Kyrios Jesus Christos*. Addition of the 149th psalm permitted to specify the meaning in more than one way. The praise of the Lord shall be performed ἐν ἐκκλησίᾳ ὁσίων (Ps *149*, 1), *in the church of the Faithful* in Christian interpretation.[147] Read across the border to verse 2, a new sentence emerged, ἐν ἐκκλησίᾳ ὁσίων εὐφρανθήτω Ἰσραὴλ ἐπὶ τῷ ποιήσαντι αὐτόν, *in the church of the Faithful Israel [God's new people, the Orthodox Christians] shall be glad in the one who made it*.[148] Ps *149*, 8 assured that even the rulers of the unbelievers eventually must submit to the Pantokrator (the prospect may be eschatological or Messianic or political[149]). In some *laud psalms* cycles, this aspect has been taken into account by the participation of the kings and nobles of Ps *149*, 8a,b in the procession of the *Faithful* to the church (and thus to the *Kyrios Jesus Christos*).[150] Ps *149*, 4-5 is the promise that all oppression will come to an end. Ps *149*, 3 is devoted to the feast of victory in which the Lord is worshipped by dance and music; addition of Ps *150*, 3-5 could serve to enhance its impact.

All this is summarized in Ps *150*, 6, but the verse contains nothing what has not been said and illustrated before. Therefore an independent illustration was dispensable. Occasionally, it was incorporated into the feast of victory (Galataki,[151] Hagios Nikolaos Vathias, Tsepelovo). The message of Ps *150*, 6 is the same as that of Ps *148*, 1; Ps *64*, 2a, σοὶ πρέπει ὕμνος τῷ θεῷ, and Ps *148*, 14b, ὕμνος πᾶσι τοῖς ὁσίοις αὐτοῦ, are essentially synonymic, too. In this view both verses cease to be alien elements in the circular inscriptions: It does not matter which particular hymn is chosen to praise *Kyrios Jesus Christos*, whether a hymn sung in the ὄρθρος or the *Hymn of Christ* of Phil *2*, 8-11. The title of the composition, Ps *148*, 1 and Ps *150*, 6 respectively, has the same meaning at Lesnovo and at Kleidonia. The final word of the *laud psalms*, *Kyrios*, is a synonym of *Pantokrator*.[152] At Bombokou and at Kozani, the quotation of Ps *150*, 6 instead of the word *Pantokrator* testifies this synonymity.

»Omnis spiritus laudet dominum«
Psalm *150*, 6 and the Realm of Spirits
in the Illustration of the *Laud Psalms*

Contents

Introduction
The *laud psalms* in 14th and 16th centuries wall
painting
ADOLPHE N. DIDRON and the *Hermeneia*
The chronicle of a misapprehension
The *laud psalms* paintings – literal text
illustration or more?
The Ps 150 miniature in the Carolingian Stuttgart
psalter
From τὸ πᾶσα πνοή to the realm of spirits
The singers and their chant
The role of Ps *149*, 1-2 in the illustration of the *laud
psalms*
Illustration: The Stuttgart Psalter, Ps 150

Introduction

The last three psalms, the *laud psalms*,[1] have been extensively illustrated in two, possibly three churches
decorated during the reign of the Serbian Tsar Stefan
Dušan.[2] From the 16th century on, *laud psalms* paintings are known in all Orthodox countries except Russia, though not widespread and initially restricted to

the 148th psalm.[3] In miniature painting, *laud psalms* illustration begins earlier, but in illuminated psalter manuscripts, all psalms have been illustrated[4] more or less evenly.[5] The question why only the last psalms found access to wall painting has attracted scholarly attention, but proposed explanations made use of insufficiently supported hypotheses which were at variance with some facts and not always compatible with each other. The result suggests that the key for the lock of proper understanding has not yet been found. A new look at the facts and the arguments seems, therefore, desirable. In the previous discussion, the final verse of the psalter, Ps *150*, 6, plays a key role. The following analysis focusses on this verse, πᾶσα πνοὴ αἰνεσάτω τὸν κύριον, *omnis spiritus laudet dominum*, *let all breath praise the Lord*.

The Laud Psalms in 14th and 16th Centuries Wall Painting

The earliest *laud psalms* paintings on Greek soil are in the *lite* of the monastic churches of Dousiko (1557/58) and Roussanou (1560), both in Thessaly, and of Dochiariou (1568), Mount Athos; all of them end with Ps *148*, 14.[6] In Chrelju's tower in the Rila monastery (after 1334/35) and in the narthex of the catholicon of Lesnovo (1349), psalms 148 and 149 are illustrated, but there is no detail which can unambiguously be assigned to Ps 150.[7] An illpreserved series of scenes in the catholicon of Kučevište is believed to be an illustration of the *laud psalms*[8] because of a scene of singers and musicians playing wind and string instruments.[9] This does not permit to identify the scene as an illustration of Ps 150, because at Lesnovo, a round dance performed with accompanying music is, according to an inscription, the illustration of Ps *149*, 3.[10] A detailed assignment of the panels in Kučevište to individual verses of the *laud psalms*[11] lacks convinving arguments and leaves doubts whether in Kučevište the *laud psalms* are at all depicted. In conclusion, a privileged role of Ps 150 and particularly of its final verse is not discernible in these early paintings.

Adolphe N. Didron and the Hermeneia

Ps *150*, 6 owes its special role to a remark of ADOLPHE NAPOLÉON DIDRON. During his visit of the Holy Mountain Athos in 1839, DIDRON had discocered the *Painters' Guide*, Ἑρμηνεία τῆς ζωγραφικῆς τέχνης (henceforth: *Hermeneia*). A French translation was printed in 1845.[12] In the book, *ca.* 380 compositions are described (plus many individual saints). It is, though, not comprehensive; the illustration of the *laud psalms* is not described. On the other hand, the Communion of the Apostles is followed and the Revelation preceded by a composition whose Greek title is τὸ πᾶσα πνοή.[13] This is the beginning of verse Ps *150*, 6. A misinterpretation of a note of DIDRON generated the opinion that the τὸ πᾶσα πνοή chapter is the description of the *laud psalms* composition. The *opinion* gradually developed into a generally accepted fact. Both compositions are praises of the Lord who is surrounded by the Hosts of Heaven. More than the *laud psalms* illustration, the πᾶσα πνοή chapter is indebted to the iconography of the Pantocrator in the *Second*

Coming and the *Last Judgment*.[14] *E. g.*, only the πᾶσα πνοή chapter includes the Mother of God and St. John Prodromos, the minor figures of the Deesis. In the terrestrial sphere of the praise of the Lord, both compositions are entirely different.[15] In the chapter on the *Second Coming* of the *Hermeneia*, nine *choruses* of *All Saints* praise the Lord;[16] in the πᾶσα πνοή chapter, they show up under the name τὰ τάγματα τῶν ἁγίων πάντων.[17] In the *laud psalms* illustrations, Ps *148*, 6-14, the 149th psalm and in many cases verses 1-5 of the 150th psalm are depicted in a detailed, literal way (Ps *148*, 6, devoted to the unalterable course of the stars, by the zodiac[18]), while verses of more abstract contents including Ps *150*, 6 are often disregarded.[19] Equating the *laud psalms* compositions with the πᾶσα πνοή chapter was facilitated by the fact that both contain inscription bands with related texts. In the *Hermeneia* chapter, such a band separates the celestial from the terrestrial sphere. It quotes Ps *150*, 6, *148*, 1, *64*, 2[20] and can be interpreted as the text of the hymn which the Hosts of Heaven and the terrestrial *Just* sing in praise of the Lord. The beginning serves as the title of the composition which meets all criteria of the illustration of *All Saints* (Sunday after Pentecost[21]) mentioned at the end of the *Hermeneia*.[22] Russian icons, painted tablets as well as ivory carvings, comply well with the πᾶσα πνοή chapter[23] and frequently include extended quotations of the *laud psalms*, often beginning with Ps *148*, 1, in Russian ХВАЛИТЄ ГОСПОДА С НЄБЄСЪ (Ps *148*, 1a, b, 2a on an ivory tablet in Weimar, Ps *148*, 1a, b, 2a + the beginning of 2b on an almost identical tablet in Baltimore, Ps *148*, 1a, b, 2b on a tablet in St. Petersburg, Ps *148*, 1 - 4 on a tablet in Sergiev Posad, ending abruptly after и вода), which again may represent the hymns sung by *All Saints* in praise of the Lord.[24] The omission of Ps *148*, 2a in the St. Petersburg tablet may indicate that the choice of these hymns enjoyed some flexibility. Ps *150*, 6, which provided the title of the chapter in the *Hermeneia*, thus proved characteristic, but not essential.

The verses Ps *150*, 6, *148*, 1, *64*, 2, mentioned in the πᾶσα πνοή chapter, were used as a hymn sung on Sundays and holidays at the end of the matins (ὄρθρος).[25] Here, too, some flexibility existed in so far as on weekdays, the full text of the *laud psalms*, beginning with Ps *148*, 1, was sung.[26] The ὄρθρος thus draws from the same sources as *All Saints*, occasionally the same, frequently different verses, and it cannot be surprising that these sources were also used for their own sake, the illustration of the *laud psalms*. In the Koukouzelissa chapel of the Great Lavra (Athos) and in the *lite* of the catholicon of Dochiariou (as well as in Dousiko, Roussanou and elsewhere, e. g. in Karakallou (Athos)), this circular inscription is situated between the central picture of the Pantocrator (Ps *148*, 1) and the circle of the angels (Ps *148*, 2), arranged in the nine τάγματα of Pseudo-Dionysios Areopagites; it consists of Ps *148*, 1 + 2a (Lavra), Ps *148*, 1 + 2 (Dousiko, Roussanou, Dochiariou, Karakallou).[27] In these cases, the circular inscription lacks features indicating a hymn; it is in full accord with the neighbouring illustrations, and analogous to the annotations explaining the illustrations of other verses here and elsewhere. It consequently can be viewed as a legend. In Dochiariou, in the Thessalian paintings and in Karakallou, the addition of Ps *148*, 2b is motivated by the word δυνάμεις,[28] the name of one of the τάγματα of Pseudo-Dionysios Areopagites.[29] In many later *laud psalms* cycles, this concise legend has been replaced by a longer quotation. It frequently begins with Ps *150*, 6, quotes verses of Ps 148 with some liberty regarding their number and selection, and often includes Ps *64*, 2. Occasionally, this verse is quoted twice,[30] indicating a hymn text.[31] In these cases the inscription band is likely to represent the chant sung by the celestial part of the creation in praise of the Lord.

The humans praising the Lord (Ps *148*, 11 sqq., Ps 150) are not always singing the same hymns as the Hosts of Heaven: The first king of Ps *148*, 11 as well as King David when depicted in the illustration of Ps *150*, 3-5, often hold a scroll inscribed with the beginning of the hymn which they and their companions sing.[32] While many of these scroll texts begin with Ps *150*, 6,[33] others consist of different verses, sometimes even not taken from the *laud psalms*.[34] Neither the scroll texts beginning with πᾶσα πνοή nor the circular inscriptions correlate with the figurative paintings which in their turn do not exhibit any influence of the liturgy. The circular inscriptions are never identical with one of the two ὄρθρος chants,[35] and Ps *64*, 2 has never been illustrated. It follows that the circular inscriptions which feature liturgical characteristics are not legends of the figurative paintings and therefore do not suggest to interpret these paintings as *painted liturgy*, in particular as an illustration of the Sunday version of the final hymn of the ὄρθρος.[36]

The Chronicle of a Misapprehension

DIDRON adequately called the πᾶσα πνοή composition *a sort of tedeum* sung by Paradise, the various choruses of saints and almost by the entire nature in honour of Christ.[37] Intending to mark out the vast realm
of the glorification of God, he adduced a number of
examples, but most of them are vague and far-fetched.
Only one of them, the so-called dalmatic of Charlema-
gne in Rome, is really pertinent.[38] In this context, he
extensively described the *laud psalms* paintings in the
monastery Iviron on Mount Athos. DIDRON's phrasing clearly shows that he did *not* present the paintings in Iviron as a realization of the πᾶσα πνοή prescriptions of the *Hermeneia*. Later authors, however,
alleged that he did. The protagonist of the misapprehension is JOSEF STRZYGOWSKI who in 1888[39] saw
several *laud psalms* paintings on Mount Athos. He
summarized "*τò πᾶσα πνοή. Das Malerbuch... nennt
so eine große zyklische Darstellung, die sich öfter in
den Vorhallen der Kirchen des Athos gemalt findet.*"[40]
From the quotation of Ps *150*, 6 in the circular inscription of Koutloumousiou and the title of the *Hermeneia* chapter he concluded that these compositions included Ps 150; he mentioned the *Engelchöre* (choruses of angels, Ps *148*, 2) and the *Planetenkreis* (*the
circle of the planets*, Ps *148*, 6, actually the zodiac)
and remarked *Man vergleiche dazu das Malerbuch*[41]
which, however, does not mention the zodiac. STRZY-
GOWSKI also referred to the *russischen Analogien.*

Shortly before STRZYGOWSKI, HEINRICH BROCK-
HAUS visited Mount Athos.[42] He, too, treated the *laud*

psalms paintings, in particular those in the *lite* of Dochiariou, and the *Hermeneia* chapter as equivalent.[43] He failed to notice that in Dochirariou, Ps 150 is neither illustrated nor quoted in the inscriptions.[44] In somewhat vague phrasing, he correlated the *laud psalms* paintings with the πᾶσα πνοή chapter and the two ὄρθρος hymns though he did not expressly say that they are their direct illustration. In 1894, FRANZ WICKHOFF called, in disregard of its title, the πᾶσα πνοή chapter, *eine Composition ..., die nichts anderes ist als eine Darstellung des 148. Psalms*, equivalent with the *laud psalms* paintings in Iviron. WICKHOFF adopted DIDRON's opinion that the central part is surrounded by a circular inscription in which *die Worte des 148. Psalms geschrieben sind*.[45] In fact, the paintings which DIDRON had seen, were not restricted to the 148th psalm. Parts of the paintings of 1795[46] still exist and illustrate Ps *149*, 6-8.[47] The new paintings of 1888[48] conform so well with DIDRON's description that they are likely to be a copy of the earlier ones. Other verses of Ps 149 are illustrated; *e. g.* Ps *149*, 1-2a by a church.[49] Ps 150 is taken into account by the text of Ps *150*, 1-2a written on a book displayed on a table (STRZYGOWSKI: an altar[50]) situated beside the *prophetanax* David.[51] Already DIDRON and then STRZYGOWSKI assigned David, Solomon and the musicians accompanying the kings to the 150th psalm.[52] Two round dances are part of the praise of the Lord by the terrestrial creation. STRZYGOWSKI assigned both of them to Ps *150*, 3-5.[53] However, one of them is performed by boys, the υἱοὶ Σειὼν, and thus illustrates Ps *149*, 2-3.[54] The other one, performed by women, can be assigned to Ps *150*, 4. For the inscription separating the celestial from the terrestrial sphere, the paintings of 1888 do not conform with DIDRON's description. According to DIDRON, there are *écrits en grec les versets du psaume CXLVIII* whose verses 2-4 and 7-12 are discussed in detail.[55] In the paintings of 1888, the signs of the zodiac are interspersed among the verses Ps *148*, 1, 2, *64*, 2, *150*, 4, 6. The cyclic arrangement permits to read the text in the sequence Ps *150*, 6, *148*, 1, 2, *64*, 2, *150*, 4, hence as the Sunday version of the ὄρθρος hymn,[56] but extended by Ps *148*, 2 and Ps *150*, 4. The round dance of the women is placed below the quotation of Ps *64*, 2 rather than that of Ps *150*, 4; hence, this verse did not serve as a legend. The insertion of a verse not illustrated, *viz.* Ps *64*, 2, indicates that the inscription does not refer to the pictures, but renders a chant which, however, is not one of the ὄρθρος hymns.

In 1895, EGOR RJEDIN judged the *Hermeneia* chapter, one of the Russian *Chvalite gospoda* icons and a wall painting of the same subject at Jaroslavl as equivalent, but included the *laud psalms* paintings in the Koukouzelissa chapel, and regarded all of them as illustrations of Ps 148.[57] However, in the Koukouzelissa chapel, verses of all three *laud psalms* have been illustrated.[58] Ps *150*, 6, the title verse in the *Hermeneia* chapter, is illustrated neither in Iviron nor in the Koukouzelissa chapel.

In 1927, GABRIEL MILLET, obviously inspired by the *Hermeneia* chapter, published photographs of the Ps 148 paintings in the catholicon of Dochiariou (with the circular inscription Ps *148*, 1-2) and of the praise of the Lord by the humans (ending with Ps *150*, 4) in the Koukouzelissa chapel with the legend *Que tout ce qui respire loue le Seigneur* (= Ps *150*, 6).[59] Four years later, FRITZ FICHTNER equated the *laud psalms* paintings in Dochiariou and Karakallou with the πᾶσα πνοή chapter[60] (the paintings in Karakallou include the 149th psalm, but not Ps 150[61]). A connection with liturgy was addressed, but remained vague (*Die Darstellung Christi nimmt Bezug auf den Lobpreis Gottes "Alles, was Odem hat, lobe den Herrn"*). In 1973, KONSTANTINOS D. KALOKYRIS called the *laud psalms* paintings at Mardaki, Melé (Messenia) and elsewhere summarily τὸ θέμα «Πᾶσα πνοή».[62] Later, PAUL HUBER regarded the *laud psalms* paintings in the porch of Koutloumousiou and at the entrance to the icon chapel between the catholicon and the trapeza in Dochiariou without reservation as realizations of the *Hermeneia* prescriptions.[63] In both cases, the circular inscription begins with the verse Ps *150*, 6 which, however, has not been illustrated; in Koutloumousiou, it is continued with Ps *148*, 1a, 2a, 3a, 3b, 4a, 4b, in Dochiariou with Ps *148*, 1a, 2, 3: Only the beginning is as recommended by the *Hermeneia*. In either case, the illustrations have nothing in common with the circular inscriptions; they are not restricted to the verses Ps *148*, 1-4 and include verses of the 149th psalm. Details not in compliance with the psalm text which require the assumption of a dependence from liturgy, are non-existent. In 1986, the singers and the musicians playing their instruments in Kučevište, compatible with Ps *149*, 3 as well as with Ps *150*, 3-5, but neither with Ps *150*, 6 nor with the πᾶσα πνοή chapter of the *Hermeneia*, have been called *Pasa Pnoe*.[64]

In the *Chvalite gospoda* icons, the *laud psalms* inscriptions accompanying the figurative paintings are situated occasionally in the centre, though in most cases below the upper edge, sometimes in the shape of curved inscription bands.[65] The shape reflects their origin from cupola decorations, as described in the *Hermeneia* for the πᾶσα πνοή composition,[66] and thus indicates that the inscriptions serve the same purpose. A *podlinnik* of the icon painters of Mstera contains the sketch of such an icon with a calligraphic headline of Ps *150*, 6, *148*, 1, hence, as in the *Hermeneia*, albeit Ps *64*, 2 omitted.[67] Two painted *Chvalite gospoda* icons have been presented with the title *Alles was Odem hat, lobe den Herrn* (Ps *150*, 6) ;[68] their description aptly mentions first the deesis (which is not part of the iconography of the *laud psalms*), and groups of kings and *Just*, but then increasingly adopts the phrasing of Ps 148 (*virgins* [Ps *148*, 12]... *with mountains, hills and cedars* [Ps *148*, 9]... *wild beasts, creeping things and birds* [Ps *148*, 10], even a *verbatim* quotation of Ps *148*, 4 (German translation), *die Himmel allenthalben*, followed by *stars, sun and moon* [Ps *148*, 3]), while for the choice of the title, Ps *150*, 6, no reason is given. Elsewhere, Ps 148 quotations of varying length on carved ivory tablets led to the opinion that their figurative carvings were illustrations of this psalm.[69] ARNE EFFENBERGER[70] held that the tablets in Weimar and in Sergiev Posad (*vide supra*) represent the *Lobpreis Gottes durch seine ganze Schöpfung gemäß den Versen des 148. Psalms.* Striking discrepancies failed to raise doubts but were taken into account by *ad hoc* hypotheses such as a symbolic meaning of the respective details or a progressive emancipation of the artisans from the scripture texts.[71]

Details of the iconography of the *Second Coming* or the *Last Judgment* were reinterpreted accordingly. *E. g.*, the upper part of the tablets in Weimar and in Sergiev Posad is occupied by a curved representation of the firmament studded with the sun, the moon and many stars; it has been interpreted as the illustration of Ps *148*, 3-4.[72] On the *Chvalite gospoda* tablet in St. Petersburg, it appears in somewhat modified shape which has been aptly described as an unfurled scroll.[73] Its obvious iconographic prototype is the scroll dotted with stars rolled up by angels illustrating Apc *6*, 14, *the sky vanished, as a scroll is rolled up*, in many *Last Judgment* compositions.[74] The animals depicted in the lower part of the *Chvalite gospoda* icons were ascribed to Ps *148*, 9-10, the pious kings – one of the nine *chorusess* of *All Saints* in the *Second Coming* – to Ps *148*, 11.[75] In Russian *Last Judgment* icons, the snake of sin curling up from the bottom to the celestial sphere is common.[76] It reappears in the *Chvalite gospoda* tablets where it has been believed to symbolize fire, hail, snow, mist[77] and the stormy wind of Ps *148*, 8. *Die Poesie des Psalms ist sozusagen wortwörtlich ins Bildhafte übertragen worden.*[78] However, the interpretation of the *Chvalite gospoda* tablets as illustrations of the 148th psalm eventually failed to eliminate all inconsistencies[79] and thus remained unsatisfactory.[80]

Only exceptionally, the topic was addressed from an altogether different point of view. BORIS ROTHEMUND noticed that the $\pi\tilde{\alpha}\sigma\alpha$ $\pi\nu o\acute{\eta}$ chapter of the *Hermeneia*, though dealing with wall paintings, was, in fact, an adequate description of Greek *All Saints* icons.[81] Though he mentioned Abraham and the souls of the *Just* in his lap and the good thief, he did not state expressly that the scene takes place in Paradise. On the other hand, RICHARD RANDALL *et al.* called the *Chvalite gospoda* tablet in Baltimore *the rare subject of Christ Enthroned in Paradise, ... Paradise is indicated by trees and animals flanking a single river which flows from above the throne of Christ; below* [the throne] *stand the saints, and kings, women, and children.*[82] The assessment amounts to an apt characterization of an *All Saints* icon. The location marks the fundamental difference between the πᾶσα πνοή chapter and the *Chvalite gospoda* icons on the one hand and the *laud psalms* wall paintings on the other: Paradise in the former, the earth in the illustration of Ps *148, 7 – 150,* 6 (αἰνεῖτε τὸν κύριον ἐκ τῆς γῆς).

The Laud Psalms Paintings – Literal Text Illustration or More?

RAINER STICHEL followed the mainstream and sometimes went even further. He chose Ps *150,* 6 as the title of his analysis of *laud psalms* illustrations.[83] His considerations are based on several hypotheses: 1) The last three psalms form a unit.[84] 2) The miniatures in illuminated psalters, the wall paintings and the *Chvalite gospoda* tablets are equivalent; hence, the Russian tablets, too, are illustrations of the *laud psalms.*[85] 3) In the wall paintings as well as in the *Chvalite gospoda* tablets, the pictures and the psalm quotations accompanying them have the same meaning; consequently the meaning of the pictures can be deduced from the quotations.[86] 4) All illustrations are visual versions of liturgical chants as sung in the ὄρθρος. No adequate understanding of the wall paintings is possible if this dependence is ignored.[87] 5) The painters emancipated themselves from the strict wording of the verses to be illustrated and thus transferred them into less literal illustrations.[88] 6) The painted scenes are not only literal illustrations of the respective verses, but express as well symbolic or spiritual connotations.[89]

A number of obvious inconsistencies call for a reconsideration of these hypotheses. The segregation of the last three psalms is problematic, because strictly speaking, the group of the *laud psalms* includes psalms 146 and 147.[90] In the illustrated psalters, Ps 148-150 are in no way separated from the preceding psalms and thus do not form an entity of its own right. Here, the miniatures of all psalms are additions to the text. Unlike most of the wall paintings, not a few of them serve the purpose of interpreting the texts according to Christian exegesis of the Bible. Their sequence according to the psalm numbers 1-150[91] does not permit to infer an influence of the liturgical use of the *laud psalms*. The miniatures fail to explain why only the last psalms have been chosen for wall painting. In search of the reason for their choice, it must be taken into account that sometimes only Ps 148 is illustrated, and elsewhere Ps 150 is ignored. As a specimen of manuscript illumination, STICHEL discussed the Slavonic *Simon psalter* (end of 13th century[92]). Here, the respective miniature accompanies the title of Ps 148[93] and refers only to this psalm. The elements of this psalm are arranged according to the available space and illustrate the essentials of the first verses as well as of verses 7-11, the praise of the Lord by the terrestrial creation. Brief legends provide the key words for proper understanding. References to Ps 150 and in particular to its 6th verse would be out of place and are, indeed, absent. A reference to Ps *64*, 2, the final verse of the Sunday ὄρθρος, would prove a liturgical provenance of the miniature, but is likewise absent.

The *Chvalite gospoda* tablets conform well with the πᾶσα πνοή chapter, but very poorly with the *laud psalms* wall paintings.[94] The circular inscription as given in the *Hermeneia* is the same as the final hymn in the Sunday ὄρθρος, but is not met in the *Chvalite gospoda* icons whose psalm quotations are not subject to fixed rules. As well as the circular inscriptions in the wall paintings, they do exhibit marks of liturgical provenance, but not specificly the ὄρθρος. Furthermore, they never correlate with the pictures and can, therefore, obviously not contribute to the understanding of the latter. The circular inscriptions of the wall paintings never contain verses of Ps 149 though in most churches, this psalm is extensively illustrated.

A symbolical meaning of certain details of the *laud psalms* wall paintings was first proposed by DIDRON and then by STRZYGOWSKI.[95] In Iviron and frequently elsewhere, the *stormy wind* of Ps *148*, 8, τὸ πνεύμα καταιγίδος, is represented as a half-naked man protruding out of a cave and blowing a horn. DIDRON compared him with Hercules and believed him to be the personification of the earth which, in its turn, symbolizes *space*, while the zodiac represents *time*. It was concluded that *space* and *time* are exhorted to praise the Lord.[96] STRZYGOWSKI adopted this interpretation; in Koutloumousiou, he correctly read part of the legend, πνεύμα κατ[αιγίδος], but misunderstood it as *the designation of one of the four winds of the compass points*.[97] A church building, which in Iviron as frequently elsewhere serves to illustrate Ps *149*, 1b, ἡ αἴνεσις αὐτοῦ ἐν ἐκκλησίᾳ ὁσίων, according to DIDRON, *représente et figure le ciel animé par Jésus-Christ*.[98] A marble sculpture resembling a Hadrianic coin[99] was called Jupiter Cosmocrator and claimed to be the prototype of a Maiestas Domini which, in its turn, was called *Christ Cosmocrator*; [100] SRDJAN DJURIĆ applied this term to the Lord of Ps *148*, 1, 7 at Lesnovo because of the personifications of the planets and the signs of the zodiac surrounding him.[101] In all these cases, the scholastic principle known as *Ockham's razor* applies: *non sunt multiplicanda entia praeter necessitatem*:[102] If there is a choice between various interpretations, that which requires the smallest number of hypotheses deserves preference. Throughout, it suffices to regard the paintings as literal illustrations of the respective psalm verses, Ps *148*, 1, 7, Ps *148*, 8 and Ps *149*, 1, the zodiac at Lesnovo of Ps *148*, 3, 6; there is no detail which justifies any additional meaning. This is also true for the illustration of Ps *149*, 1 in the Koukouzelissa chapel which MILLET proposed to represent the transfer of the Ark of he Covenant to Jerusalem.[103]

STICHEL's hypotheses of an emancipation from literal illustrations towards a symbolic or spiritual meaning have been conceived in order to make the *Chvalite gospoda* tablets amenable to an interpretation as *laud psalms* illustrations. They permit a check: STICHEL justly pointed out that one first has to look for details in which the painters deviate from tradition. *Erst solche würden andeuten, dass Abweichungen vom traditionellen Bildinhalt gemeint sind.*[104] In the wall paintings, the text of the *laud psalms* was occasionally illustrated rather liberally. The *entire* creation is exhorted to praise the Lord, and therefore, the dragons and animals of Ps *148*, 7, 10 serve only as representatives of all (non-human) breathing beings. To achieve comprehensiveness, those fabulous creatures reportedly living at the outskirts of the inhabitable world, were added.[105] The first king of Ps *148*, 11 or the leader of the musicians of Ps *149*, 3 and Ps *150*, 3-5 was often personalized as King David.[106] But details which cannot be explained unless by a symbolic or spiritual meaning do not exist. STICHEL inferred such a meaning for the monks carrying swords in the *laud psalms* composition in the cathedral of Nicosia,[107] but without necessity.[108] When the *laud psalms* illustrations are located in cupolas, the central picture of the Lord of Ps *148*, 1 is surrounded by circular bands in which the psalms are illustrated verse by verse. In Nicosia, however, the composition consists of one large panel in which the divisions between the individual verses are disregarded.[109] The ὅσιοι, *the Faithful*[110] of Ps *149*, 5 are identical with those of verses 1 and 9; as elsewhere, they are depicted as monks.[111] Verses 5 and 6 consist of one coherent sentence according to which *the Faithful* hold two-edged swords in their hands: *The Faithful will boast in glory, and they will rejoice on their beds. The exaltations of God are in their throats, and two-edged swords in their hands.*[112] Hence, the monks (Ps *149*, 1, 5, 7) approaching a church (Ps *149*, 1) and holding swords (Ps *149*, 6) are a painstakingly literal illustration of Ps 149 not amenable to a symbolical interpretation.

Unlike the illuminated psalter manuscripts, the *laud psalms* wall paintings do not interpret the psalms christologically. In his description and interpretation of the allegedly equivalent three categories, STICHEL discussed only the Ps 148 miniature of the *Simon psalter* and one of the *Chvalite gospoda* tablets. In the latter, he believed to recognize *alles was Odem hat* (Ps *150*, 6)[113] and all groups of Ps *148*, 11; *the band winding down from heaven represents the atmospheric phenomena, fire, hail, snow and ice* (Ps *148*, 8).[114] Since the tablets are not illustrations of the *laud psalms* and since the miniatures do not serve the same purposes as the wall paintings, neither can contribute to the problem of the meaning of the wall paintings.

The Ps 150 Miniature in the Carolingian Stuttgart Psalter

The title of the πᾶσα πνοή chapter in the *Hermeneia* was even used in the literature on *laud psalms* paintings which precede the *Chvalite gospoda* icons by many centuries and, furthermore, belong to the occidental realm. In the Carolingian Utrecht psalter, each psalm, including the *laud psalms*, is accompanied by one miniature,[115] This way, the miniature devoted to Ps 148 is not at all indebted to Ps 150. And yet, it has occasionally been published with the legend *Ps 148. - Pasapnoë*, while, on the other hand, the legend of the Ps 150 miniature does not refer to the final verse of the psalm.[116] Such emancipation of the word from its origin contrasts with the opinion that in the Ps 150 miniature in another Carolingian manuscript, the Stuttgart psalter, the concluding verse was ignored.[117] The Stuttgart miniature would thus anticipate most Orthodox wall paintings in which Ps *150*, 6 is not illustrated.

In the Utrecht psalter (as well as in the Greek psalter Vat. gr. 1927[118]), each miniature is the comprehensive illustration of a whole psalm. In the Stuttgart psalter, on the other hand, the miniatures selectively illustrate single verses (occasionally several verses), and focus on their key words. Exceptionally, the miniatures of the 148th and the 149th psalm are, in principle, illustrations of the whole psalms, but in fact only of selected verses (Ps *148*, 1-4, 7, 10; Ps *149*, 1, 6, 8-9[119]), and again in a highly succinct manner. The Ps 150 miniature (fig. on p. 140)[120] is different.

Its description by ERNEST T. DE WALD is rather general and vague and sometimes inadequate: *Psalm 150, which contains injunctions to praise the Lord. The picture illustrates the various methods of praise. In the upper centre is the sanctum. At the extreme left a man with a book in which is written, Laudabo Dominum meum in vita mea. David, crowned, is playing the cythara in the centre of the picture. About him are dancers* [plural!] *and musicians performing on tuba* [*recte*: horn!]*, cymbals, and organ. The organ with the three men managing the bellows is of special interest.*[121] DE WALD did not correlate the details with the individual verses. JAKOB ESCHWEILER, BONIFATIUS FISCHER, HERMANN JOSEF FREDE and FLORENTINE MÜTHERICH described the miniature in more detail, but included hypothetical interpretations and occasionally lacked precision.[122] *Oben in der Mitte steht das Heiligtum auf dem Berg Sion. Darum gruppieren sich ein Hornbläser, ein Sänger mit geöffnetem Psalterium (laudabo Deum meum in vita mea Ps 145, 2), König David mit der Cithara und eine Tympana-Spielerin.[123] Unten steht links der huldigende Psalmist, in der Mitte ein kleiner nackter Tänzer (ursprünglich David, der nackt vor der Bundeslade tanzt, vgl. 2 Sam 6, 20), rechts eine große Orgel mit drei Balgtretern. In the middle of the upper part, the sanctuary stands on Mount Sion*: PETER BURKHART questioned the interpretation of the building on top of a hill as the *sanctum* (= the temple; Ps *150*, 1; *cf.* DE WALD)[124] and preferred to view it as the Ark of the Covenant.[125] Ps *150*, 1 exhorts the Faithful to praise the Lord '*in* sanctis' and thus decides the issue in favour of the temple. Furthermore, the Ark of the Covenant, as depicted elsewhere in roughly contemporaneous paintings, is different. In two miniatures in the Utrecht psalter[126] as well as in the mosaic in the oratory of Theodulf of Orléans in Germigny-de-Prés (799-818 A.D.),[127] it is house-shaped but equipped with sticks for carrying; it is placed below a tent on a table draped with clothes.[128] *At the bottom to the left, the worshipping psalmist is standing,* in fact, a man with outstretched arms looking up. His interpretation as the *worshipping psalmist*[129] is adopted from the Utrecht psalter, where *the psalmist* is ubiquitous;[130] he is not typical for the Stuttgart psalter. According to BURKHART, *the singer to the left of the upper part and the worshipping man below him cannot directly be traced back to the [psalm] text nor to Patristic exegesis. This confirms the impression that this picture, originally a literal illustration [of the psalm], has later been extended by interpretative additions*.[131] The interpretation of the small naked figure to the right of the *worshipping psalmist* as a *dancer (originally David who dances undressed in front of the Ark of the Covenant)* illustrating verse 4a, *laudate eum in tympano et choro, Praise him with drum and dance*,[132] is unsatisfactory. Much later, in the *laud psalms* paintings of Orthodox churches, the *chorus* (LXX: χόρος) of Ps *150*, 4 is almost always performed by several dressed women; a single naked figure would be a highly inappropriate abstraction of a round dance. Frequently, King David is the band leader of the musicians; occasionally, he crosses his legs in the gesture of dancing,[133] but he is always the aged king in royal attire and never the naked youth of 2Sam (LXX: 2Kings) *6*, 20. Though not mentioned in the *laud psalms*, he unites all three aspects of Ps *149*, 3, *150*, 3-5, the aspects of singing, of playing music on instruments and of dancing. Even here, no iconographic dependence from LXX 2Kings *6*, 20 is discernible. In the Stuttgart miniature, the nudity of the *dancer* cannot be rationalized this way, because in medieval occidental miniatures[134] as well as in later postbyzantine wall paintings,[135] the scene of the transfer of the Ark of the Covenant to Jerusalem on an oxcart shows David consistently in long royal clothes. In the Stuttgart miniature, the naked figure holds with both hands a long red cloth conceiling its genitals. This is not the gesture with which elsewhere in Carolingian miniatures dressed dancers accompanying King David whirl a large cloth above their heads,[136] a gesture dating back to antiquity[137] and met elsewhere in the Stuttgart psalter, *e. g.* in the personification of *terra* in

Ps *41*, 7,[138] again following an ancient prototype.[139] According to ESCHWEILER, FISCHER, FREDE and MÜTHERICH as well as to BURKHART, the Ps 150 miniature of the Stuttgart psalter is restricted to the verses 1-5 of the psalm.[140]

We prefer to view the miniature as a highly succinct literal albeit selective illustration of all verses of the 150th psalm. Verse 1a, *laudate dominum in sanctis eius*, is represented by the building standing on top of a mountain which signifies the temple on Mount Sion as mentioned in Ps *149*, 2. King David with the cithara in the centre and the hornblower further left stand for verse 3a, b, *laudate eum in sono tubae, laudate eum in psalterio et cithara*. Verse 5a, b, *laudate eum in cymbalis bene sonantibus, laudate eum in cymbalis iubilationis*, is taken into account by the woman standing to the right of Mount Sion and holding cymbals of the *Gabelbecken* type[141] in her hands. The large organ below her is – *pars pro toto* – the adequate representative of verse 4, *laudate eum in tympano et choro, laudate eum in cordis et organo*.[142] Verse 2, *laudate eum in virtutibus eius, laudate eum secundum multitudinem magnitudinis eius*, as well as verse 1b, *laudate eum in firmamento virtutis eius*, lack a tangible object, but since the psalms are chants, both verses could be illustrated by the action of singing. The man holding a book in his left hand to the left of the hornblower, then, is a singer who holds his music; the words written on the book are the text of his chant. DE WALD's decipherment (*vide supra*) is Ps *145*, 2, *laudate dominum in vita mea*, extended by the word *meum*. The digitalisate of the Stuttgart psalter[143] permits to check DE WALD's reading. The word *domi-*

num is abbreviated as *dm* (with a bar on top of the letter *m*). The thumb and one finger of the singer's left hand cover parts of both pages of the book, so that to the right, the third line (after *me* of the second line, of *vita mea*) is not visible. The concealed *a* of *mea* is followed by illegible letters, indicating that the quotation is meant to continue:[144] *psallam Deo meo quamdiu ero. Nolite confidere in principibus, in filio hominis cui non est salus*. In the Stuttgart psalter, Ps 145 is not illustrated by this verse, but by verse 4.[145] If the singer is viewed as the illustration of verse 1b, the man with outstretched arms below him, in an attitude of singing as well, is left to illustrate verse 2.

Thus, all verses 1-5 would have been illustrated individually, or even their halves: 3a / 3b and either 1a / 1b and 2, or 1 (by the temple) and 2a / 2b (by the singer and the man below him), though only succinctly: neither comprehensively nor redundantly. *E. g.*, two string instruments are mentioned in verse 3b (*psalterium* and *cythara*), and they are again referred to in verse 4b (*in cordis*), but only one of them is depicted as King David's instrument. Of the three musical instruments enumerated in verse 4, only the largest, the organ, is depicted. Neither an influence of patristic exegesis nor interpretative additions are recognizable.

The proposed interpretation of the naked figure below King David as a dancer representing the round dance of verse 4a (*in tympano et choro*) is hardly compatible with the concept of the miniature. As verse 4 has otherwise adequately been taken into account, the *chorus* required no illustration. If the building in the upper part is a straightforward illustration of *in sanc-*

tis eius rather than the Ark of the Covenant, it is too far-fetched to explain the nakedness by reference to 2Sam *6*, 20. In the centre of the miniature, King David is clad in noble attire; his doubling in an altogether different shape seems unacceptable.

On the other hand, the thorough consideration of the verses 1-5 calls for an illustration of verse 6. All inconsistencies become immaterial, if the figure is interpreted as *spiritus*, hence *pars pro toto* as the illustration of verse 6, *omnis spiritus laudet Dominum*. Thus, the 150th psalm would have been illustrated completely, adequately and consistently. The Stuttgart psalter contains the Gallicanic version of the psalms[146] which is based on the Septuagint.[147] Here, Ps *150*, 6 begins with πᾶσα πνοή, *all breath [praise the Lord]*: it is the breath emanating from the mouth, as the soul does at the time of death – the soul which is reunited with the body when, at the *Last Judgment*, the dead are resurrected. For the soul, as incorporeal as the breath, a small, naked, anthropomorphic figure is common iconography.

In the LXX, πνοή is the Greek equivalent of five Hebrew words, 13times the same as in Ps *150*, 6.[148] The Latin translations in the Vulgate are varying, *e. g.* Gen *2*, 7, Iob *33*, 4 and Prov. *20*, 27 *spiraculum*, 1 [LXX 3] Kings *15*, 29 *anima*, Iob *26*, 4 *spiramen*, Iob *27*, 3 *halitus*, Jes *42*, 5, *57*, 16 and Dan. *5*, 23 *flatus*, rarely *spiritus* (2 [LXX 4] Kings *22*, 16). *spiritus* is frequent in the Gallicanic psalter, almost exclusively as the equivalent of τὸ πνεῦμα or derivatives thereof; conversely, however, τὸ πνεῦμα of the LXX, in the meaning of *the soul*, is not consistently translated as *spiri-*

tus, but also as *anima*. In the Stuttgart psalter, *anima* is depicted differently: In Ps *42, 5* (fol. 55r), *quare tristis es anima mea et quare conturbas me*,[149] as a dressed woman, but *spiritus*, spirits of various kind, and similar creatures appear at different places as small, frequently naked figures.[150] Wicked demons are characterized by additional details such as bristled hair and chicken feet. In the miniature of Ps *145, 4, exibit spiritus eius et revertetur in terram suam, the soul* has not been illustrated.[151] On fol. 38r, the *wicked souls* of Ps *30, 18 (31, 19), erubescant impii et deducantur in infernum*, are small humans with normal hair.[152] On fol. 56r (Ps *43, 8, salvasti enim nos de adfligentibus nos et odientes nos confudisti*),[153] five small naked, brown devils with wings and tousled hair kindle the fire of hell. Similar devils are depicted on the miniatures of Ps *20, 9-10, inveniatur manus tua omnibus inimicis tuis dextera tua inveniat omnes qui te oderunt. Pones eos ut clibanum ignis in tempore vultus tui Dominus in ira sua conturbabit eos et devorabit eos ignis*,[154] and *108, 6, 19, constitue super eum peccatorem et diabolus stet a dextris eius; fiat ei sicut vestimentum quo operitur, et sicut zona qua semper praecingitur*.[155] On fol. 30r, a naked, winged, anthropomorphic figure devoid of 'wicked' attributes holds the ornamental first letter of Ps 24.[156] In the miniature of Ps *105, 37-38, et immolaverunt filios suos et filias suas daemoniis*, the son and the daughter are naked and smaller than their father, but the demons (with wings and with claws on their feet) are as well.[157] In Ps *126, 3, Ecce hereditas Domini filii mercis fructus ventris, thy childrens' children*[158] are not yet born and therefore depicted as the souls of unborn children, hence naked and smaller than the real children at the table.

The 13th century mosaics of San Marco are indebted to older iconography.[159] Here, the *breath of life* (LXX: ἡ πνοὴ ζωῆς; Vulgate: *spiraculum vitae*) which the Lord God (depicted as the pre-existent Christ) breathed into Adam's nostrils (Gen. *2, 7*),[160] is a small, naked human with the wings of a dragonfly. In the Vulgate,, the phrasing is different in Gen *2, 7* and in Ps *150, 6* (*spiraculum vitae / spiritus*); in the LXX, it is identical and thus shows more clearly that the breath received by the first man[161] is the same as the breath with which his descendants shall praise the Lord in Ps *150, 6*.[162] The end of Gen *2, 7*, *et factus est homo in animam viventem*, is a case of *parallelismus membrorum* demonstrating that *spiritus* and *anima* are virtually synonyms.[163]

The verb *exspirare*, *to expire*, *to die*, literally *to breathe out*, as a derivative of *spiritus*, is expressed by a small anthropomorphic soul leaving the body through the mouth. In the parable of the rich glutton and the poor Lazarus[164] in the *Codex aureus* of Echternach,[165] the soul of the dying Lazarus leaves his body through the mouth; it is depicted as a small, dressed anthropomorphic, winged creature, received by two angels. To the right, in Paradise, the soul, now naked and devoid of wings, sits on Abraham's lap. Both from the right and from the left, six similar souls are approaching. Below, the glutton is passing away. His soul, too, leaves the body through the mouth. The naked, anthropomorphic creature is seized by two black devils. Further to the right, a brown devil has put it on his shoulder and carries it to hell. Below the scene of *Abraham's lap*, his naked soul stands on the thigh of a many-headed devil amid the flames of hell with raised arms;[166] the heads and chests of seven other souls rise from the flames. This iconography is also met in an illustration of the psalms, *viz.*in the miniatures of the psalter Paris B. N. lat. 8846, painted *ca.* 1300. Ps *61, 11, nolite concupiscere divitiae si affluant, nolite cor adponere,* is illustrated by two men. One of them sits at a table and distributes his money to the poor; the other one pours his money into a large chest. In another scene, this chest stands beside the deathbed of the man whose small, naked soul has just left through his mouth. Two devils grasp it; its left foot is still within. The death of the charitable man is similar, though his soul is dressed and received by two angels.[167] *My soul*, ἡ ψυχή μου, *anima mea*, occurs in the verses 2 and 6, hence, the miniature may also illustrate these verses.

In the respective NT healings, the maniacs are possessed by evil spirits, in Greek consistently πνεύματα, *spiritus* in the Vulgate: Mt *8,* 16 *et eiciebat spiritus verbo*; Mk *1,* 12 *et statim Spiritus expellit eum in desertum*; Mk *1,* 23 *et erat in synagoga eorum homo in spiritu immundo*; Mk *3,* 11 *et spiritus immundi cum illum videbant procidebant ei*; Mk *6,* 7, *et dabat illis potestatem spirituum immundorum*; Mk *9,* 16 *filium meum ad te habentem spiritum mutum*; Mk *9,* 19 *et cum vidisset illum statim spiritus*; Mk *9,* 25 *comminatus est spiritu immundo... surde et mute spiritus*; Lc *8,* 2, *et mulieres aliquae quae erant curatae ab spiritibus malignis et infirmitatibus*. In an Ottonian ivory plate of the so-called antependium of

Magdeburg,[168] in the wall painting of St. George's church at Oberzell[169] and in the miniatures of the Reichenau gospels[170] and in the Hitda gospel,[171] the *unclean spirit, τὸ πνεῦμα τὸ ἀκάθαρτον, spiritus immundus*, of the maniac of Gerasa (Mk *5, 2, 8*, Lc *8, 29*) is a small, naked, anthropomorphic, winged creature which leaves its victim through his mouth, in that respect resembling the breath, *omnis spiritus*, of Ps *150*, 6. In the miniatures, its dark skin characterizes it as a demon. Somewhat later, *ca.* 1045, similar demons occur in the Codex aureus of Echternach[172] and in the gospels of Otto III in Munich[173] and in Aachen.[174] This iconography is also common in Orthodox wall painting. In the composition of the archangel healing a possessed monk at Lesnovo, the naked, winged and dark-skinned demon comes out of the mouth of the monk who is lying on his back.[175] *Spiritus sanctus*, the *Holy Spirit*, marks the other end of this vast semantic field.

Viewed as the *spiritus* of verse 6, the naked dancer of the Ps 150 miniature of the Stuttgart psalter fits well into this scheme. The iconography as a small, naked figure is derived more from the *word spiritus* than from its *meaning* in Ps *150*, 6, *viz.* the breath coming out of the mouth. In later wall paintings, both aspects are combined in the *stormy wind* of Ps *148*, 8, πνεῦμα καταιγίδος / *spiritus procellarum*. At Lesnovo, it is a naked, anthropomorphic, winged creature riding on a two-headed monster.[176] Elsewhere, it is iconographically derived from the incorporeal angels.[177] In the Ps 148 miniature of the Stuttgart psalter, verse 8 was ignored, but on fol. 124r, Ps *106*, 29 has been illustrated by Jesus Christ appeasing the storm (Mt *8*, 23-27; Mk *4*, 35-41; Lc *8*, 22-25);[178] according to common iconography,[179] the storm, *spiritus procellae* in verse 25, is represented as a human head blowing air out of its mouth.

After all, the Ps 150 miniature of the Stuttgart psalter can be viewed as a selective verbal illustration of all verses of the last psalm. It is no precedent for the phenomenon that in Orthodox wall paintings of the *laud psalms*, Ps *150*, 6 is seldom illustrated.

From τὸ πᾶσα πνοή to the Realm of Spirits

The *spiritus* of verse 6 connects the Ps 150 miniature with the realm of spirits. While in the 148th psalm, the entire creation is exhorted to praise the Lord, Ps 150 restricts the praise to mankind.[180] *All breath* does not refer to *all* breathing creatures, but only to humans – to all those who have the gift of language; it is the πνεύμα which Adam had received from the Lord God[181] (*vide supra*). When PAUL DURAND translated DIDRON's copy of the *Hermeneia* into French, the most popular French Bible was the translation of LOUIS ISAAC LEMAISTRE DE SACY (1613-1684). Ps *150*, 6 had been adequately translated as *Que tout ce qui vit et qui respire, loue le Seigneur*.[182] But LEMAISTRE DE SACY had added a comment: *ce que quelques-uns restreignent aux hommes seuls, d'autres l'entendent également & des anges & des hommes; & plusieurs, generalement de tout ce qui vit, soit des anges, soit des hommes, soit des animaux*, and he repeatedly called the angels, the ἀσώματοι, *les Esprits Celestes*.[183] Ἡ Σύναξις τῶν Ἀσωμάτων, the *assembly of the incorporeal* (= the *celestial spirits*) became *La réunion de tous les esprits* in DURAND's French translation and thus the title of the chapter τὸ πᾶσα πνοή in DIDRON's *Hermeneia*.[184] The first verse of the circular inscription, *Que tout esprit loue le Seigneur*,[185] is an exact translation of the text of the Vulgate, *omnis spiritus laudet Dominum*. The lauds sung by mankind were thus transmuted into a hymn of the Hosts of Heaven.

For his translation of DURAND's French version into German, GODEHARD SCHÄFER consulted the Greek original which is devoid of an equivalent of the words *La réunion* in the French title. He omitted the addition and translated the title as *Die ganze Geisterwelt*[186] (*the whole realm of spirits*) and, consequently, the beginning of the circular inscription as *Die ganze Geisterwelt möge den Herrn loben*. He thus failed to grasp that the circular inscription begins with the quotation of Ps *150*, 6. It is obvious that he believed *die ganze Geisterwelt* to be an adequte translation of πᾶσα πνοή. On the one hand, he thus entirely misunderstood the real meaning of the 150th psalm. On the other hand, SCHÄFER's title is an excellent summary of the chapter whose essence is the praise of the Lord by *All Saints*: Already DIDRON hat noticed that the scene is located in Paradise: in the timeless Paradise after the expulsion of Adam and Eve and, as borne out by the mention of the OT *Just* whom Christ liberates from Hades in the *Anastasis*,[187] and of Christian saints, even after Easter, but before the end of days when their souls are reunited with their resurrected bodies. In the Greek icons of *All Saints*, this Paradise is depicted, with the patriarchs, the Mother of God and the good thief who came into Paradise on Good Friday;[188] in the Russian tablets it is intimated by the animals and trees which have been misinterpreted as an illustration of Ps *148*, 9-10. *Die ganze Geisterwelt*, the whole realm of spirits, then, is the collective term of all those who praise the Lord in Paradise, the Hosts of Heaven and the souls (*spiritus*) of the terrestrial *Faithful*.

SCHÄFER's choice of words thus mirrors the *spiritus* of the Vulgate, but it was a dangerous choice. The Age of Enlightenment had been followed by a period in which occultism throve. When SCHÄFER's book appeared, the meaning of the word *Geisterwelt* was no longer restricted to the (incorporeal) angels, but encompassed *all* creatures believed to live in a supernatural world, which were able to communicate in many ways with the real world. Books on them were in vogue in SCHÄFER's time, such as *Aus der Geisterwelt* by FRIEDRICH HEINRICH KARL VON FOUQUÉ (Erfurt 1818), *Die Seherin von Prevorst. Er-öffnungen über das innere Leben der Menschen und über das Hereinragen einer Geisterwelt in die unsere* by JUSTINUS KERNER (Stuttgart and Tübingen 1829), *Schlüssel zur Geisterwelt oder die Kunst des Lebens* by the freemason J. KERNNING (*alias* J. B. KREBS) (Leipzig and Stuttgart 1833), *Blicke in die Traum- und Geisterwelt. Erzählungen und Thatsa-chen von der Nachtseite der Natur, über Träume, Ah-nungen, Vampyre und das Gespenst des Alpes* (anony-mous, Leipzig 1854), *Die neuesten Manifestationen aus der Geisterwelt* by D. HORNUNG (Berlin 1859), *Clara, oder über den Zusammenhang der Natur mit der Geisterwelt* by F. W. J. VON SCHELLING (posthumous publication 1860/61). The spirits of these books as well as those of SWEDENBORG,[189] in GOETHE's *Faust*,[190] of the orders of the *Illuminati* and the *Rosicrucians* and of the *Romantics* have next to nothing in common with the Hosts of Heaven.

The Singers and their Chant

In the Greek *Hermeneia*, hence without the influence of the *spiritus* of the Vulgate, τὸ πᾶσα πνοή could hardly have the meaning which DURAND and – more clearly – SCHÄFER assigned to it. Here, the title of the chapter must refer to the chant which *All Saints* sing in praise of the Lord. However, the composition as described in the *Hermeneia* is not devoted to the verses Ps *150, 148*, 1, *64*, 2, but to those who sing them. In the translations, the meaning of the title shifted from the chant to the singers; only in them the title correlates with the description. Similarly, in the Stuttgart miniature *depicted* are those who comply with the exhortation of Ps *150*, 6; the text of their chant is not illustrated. The quotation on the book of the singer is not taken from the *laud psalms*, but from a different psalm: *All breath* does not praise the Lortd with the text depicted in the miniature. Much later, this feature is met again, *e. g.* in the cathedral Sveti Cxoveli at Mcxeta, Georgia. Here, the first king of Ps *148*, 11 acts as the conductor of the people of Ps *148*, 11-12, and the singer of Ps 150 is King David. Both of them hold scrolls with verses of Ps 103. Hence, the *Faithful* praise the Lord by singing the 103rd psalm.[191] Examples like this demonstrate that the texts on the scrolls do not permit conclusions concerning the meaning of what is painted. When on the scroll of David acting as the conductor of the choir of Ps *150*, 3-5 (or Ps *149*, 3) or as the first king of Ps *148*, 11[192] πᾶσα πνοὴ αἰνεσάτω τὸν κύριον is quoted,[193] the *Faithful* praise the Lord with a chant which begins with Ps *150*, 6 and which may be the chant sung in Sunday matins and whose Latin version in a Gallicanic psalter would be *Omnis spiritus laudet Dominum. Laudate Dominum de caelis, laudate eum in excelsis. Te decet hymnus Deus in Sion, et tibi reddetur votum in Hierusalem.* However, as is the case with the 145th psalm in the Stuttgart niniature, its *contents* is not illustrated. Neither here nor in the Slavonic *Simon psalter*[194] it is necessary to refer to interpretative additions, nor is it mandatory to deduct the late wall paintings of the *laud psalms* from the liturgy of the byzantine ὄρθρος service. In the Stuttgart psalter, the Ps 150 miniature is no more than an illustration of the text, and among the miniatures of the manuscript, it does not play a privileged role. It shares this feature with all illuminated psalters, Latin as well as Greek, in striking contrast with the emphasis which the *laud psalms* enjoy in Orthodox wall paintings.

The Role of Ps 149, 1-2 in the Illustration of the Laud Psalms

Details in which the painters deviate from tradition and which, according to STICHEL, might indicate connotations beyond the immediate text of a psalm, can be found in wall paintings of the 149th psalm, *viz.* in the illustration of Ps *149*, 1 and in the accompanying inscriptions. In the *laud psalms* wall paintings at Lesnovo, illustration of Ps *149*, 1 is restricted to its first part, *Sing to the Lord a new song.*[195] In all later paintings, it is exclusively the second part which is illustrated: *Sing his praise in the assembly of the Faithful.*[196] The passage ἐν ἐκκλησίᾳ ὁσίων is rendered as a church approached by nimbed men (monks); occasionally this picture is in the centre of the terrestrial part of the praise of the Lord[197] (*e. g.*, in Nicosia; *vide supra*). On the other hand, the final words of Ps *149*, 1 and the beginning of verse 2, *let Israel rejoice* [*in his master*], were used to form a new sentence, ἐν ἐκκλησίᾳ ὁσίων εὐφρανθήτω Ἰσραέλ, *Israel*, identical with the ὅσιοι of Ps *149*, 1, 5, 9, *shall rejoice in the Church of the Faithful.*[198]

For an adequate appreciation, the comments of the psalms by HERMANN GUNKEL and by FRANK-LOTHAR HOSSFELD and ERICH ZENGER are helpful: Psalm 149 *outlines... the vision of the salvation of the persecuted and despised »poor« Israel by its king JHWH and, concomitantly, the dethronement of all kings and rulers of this earth, with the universal establishment of his legal system as the goal – for the benefit of the whole universe, as is displayed in Ps 150 which follows... Ps 149 is... a hymn, which in its first part celebrates the salvation of Israel by JHWH as evidence of his royal rule and which in its second part relates the dethronement of all kings of the peoples with assistance of the rescued Israel as a consequence of the universal royal rule of JHWH.*[199] *The psalm is important because it demonstrates most clearly the political hopes of the Jews. Having passed through several empires, the Jews get excited by the fervent yet unrealistic dream to defeat some day the pagan tyrants and to rise themselves to universal rule... This hope is religious only in so far as Israel, being unable to rely on itself, asks its God for just retaliation and universal glory and expects them confidently.*[200] The (Orthodox) Christians considered themselves to be the *New Israel*, the new *Chosen People* of the Lord,[201] and in all countries in whose churches Ps *149*, 1 was illustrated by the ἐκκλησία ὁσίων, their living conditions resembled those of the Israelites at the time when the *laud psalms* were composed. They could make use of Ps 149 without any reinterpretation to express their hopes for salvation.[202] Ἐκκλησία ὁσίων, the *assembly of the Faithful*,[203] is the Orthodox Church; she vouches for this promise. The sentence *The Faithful shall rejoice in their Church* is the exhortation not to convert to Islam in search for a better life, but to remain faithful to the Orthodox Church.[204] In the cathedral of Nicosia, a church building is placed below *the Lord* of Ps *148*, 1, 7; it acts as a symbol of the Church as an institution.

In many *laud psalms* compositions, *the Lord* is the Pantocrator who has raised his right hand in the gesture of speaking, while his left hand holds a book or a scroll with the text of what he is speaking. In Nicosia, both hands are outstretched in a gesture of invitation towards those who approach him and his Church, the ἐκκλησία ὁσίων.[205]

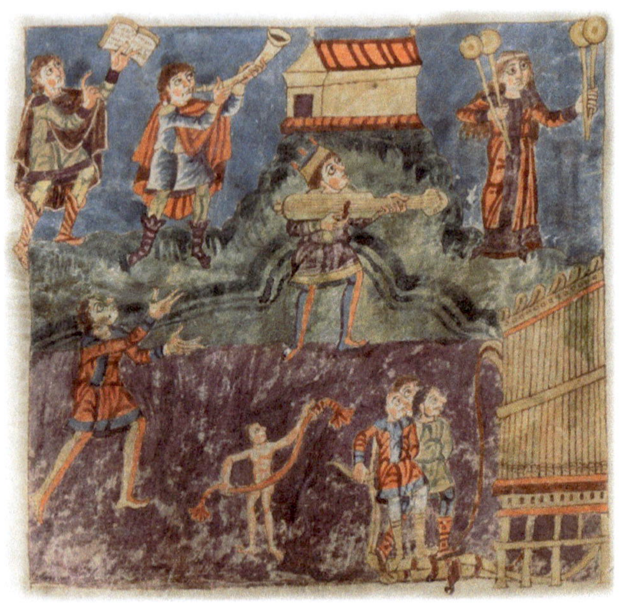

The Stuttgart Psalter, Ps 150

Abstracts

The Peoples in the Slavonic *Last Judgment*
Matthew, Chapter 25, Daniel's Vision and
Saint Peter's Speech at Pentecost

In the conventional interpretation of the *Last Judgment*, those standing *on the right hand* of the judge are *the Blessed* while those standing *on the left hand* are *the Damned*. M. GARIDIS and A. GRABAR observed that some Russian icons defied this characterization but confessed to be unable to propose a plausible explanation. A detailed analysis of Russian *Last Judgment* icons and the *Last Judgment* in Voroneţ (Rumania) focusses on the alien peoples standing *on the left hand*. A semantic investigation of the terms λαοί, ἔθνη *etc.* and their Slavonic translations in the Book of the prophet Daniel and in the Revelation of St. John aims at establishing the criteria according to which mankind is organized in the groups which face judgment. It emerges that those approaching the judge *from the left* represent all those groups whose fate has not yet been decided, unbelievers as well as heretics and among the Orthodox Christians the *social sinners etc.* Moses, anticipating St. Peter's address to the Jews at Pentecost, is trying to make them confess that Jesus Christ is the Lord as a prerequisite to be granted remission of their sins and admission to Paradise. Paying homage to the Lord, all those for whom a favourable sentence is a matter of course, stand *on the right hand* of the judge. In Voroneţ, the judgment is viewed by the **ВЄТХИ ДЄНЬМИ**, labeled IC XC. The intriguing doubling of Christ as the *Ancient of Days* and the judge is discussed.

The Role of the Inscription Bands in Wall
Paintings of the *Laud Psalms*

Many wall paintings of the *laud psalms* include a circular inscription band. Initially restricted to verses taken from Ps *148*, 1-6, they could serve as legends for the illustrations of the praise of the Lord by the celestial part of the creation. Later, Ps *150*, 6 and / or Ps *64*, 2a were added. Comparison with the texts on the scrolls of the protagonists of mankind praising the Lord (Ps *148*, 11-14) suggests that the extended versions represent the hymns sung by the entire creation. Their essence is the creed that *Jesus Christ is the Lord*.
The study is based on the post-Byzantine *laud psalms* paintings of *ca*. 70 churches.

»Omnis spiritus laudet dominum«.
Psalm *150*, 6 and the Realm of Spirits in the
Illustration of the *Laud Psalms*

Wall paintings of the psalms 148 and 149 are met in 14th century Serbian churches, elsewhere only in Post-Byzantine time. Only later, the 150th psalm was included. Ever since ADOLPHE N. DIDRON's discovery of the *Painter's Manual* of Dionysios of Phourna, the *Hermeneia*, it has intrigued scholars why only these psalms, the *laud psalms*, were chosen for wall painting. A chapter entitled τὸ πᾶσα πνοή (reminiscent of Ps *150*, 6), believed to describe the *laud psalms* paintings in spite of serious discrepancies, gave rise to a focus on the final verse of Ps 150 though this verse has, in fact, only seldom been illustrated. Along these lines, no satisfactory explanation for the special role of the *laud psalms* in wall painting has emerged. A new assessment of πᾶσα πνοή, *omnis spiritus* in the Vulgate, starts with an analysis of the Ps 150 miniature in the Carolingian Stuttgart psalter which, though western, is pertinent, because it slightly antedates the Photian schism. Revising previous interpretations, it is proposed that the miniature is a painstaking illustration of all verses of the psalm; a naked figure so far identified as a dancer, is, in fact, a personification of the *spiritus* and serves to illustrate verse 6. The proposal is backed by a survey of the iconography of the *spiritus* elsewhere.

The new identification has been found helpful for a better understanding of the *Hermeneia* and its 19th century translations which reflect the contemporaneous revival of the preoccupation with *spirits* and thereby became the source of misunderstandings. In fact, the πᾶσα πνοή chapter of the *Hermeneia* is not a description of the *laud psalms* paintings but an illustration of *All Saints* singing hymns in praise of the Lord. On the other hand, in Post-Byzantine time, the *laud psalms* have not been illustrated for their own sake, but serve to convey the message that the Christians shall remain faithful to the Church and are assured that eventually oppression will come to an end.

Notes

The Peoples in the Slavonic *Last Judgment*
Matthew, Chapter 25, Daniel's Vision and
Saint Peter's Speech at Pentecost

[1] M. Garidis, *Byzantion 39* (1969) [1970] 86-103 (based
on his *Thèse de Doctorat de 3ème cycle*, Université de Paris
1966, printed: M. K. Garidis, *Études sur le Jugement
Dernier post-byzantin du XVe à la fin du XIXe siècle.
Iconographie – Esthétique* [Ἑταιρία Μακεδονικῶν
Σπουδῶν, σειρά φιλ. καὶ θεολ., 16], Θεσσαλονίκη 1985
(chapter IV, esp. pp. 91-117).
[2] A. Grabar, *Byzantion 50* (1980) 186-197.
[3] In this study, *on the right hand* and *on the left hand*
refers to Christ; otherwise, *right* and *left* means *as seen by
the beholder.*
[4] Garidis, *La représentation,*[1] p. 94.
[5] Grabar, *La représentation,*[2] p. 191.
[6] Grabar, *La représentation,*[2] title and note 1. For the
topicality of the problem *cf.* C. Märtl, P. Schreiner (eds.),
*Jakob Philipp Fallmerayer (1790-1861). Der Gelehrte und
seine Aktualität im 21. Jahrhundert* [Bayer. Akad. Wiss.,
Phil.-hist. Kl., Abhandlungen, N. F., 139], München 2013,
in particular C. Voss, "Slavische Sprache(n) und slavische
Ethnizität in Griechenland. Jakob Philipp Fallmerayer aus
der Sicht der heutigen Minderheiten", 121-132; W. Pohl,
"Ethnische Identitäten in Südosteuropa als
Forschungsproblem", 143-153.
[7] *La Sainte Bible* traduite par Lemaistre de Sacy, Paris
1841.
[8] *A New English Translation of the Septuagint*, Oxford
University Press, New York, Oxford 2009 (electronic
edition with *corrections and emendations*, 2014) (with
occasional exceptions).

[9] Papadopoulo-Kérameus; Didron, *Manuel*; Schäfer, *Handbuch*; Hetherington, *Manual;* Erminia. An older edition of the Greek text, ΕΡΜΗΝΕΙΑ ΤΩΝ ΖΩΓΡΑΦΩΝ, ΩΣ ΠΡΟΣ ΤΗΝ ΕΚΚΛΗΣΙΑΣΤΙΚΗΝ ΖΩΓΡΑΦΙΑΝ, ΥΠΟ ΔΙΟΝΥΣΙΟΥ ΤΟΥ ΙΕΡΟΜΟΝΑΧΟΥ ΚΑΙ ΖΩΓΡΑΦΟΥ, τοῦ ἐκ Φουρνᾶ τῶν Ἀγράφων, ΑΘΗΝΗΣΙ 1853, is superseded by Papadopoulo-Kérameus' edition and remains out of consideration.

[10] Papadopoulo-Kérameus, pp. 140-141; Didron, *Manuel*, pp. 262-267; Schäfer, *Handbuch*, pp. 2632-266; Hetherington, *Manual*, p. 49; Erminia, pp. 214-215.

[11] Papadopoulo-Kérameus, pp. 141-142; Didron, *Manuel*, p. 268-278; Schäfer, *Handbuch*, pp. 266-269; Hetherington, *Manual*, pp. 49-50; Erminia, pp. 215-218.

[12] M. Restle, "Malerbücher", *RBK 5*, 1221-1237, esp. 1225-1236.

[13] А. Давидов Темерински, "Циклус Страшног Суда", in: В. Ј. Ђурић (ed.), *Зидно Сликарсво Манастира Дечана. Грађа и Студије*, Београд 1995, pp. 191-209; В. Todić, M. Čanak Medić, *The Dečani Monastery*, Belgrade 2013, pp. 452-453. In Armenia, the *Second Coming* excluding the *Last Judgment* had been painted as early as A. D. 930: S. Manukyan, *Tatev Monastery Frescoes, Armenia, AD 930*, paper presented at the 23rd International Congress of Byzantine Studies, Belgrade 22-27 August 2016 (24.08.2016). *Cf.* J. Engemann, "Auf die Parusie Christi hinweisende Darstellungen in der frühchristlichen Kunst", *JbAC 19* (1976) 139-156.

[14] *E. g.*, P. A. Underwood, *The Kariye Djami* [Bollingen Series, LXX], New York 1966, vol. 1, p. 199; vol. 3, pls.. 368-371, 374; D. T. Rice, *Byzantinische Malerei. Die letzte Phase*, Frankfurt/Main 1968, figs. 113, 114; G. Tzioras (ed.), *Meteora. Die heiligen Felsen und ihre Geschichte*, Kalabaka s. a., fig. on p. 64; D. Z. Sofianos, *Meteora Wegweiser*, Kloster Megalou Meteorou 1991, fig. on p. 32. – It has occasionally been questioned whether the *Second Parousia* and the *Last Judgment* refer indeed to the same

sequence of apocalyptic events; *cf. e. g.*, C. A. Auberlen, *Der Prophet Daniel oder die Offenbarung Johannis in ihrem gegenseitigen Verhältniß betrachtet und in ihren Hauptstellen erläutert*, Basel [2]1857, pp. 369-370. In the joint illustrations on icons and in wall paintings they clearly do.

[15] K. Onasch, *Liturgie und Kunst der Ostkirche in Stichworten unter Berücksichtigung der Alten Kirche*, Leipzig 1981, pp. 129-131.

[16] *Cf.* Sir Isaac Newton, *Observations upon the Prophecies of Daniel and the Apocalypse of St. John*, London MDCCXXIII, esp. Part II, chap. III: *Of the relation which the Prophecy of John hath to those of Daniel, and of the Subject of the Prophecy* (pp. 276-323); Auberlen, *Der Prophet Daniel*;[14] [A.] Bludau, "Die Apokalypse und Theodotions Danielübersetzung", *Theologische Quartalschrift 79* (1897) 1-26; Underwood, *The Kariye Djami*,[14] vol. 1, p. 200; K. Koch, *Das Buch Daniel* [Erträge der Forschung, 144], Darmstadt 1980, p. 80; M. Albani, *Daniel. Traumdeuter und Endzeitprophet* [Biblische Gestalten, 21], Leipzig 2010, p. 23.

[17] To be sure, in Christian time, βασιλεύς meant the Orthodox emperor, Christ's lieutenant on earth, but the Revelation is indebted to the OT, and in the LXX, βασιλεύς is the equivalent of Hebrew *melek* who frequently is a tribal chief (*cf.* the 70 *meleks* / βασιλεῖς of Judges *1*, 7).

[18] H. G. Liddell, R. Scott, *A Greek-English Lexicon*, vol. 2, Oxford, 9th ed. Reprinted 1951, p. 1281: *crowd, throng*.

[19] In the Greek and the Slavonic Bibles, the Book of Daniel is essentially based on Theodotion's version. Therefore, the Old Greek version will be considered only for comparison.

[20] NETS,[8] Dan (Θ) *7*, 13-14.

[21] Dan (Θ) *3*, 4.

[22] Dan (LXX) *3*, 4: ἔθνη as well as λαοί; χῶραι instead of φῦλαί.

[23] Dan (Θ) *3*, 7; LXX: πάντα τὰ ἔθνη, φῦλαί καὶ γλῶσσαι.

[24] Dan (Θ) *3*, 96: πᾶς λαός, φυλή, γλῶσσα; in the LXX version ἔθνος instead of λαός.

[25] NETS,[8] Dan (Θ) *3*, 98 (*4*, 1).

[26] Dan (Θ) *5*, 19.

[27] Dan (Θ) *6*, 25 (26).

[28].Dan (LXX) *6*, 25 (26).

[29] Dan (LXX) *6*, 26 (27).

[30] J.-P. Deschler, *Kleines Wörterbuch der kirchenslavischen Sprache*, München 1987, p. 156: преподобный *ehrwürdig, fromm, heilig. Cf.* T. A. Lysaght, *Old Church Slavonic (Old Bulgarian) – Middle Greek – Modern English Dictionary*, Wien 1983, p. 335. – *Cf.* J. G. Deckers, "Göttlicher Kaiser und kaiserlicher Gott. Die Imperialisierung des Christentums im Spiegel der Kunst", in: F. A. Bauer, N. Zimmermann (eds.), *Epochenwandel? Kunst und Kultur zwischen Antike und Mittelalter*, Mainz 2001, 3-16, p. 8.

[31] Papadopoulo-Kérameus, pp. 140, 141; Didron, *Manuel*, pp. 263, 268: *Tous les saints*; Schäfer, *Handbuch*, pp. 263, 267: *Alle Heiligen*; Hetherington, *Manual*, p. 49: *All the Saints*; Erminia, p. 214: *toţi sfinţii*. UNDERWOOD called them the *choirs of the Elect*, but in the Entry into Paradise, *the Elect* have the broader meaning of *all people* who enjoyed a favourable sentence: Underwood, *The Kariye Djami*,[14] vol. 1, pp. 200, 203, 210-212 (pls. 404-406: in the first picture plane, the *choirs of the Elect* are depicted, but behind them, there is an undefinable but large crowd of people intimated by their heads). UNDERWOOD regarded the *choirs of the Elect* as the *representatives* of *the elect from all 'nations', or categories, of men who are to be on the King's right hand and to whom he addresses the words of acceptance inscribed* [in the Kahriye Cami] *at his right* (Underwood, *The Kariye Djami*,[14] vol. 1, p. 203).

[32] *Cf.* Catalogue *1000-Летие Русской Художественной Культуры, 1000 Jahre russische Kunst*

– Zur Erinnerung an die Taufe der Rus im Jahr 988,
Москва, Schleswig, Wiesbaden, 1988/89, No. 124 (p. 102);
in the Greek realm, *e. g.*, N. K. Μουτσόπουλος, *Καστορία,*
Παναγία ἡ Μαυριώτισσα, Ἀθῆναι 1967, figs. 52, 53, 55; A.
W. Carr, A. Nicolaïdès (eds.), *Asinou Across Time. Studies*
in the Architecture and Murals of the Panagia
Phorbiotissa, Cyprus [Dumbarton Oaks Studies, 43],
Washington DC 2012, figs. 5.26, 5.27, 5.30, 5.33.
[33] *ThWbNT* 1 (1933) 719-726 ([J.] Behm, γλῶσσα), 2
(1935) 362-370 (K. L. Schmidt, ἔθνος), 4 (1942-1943) 34-
37, 49-57 ([H.] Strathmann, λαός), 5 (1954) 582-590 (R.
Meyer, P. Katz, ὄχλος), 9 (1969-1973) 240-245 (Maurer,
φυλή). *Cf.* I. F. Schlevsner, *NOVVM LEXICON GRAECO-*
LATINUM IN NOVVM TESTAMENTUM, Lipsia [4]1819,
vol. 1, 532-533, 702-703, *2*, 13, 369-370, 1307-1398.
[34] J. Lavy, *Langenscheidts Handwörterbuch Hebräisch-*
Deutsch, Berlin, München, Wien, Zürich 1975, p. 91: *Volk,*
Fremder, Nichtjude.
[35] Lavy, *Handwörterbuch*,[34] p. 426: *Volk.* The singular is
the standard word for *God's Chosen People*, the Israelites,
but, as a matter of course, the plural is not.
[36] E. Hatch, H. A. Redpath, *A Concordance to the*
Septuagint, Oxford 1897, pp. 368-373, 853-862.
[37] Lavy, *Handwörterbuch*,[34] p. 245: *Nation, Volk.*
[38] Gen *27*, 29, Is *34*, 1, *41*, 1, *43*, 4, 9, most in
parallelismi membrorum (in Gen *27*, 29 with ἔθνη < ʿami,
in Is *34*, 1; *43*, 9 with ἔθνη < goji).
[39] Is *51*, 4 (in a *parallelismus membrorum* with λαός <
ʿam).
[40] Prov. *14*, 34 (in an antithetical *parallelismus*
membrorum with ἔθνος < goj).
[41] *E. g.*, Ps *2*, 1; *17 (18)*, 43; *32 (33)*, 10, 12; *43 (44)* 3;
46 (47), 4; *56 (57)*, 10; *66 (67)*, 3-6; *67 (68)*, 31; *95 (96)*,
10; *104 (105)*, 13, 44; *107 (108)*, 4; *116 (117)*, 1; *149*, 7; Is
1, 4; *2*, 4; *10*, 6; *18*, 2, 7; *33*, 3; *55*, 5; *60*, 5, 21-22; *61*, 9.
[42] Ps *67 (68)*, 30, NETS.[8]

[43] M. Altbauer, *Der älteste serbische Psalter*
[Slavistische Forschungen, 23], Köln, Wien 1979.
[44] Belting.
[45] It thus depends entirely on the context whether
ІАЗЫКЪ means *language* or *nation*. An Old Russian Bible,
БІБЛІА ИЛИ КНИГИ СВАЩЕННАГѠ ПИСАНІА
ВЕТХАГѠ И НОВАГѠ ЗАБѢТА, [Sanktpeterburg 1816],
makes a distinction (though not entirely consistently) by
using different characters, **АЗЫКЪ** = *language*, **ІАЗЫКЪ** =
nation . In the Serbian psalters at Sinai (throughout
ІЕЗЫКЪ) and Munich (**ІЕЗЫКЪ** as well as **ЄЗЫКЪ**) no such
differentiation has been made.
[46] Gen *10*, 20, 31.
[47] Interestingly, in the Russian Bible of 1816,
ІАЗЫКЪ rather than **АЗЫКЪ**; *cf.* note 45.
[48] φῦλή > **ПЛЕМА**: Apc *11*, 9; φῦλή > **КОЛѢНА**: Apc *5*,
9, *7*, 9, *13*, 7: F. Miklosich, *Lexicon Palaeoslovenico-
Graeco-Latinum*, Vindobonae 1862-1865, p. 571,
ПЛЕМА... φῦλή tribus; p. 299: **КОЛѢНО**... φῦλή tribus.
[49] For ἔθνος: Apc *5*, 9, *10*, 11, *13*, 7, *14*, 6, *17*, 15; for
γλῶσσα: Apc *7*, 9.
[50] For ἔθνος: Apc *11*, 9; for γλῶσσα: Apc *14*, 6 (here,
φυλή has formally been translated by **ІАЗЫКЪ**.
ἔθνος:/**ПЛЕМА** and φυλή/**ІАЗЫКЪ** may indicate that the
translator simply disregarded the canonical order).
[51] ΚΙΤΑΠΗ ΣΕΡΙΦ ΓΙΑΝΙ ΑΧΤΗΛ ΤΖΕΤΙΤ,
ΣΤΑΜΠΟΛΤΑ 1869.
[52] *Langenscheidts Universal-Wörterbuch, Türkisch*,
Berlin [6]1958, p. 73: *kavm Volk*; K. Steuerwald, *Türkisch-
Deutsches Wörterbuch – Türkçe-Almanca Sözlük*,
Wiesbaden [2]1988, p. 1092: *taife Gruppe od. Klasse von
Menschen; Volksstamm.*
[53] Steuerwald, *Wörterbuch*,[52] p. 579: *kabile
(Nomaden-)Stamm, primitive Völkerschaft.*
[54] Steuerwald, *Wörterbuch*,[52] p. 588 : *kalabalık
Menschenmasse.*

[55] Steuerwald, *Wörterbuch*,[52] pp. 286-288: *dil Zunge, Sprache.*

[56] Steuerwald, *Wörterbuch*,[52] p. 454: *halk Volk, Bevölkerung, Bewohner, Einwohner, Leute, Publikum, das einfache Volk.*

[57] *Cf.* Sch-11, pp. 149, 162.

[58] F. M. Denny, *Umma*, in: Encyclopaedia of Islam, 2nd ed. *Cf.* J. Horovitz, *Jewish proper names and derivatives in the Koran* [Hebrew Union College Annual, 2], Cincinnati, Ohio 1925 (reprint Hildesheim 1964), pp. 46-47.

[59] *E. g.*, ἔθνος > *goj*: Ps *43* (*44*), 3, 15; *46* (*47*), 4; *56* (*57*), 10; *66* (*67*), 5; *107* (*108*), 4; Prov. *24*, 24 (*30*, 39); Is *17*, 12; *51*, 4; *55*, 4; *60*, 2-3 (antithetical); Jer *28* (*51*), 58; Hab *2*, 13.

[60] Lavy, *Handwörterbuch*,[34] p. 45: *die Völker der Welt, Nichtjuden.*

[61] Papadopoulo-Kérameus, p. 45; Didron, *Manuel*, p. 71; Schäfer, *Handbuch*, p. 99; Hetherington, *Manual*, p. 18; Erminia, p. 67; G. Heil, Pseudo-Dionysius Areopagita, Über die himmlische Hierarchie. Über die kirchliche Hierarchie [Bibliothek der griechischen Literatur, 22], Stuttgart 1986, pp. 42-43; G. Heil, A. M. Ritter (eds.), Corpus Dionysiacum, vol. 2, Pseudo-Dionysius Areopagita, De Coelesti Hierarchia, De Ecclesiastica Hierarchia, De Mystica Theologia, Epistulae [Patristische Texte und Studien, 67], Berlin, Boston ²2012, pp. 26-27.

[62] Papadopoulo-Kérameus, p. 140; Didron, *Manuel*, pp. 263-264; Schäfer, *Handbuch*, p. 263; Hetherington, *Manual*, p. 49; Erminia, p. 214.

[63] Hetherington, *Manual*, p. 49; *cf.* Papadopoulo-Kérameus, p. 141; Didron, *Manuel*, p. 268; Schäfer, *Handbuch*, p. 267; Erminia, p. 216. Correspondingly, in early Russian wall paintings of the *Last Judgment*, they are depicted on the same level as the enthroned apostles: Garidis, *Études*,[1] pp. 83-84.

[64] Mt *19*, 28.

[65] Catalogue *Kunstschätze in Bulgarischen Museen und Klöstern*, Essen 1964, p. 183 (No. 360 with fig.; erroneously believed to be the Mother of God). *Cf.* Didron, *Manuel*, p. 263, note 1.

[66] ДавидовТемерински, Циклус,[13] figs. 7, 8; Todić, Čanak Medić, *The Dečani Monastery*,[13] p. 452, fig. 336. In Dečani, eight of the twelve *choruses* of *All Saints* are depicted below arches. In the *Last Judgment* in the narthex of the churches of the monastery of Saint John Lampadistis in Kalopanayiotis (Cyprus) (15th cent.), seven *choruses* of *All Saints* approach the Judge and the Hetoimasia under arches of the same kind. On the other side, four donors turn to the Judge with imploring gestures of their hands. (As they do not belong to the iconography of the *Last Judgment*, they are separated by a frame; otherwise they are integrated into the composition.) As a matter of course, they do not belong to the *Damned. Cf.* A. Stylianou, J. A. Stylianou, *The Painted Churches of Cyprus, Treasures of Byzantine Art*, London 1985, pp. 306-307, 310-311.

[67] Tzioras, *Meteora*,[14] fig. on p. 55; Sofianos, *Meteora*,[14] fig. on p. 77. Similar, though less elaborate illustrations in Barlaam (Meteora) (Tzioras, *loc. cit.*, fig. on p. 64; Sofianos, *loc. cit.*, fig. on p. 32) and in Mardaki (Messenia) (*cf.* Κ. Δ. Καλοκύρης, *Βυζαντιναί Ἐκκλησίαι τῆς Ἱερᾶς Μητροπόλεως Μεσσηνίας* Θεσσαλονίκη 1973, 174-200; Κ. Δ. Καλοκύρης, "Χρονολόγηση τῶν τοιχογραφιῶν καὶ ἀποκάλυψη τοῦ ζωγράφου τῆς μονῆς Μαρδακίου Μεσσηνίας", *Actes du XVe Congrès international d'études byzantines, Athènes – Septembre 1976, II. Art et archéologie, Communications, A*, Athènes 1981 [Βιβλιοθήκη τῆς ἐν Ἀθήναις Ἀρχαιολογικῆς Ἑταιρείας, 92], 229-236.). – The wall paintings of 1566 in Barlaam have been restored to an unknown extent in 1780/82: Sofianos, *loc. cit.*, p. 28; Dionyssios, metropolitan of Trikala, *Qu'est Varlaam?*, Athènes 1962, p. 20: ΑΨΠ, ΑΨΠΒ. *Cf.* R. Hootz (ed.), F. Kyrieleis, Kunstdenkmäler in Griechenland.

Festland ohne Peloponnes, Darmstadt 1982, p. 431; Sch-27.
The quotations of Mt 25 show considerable overpainting.
[68] *E. g.*, in Torcello (G. Perocco, *L'isola di Torcello*, Ve-
nezia 1956, fig. without number; A. Niero, *Die Basilika
von Torcello und Santa Fosca*, Venezia s. a., figs. 24, 29; I.
Andreescu, "Torcello. I. Le Christ inconnu, II. Anastasis et
Jugement dernier: Têtes vraies, têtes fausses", *Dumbarton
Oaks Papers 26* (1972) 183-223, pls. 15, 36; Garidis,
Études,[1] fig. 4; Y. Christe, *Das Jüngste Gericht*,
Regensburg, Darmstadt 2001, fig. 11; T. Velmans, *Byzanz.
Kunst und Architektur*, Petersberg 2009, fig. on p. 45) and
in the Panagia Mavriotissa (Kastoria) (Μουτσόπουλος,
Καστορία, [32] figs. 39, 44-48); S. Pelekanidis, M. Chatzida-
kis, "Panagia Mavriotissa", in: S. Pelekanidis, M. Chatzida-
kis, *Kastoria* [Byzantine Art in Greece. Mosaics – Wall
Paintings], Athens 1985, 66-83, figs. 14, 17, 18).
[69] Т. В. Толстая / T. V. Tolstaya, *Успенский Собор
Московского Кремля / The Assunption Cathedral of the
Moscow Kremlin*, Москва 1979, pl. 113; E. Smirnowa,
Moskauer Ikonen des 14. bis 17. Jahrhunderts, Leningrad
1989, pls. 113, 114.
[70] Garidis, *La représentation*,[1] p. 94; Garidis, *Études*,[1] pp.
43, 70, 99 (1st half of 15th cent.).
[71] Underwood, *The Kariye Djami*,[14] vol. 1, p. 202; vol. 3,
pls. 373-375.
[72] Tzioras, *Meteora,*[14] fig. on p. 64; Sofianos, *Meteora
Wegweiser*,[14] fig. on p. 32.
[73] [A. N.] Didron, "La dalmatique impériale", *Ann.
Archéol. 1* (1844) 152-167, fig. 12.
[74] В. Н. Лазарев, *Древнерусские Мозаики и Фрески XI
– XV вв.*, Москва 1973, fig. 405.
[75] Dan 7, 10.
[76] A. Grabar, G. Oprescu, *Bemalte Kirchen in der
Moldau* [UNESCO-Sammlung der Weltkunst], Paris 1962,
pl. XXI; M.A. Musicescu, S. Ulea, *Voroneţ*, Bucarest
²1971, fig. 52; V. Drăgut, P. Lupan, *Die Wandmalerei in
der Moldau im 15. und 16. Jahrhundert*, Bukarest 1983, fig.

180; Sch-11, pl. 8a. (Note that the icon is older than the paintings in Voroneţ.)

[77] Sch-11, pl. 8a; Sch-22, fig. 12 (also in Levkothea and Tsepelovo: *ibid.*, figs. 6, 7; Καπεσοβίτες Ζωγράφοι. Ἡμερολόγιο 2003, fig. illustrating the week August 25th to 31st).

[78] T. T. Rice, *Ikonen*, London 1962, pl. 23; M. B. Алпатов / M. V. Alpatov, *Древнерусская Иконопись, Early Russian Icon Painting*, Москва / Moscow 1974, pls. 119, 120.

[79] K. Onasch, *Ikonen*, Berlin 1961, pl. 55, pp. 370-371 (*cf. ibid.* pl. 26 and Rice, *Ikonen*,[78] pl. 16); T. T. Rice, *A concise history of Russian Art*, London 1963, fig. 98; Н. Г. Машковцев, *История русского искусства*, vol. 1, Москва 1957, pl. 62.

[80] K. Δ. Καλοκύρης, *Ἄθως. Θέματα Ἀρχαιολογίας καὶ Τέχνης*, Ἀθῆνα 1963, pl. 61A (bl./wh.). But also with a Jew on an icon of the Raising of Lazarus: Onasch, *Ikonen*,[79] pl. 40.

[81] Grabar, *La représentation*,[2] p. 190.

[82] K. Onasch, *Ikonen*,[79] pl. 51; I. J. Danilowa, N. J. Mnewa, *Die Malerei im 17. Jahrhundert*, in: I. E. Grabar, W. N. Lasarew, W. S. Kemenow, *Geschichte der russischen Kunst, 4*, Dresden 1965, 253-346, p. 258, fig.190; V. N. Lasarew, *Ikonen der Moskauer Schule*, Berlin 1977 / Wien, Köln, Graz 1978, figs. 62, 66; Smirnowa, *Moskauer Ikonen,*[69] pls. 151-154; L. Likhacheva, "St. Alexander Svirskii", "The Metropolitan Philip"; in: R. Grierson (ed.), *Gates of Mystery. The Art of Holy Russia*, Fort Worth TX, s. a., pp. 152, 160.

[83] Μουτσόπουλος, *Καστορία*[32] fig. 39; Pelekanidis, Chatzidakis, Mavriotissa,[68] figs. 14, 17, 18.

[84] See note 32.

[85] Grabar, Oprescu, *Bemalte Kirchen,*[76] pl. XVIII; W. F. Volbach, J. Lafontaine-Dosogne, *Byzanz und der christliche Osten* [Propyläen Kunstgeschichte, 3], Berlin 1968, pl. XXXIX; Musicescu, Ulea, *Voroneţ,*[76] fig. 45.

[86] Musicescu, Ulea, *Voroneţ*,[76] figs. 57-58; Drăguţ, Lupan, *Wandmalerei*,[76] figs. 82, 83.

[87] A. M. Ammann, "Darstellung und Deutung der Sophia im vorpretinischen Russland", *Or. Christ. Per. 4* (1938) 120-156, p. 140; W. Felicetti-Liebenfels, *Geschichte der russischen Ikonenmalerei in den Grundzügen dargestellt* [Forschungen und Berichte des Kunsthistorischen Institutes der Universität Graz, 3], Graz 1972, p.. 163. The eight corners of both squares were also called an *eight-pointed nimbus* (*achtzackiger Nimbus*: Felicetti-Liebenfels, *ibid.*, pp. 149, 163); as the lowest corner is concealed by the neck, also *siebenteilig* (Ammann, *loc. cit.*).

[88] В. И. Антонова, Н. Е. Мнева, *Государственная Третьяковская Галлерея, Каталог Древнерусской Живописи XI-начала XVIII в. в.*, vol. 1, Москва 1963, fig.72; Felicetti-Liebenfels, *Geschichte* (1972),[87] fig. 353; Alpatov, *Early Russian Icon Painting*,[78] pl. 113; D. S. Lichatschow, V. K. Laurina, W.A. Puschkarjow, *Nowgoroder Ikonen des 12. bis 17. Jahrhundert*, Leningrad 1981, pl. 72. Also on the *Last Judgment* icon in St. Petersburg: Catalogue *1000-Летие*,[32] No. 124 (p. 102).

[89] For the Universal Judge as ὁ υἱὸς τοῦ ἀνθρώπου *cf.* G. Millet, *La Dalmatique du Vatican. Les Élus, Images et Croyances*, Paris 1945, pp. 3, 17, 25-27, 29, 33; Todić, Čanak Medić, *The Dečani Monastery*,[13] p. 419.

[90] Dan (Θ) *7*, 13 (NETS[8]). Daniel's vision has justly been called a *crux interpretum* (Albani, *Daniel*,[16] p. 171).Though many details remain enigmatic, the role of Dan *7*, 9-10, 13-14 as a prophecy to Mt *24*, 30 must have been obvious for a Christian reader. *Cf.* Koch, *Buch Daniel*,[16] p. 215.

[91] Occasionally also the circular nimbus with a cross and ὁ ὤν symbolizing the consubstantiality: W. Felicetti-Liebenfels, *Geschichte der byzantinischen Ikonenmalerei*, Olten, Lausanne 1956, pl. 135B; *cf.* V. Lazarev, *Old Russian Murals & Mosaics from the XI to the XVI Century*, London 1966, p. 124.

[92] ὁ ὤν in the nimbus of Christ does not necessarily or exclusively refer to Exod *3*, 14; because of John *1*, 18 in conjunction with verse 14 it can also be a reference to the incarnation. For IC XC ὁ παντοκράτωρ Apc *4*, 8 has to be considered.

[93] *E. g.*, Catalogue *1000-Летие*,[32] No. 141 (p. 116), 181 (p. 148).

[94] Dated 1616 and *ca.* 1600, respectively (autopsy, August 28th, 2016). In the *Hermeneia*, ὁ παλαιὸς ἡμερῶν is an epithet of the first person of the Trinity: Papadopoulo-Kérameus, p. 227; Didron, *Manuel*, p. 456; Schäfer, *Handbuch*, p. 419; Hetherington, *Manual*, p. 88; Erminia, p. 225. – Felicetti-Liebenfels, *Geschichte* (1956),[91] p. 103, called *God Father* on Michael Damaskinos' NT trinity icon in the Benaki-Museum in Athens *the Ancient of Days*. There are no supporting inscriptions, while the first and the second person of the Trinity are characterized as *God Father* and Jesus Christ by the texts on the scroll of the former and the book of the latter, Mt *3*, 17 and John *14*, 6, respectively. To represent *God Father* as an old man is the obvious way to express the father/son relation (*cf.* the iconography of David and Solomon) so that it is unjustified to resort to Daniel's vision. Note that in the отечество type of the NT Trinity (W. N. Lasarew, "Die Malerei und die Skulptur Nowgorods", in: Grabar, Lasarew, Kemenow, *Geschichte der russischen Kunst*,[82] 2 (1958), 55-207, pp. 160, 164; Lichatschow, Laurina, Puschkarjow, *Nowgoroder Ikonen*,[88] p. 296, legend of pl. 55: *Vaterschoß*, elsewhere *Vaterschaft*), *God Father* is not *the Ancient of Days*, but ГОСПОДЬ САВАОѲЪ: M. Alpatov, N. Brunov, *Geschichte der altrussischen Kunst*, Baden, Wien. Brünn, Leipzig 1932, fig. 302; J. N. Dmitrijew, "Die «Stroganow-Schule» in der Malerei", in: Grabar, Lasarew, Kemenow, *Geschichte der russischen Kunst*,[82] 3, Dresden 1959, 457-478, fig. 356; Onasch, *Ikonen*,[79] fig. 9; B. Rothemund, *Handbuch der Ikonenkunst*, München [2]1966, fig. on p. 203; Alpatov, *Early Russian Icon Painting*,[78] pl. 196; Catalogue

155

1000-Летие,[32] No. 201 (p. 159; here with the double square nimbus). *God Father* without inscription **ВЕТХИ ДЄНЬМИ** also in Антонова, Мнева, *Каталог,*[88] *1*, fig. 46; Lasarew, *loc. cit.*, fig. 143 (on p. 160 called *Gott Zebaoth* because of the accompanying seraphim; *cf.* Is *6*, 2-3); Onasch, *Ikonen,*[79] pl. 24; Felicetti-Liebenfels, *Geschichte* (1972*),*[87] fig. 296; Lichatschow, Laurina, Puschkarjow, *loc. cit.*, pl. 55. Likewise, Felicetti-Liebenfels' description of *God Father* with a double square nimbus on a four-field Pskowian icon in Moscow (1547) (Alpatov, *loc. cit.*, pl. 191; М. В. Алпатов, И. С. Родникова, *Псковская Икона XIII – XVI веков,* Ленинград 1991, pl. 119) as *the Ancient of Days* (*Geschichte* (1972*),*[92] pp. 162-163) is not authenticated by an inscription.

[95] Felicetti-Liebenfels equated the *Ancient of Days* with the *Lord Sabaoth*, though on the occasion of an отечество type Trinity icon where the identification of *God Father* as the *Ancient of Days* is not epigraphically legitimized (Felicetti-Liebenfels, *Geschichte* (1972),[87] p. 149, referring to fig. 296), indirectly also Onasch, *Ikonen,*[79] p. 356 (referring to pl. 24), in so far as he deduced *God Father* from Dan *7*, 9 and the seraphim depicted beside him from Is *6*, 2, the verse preceding their praise of the *Lord Sabaoth*. *Cf.* Антонова, Мнева, *Каталог,*[88] *1*, pp. 94-95.

[96] A. W. Carr, "The Murals of the Bema and the Naos", in: *Asinou Across Time,*[32] 211-310, pp. 226, 234. *Cf.* Ch. Diehl, *Manuel d'art byzantin*, vol. 2, Paris 1926, p. 489: *«l'ancien des jours» (ὁ παλαιὸς τῶν ἡμερῶν)... est à la fois le Père et le Fils.*

[97] Lazarev, *Old Russian Murals,*[91] fig. 98, p. 124; Лазарев, *Древнерусские Мозаики и Фрески,*[74] fig. 270, p. 106.

[98] Diehl, *Manuel,*[96] 2, fig. 275, pp. 580, 582; L. Shivkova, *Das Tetraevangeliar des Zaren Ivan Alexander,* Recklinghausen 1977, pl. I.

[99] S. Pelekanidis, M. Chatzidakis, "Hagios Stephanos", in: Pelekanidis, Chatzidakis, *Kastoria,*[68] 6-21, figs. 18, 19;

Shivkova, *Tetraevangeliar*,[98] pl. III (*cf.* K. Wessel, "Christusbild", *RBK 1*, 966-1047, cols. 1028-1029).

[100] R. Hamann-Mac Lean, H. Hallensleben, *Die Monumentalmalerei in Serbien und Makedonien vom 11. bis zum frühen 14. Jahrhundert* [Osteuropastudien der Hochschulen des Lands Hessen, Reihe II, Marburger Abhandlungen zur Geschichte und Kultur Osteuropas, 3-5], Gießen 1963, fig. 23; V. Đurić, *Die Kirche der Hl. Sophie in Ohrid* [Kunstdenkmäler in Jugoslawien], Beograd 1963, fig. 26.

[101] K. Weitzmann, M. Chatzidakis, K. Miatev, S. Radojčić, *Frühe Ikonen. Sinai Griechenland Bulgarien Jugoslawien*, Wien, München 1965, pl. 19; K. Weitzmann, W. C. Loerke, E. Kitzinger, H. Buchthal, *The Place of Book Illumination in Byzantine Art*, Princeton 1975, fig. 33; K. Weitzmann, M. Chatzidakis, S. Radojčić, *Le grand livre des icônes*, Paris 1983, pl. on p. 41; Drăguţ, Lupan, *Wandmalerei*,[76] fig. 227; Papadopoulo-Kérameus, p. 211; Didron, *Manuel*, p. 456; Schäfer, *Handbuch*, p. 379; Hetherington, *Manual*, p. 82; Erminia, p. 221.

[102] F. DÖLGER, *Mönchsland Athos*, München 1943, p. 184, fig. 105, published a miniature in a 12th cent. manuscript in the monastery Vatopedi (Mount Athos) showing *the Lord* speaking to Hiob. In his opinion, *the Lord* is the *Preexistent Logos* and at the same time, on account of his old man's features, the *Ancient of Days*. In fact, *the Lord* has the circular nimbus with an inscribed cross (though without the letters ὁ ὤν) and the epithet IC XC while an epigraphic reference to Dan 7, 9, 13, 22 is lacking.

[103] Lasarew, Malerei,[94] fig. 70; ; Onasch, *Ikonen*,[79] pl. 15; Lichatschow, Laurina, Puschkarjow, *Nowgoroder Ikonen*,[88] pl. 2.

[104] Carr, Murals,[100] p. 226, note 45. *Cf.* Lasarew, Malerei,[94] p. 86.

[105] М. Чанак-Медић, Б. Тодић, *Манастир Пећка Патријаршија*, Нови Сад 2014, fig. 134.

[106] N. M. Elias, *The Divine Liturgy Explained*, Athens
[4]1984, pp. 160-161.
[107] Чанак-Медић, Тодић, *Манастир*,[105] figs. 60, 61.
[108] Sch-20, figs. 2, 3. Jesus Christ is also equated with
the *Lord Sabaoth* in Martin Luther's famous hymn *Ein feste
Burg ist unser Gott*: *Und fragst du, wer der ist – er heißt
Jesus Christ, der Herr Zebaoth, und ist kein andrer Gott...*
[109] Belting, fol. 97v.
[110] Iconographically, the arrangement resembles the
Russian отечество icons; see note 94.
[111] I. Ševčenko, "Die Bildlegenden", in: Belting, Text,
83-164, pp. 117-119; S. Dufrenne, "Die Psalmen", *ibid.*
192-250, pp. 216-217. The composition which is not a
straightforward illustration of the pertinent psalm verses
(Ševčenko, p. 119), has been interpreted as Christ, the
logos begotten in Eternity as well as the *incarnate logos*
who has risen and is enthroned in divine eternity (Dufrenne,
loc. cit., p. 216).
[112] *Cf.* Catalogue *1000-Лemue*,[32] No. 124 (p. 102), pp.
352-353.
[113] Musicescu, Ulea, *Voroneţ*,[76] fig. 46; Drăguţ, Lupan,
Wandmalerei,[76] fig. 180.
[114] Musicescu, Ulea, *Voroneţ*,[76] figs. 53, 54; Drăguţ,
Lupan, *Wandmalerei*,[76] figs. 180, 184, 186.
[115] Musicescu, Ulea, *Voroneţ*,[76] fig. 55; Drăguţ, Lupan,
Wandmalerei,[76] fig. 189.
[116] Drăguţ, Lupan, *Wandmalerei*,[76] fig. 180.
[117] I am much indebted to Dr. Marina A. Bobrik,
Moscow, who deciphered and identified the text.
[118] Grabar, Oprescu, *Bemalte Kirchen*,[76] pl. XVI (not
Moldoviţa), XXI; Garidis, *La représentation*,[1] figs. 7, 8;
Musicescu, Ulea, *Voroneţ*,[76] figs. 45, 52; Grabar, *La
représentation*,[2] figs. 1, 2; Drăguţ, Lupan, *Wandmalerei*,[76]
figs. 180, 190, 191; Garidis, *Études*,[1] figs. 96, 97; Sch-11,
pl. 8a,b.

[119] ΑΡΑΠЬСКЫ: J. Pawlowsky, *Russisch-Deutsches Wörterbuch*, Riga, Leipzig [3]1900, p. 17 (not Arabs; *cf.* Sch-11, note 26).
[120]] Drăguţ, Lupan, *Wandmalerei*,[76] figs. 180, 192, 193.
[121] Drăguţ, Lupan, *Wandmalerei*,[76] figs. 180, 192.
[122] Musicescu, Ulea, *Voroneţ*,[76] fig. 56. *Cf.*
Строгановский Иконописный Лицевой Подлинник
(Конца XVI – начала XVIII столетии) / Ikonenmaler-
handbuch der Familie Stroganow, Москва 1869, reprint
München 1965, pp. 188, 195.
[123] Musicescu, Ulea, *Voroneţ*,[76] figs. 47-49; Drăguţ,
Lupan, *Wandmalerei*,[76] figs. 180, 188.
[124] Grabar, Oprescu, *Bemalte Kirchen*,[76] pl. XXII;
Musicescu, Ulea, *Voroneţ*,[76] figs. 50-51; Grabar, *La
représentation*,[2] fig. 2; Drăguţ, Lupan, *Wandmalerei*,[76] fig.
187.
[125] Musicescu, Ulea, *Voroneţ*,[76] fig. 51.
[126] Grabar, Oprescu, *Bemalte Kirchen*,[76] p. 16, pl. XIX;
Musicescu, Ulea, *Voroneţ*,[76] figs. 45, 56; Drăguţ, Lupan,
Wandmalerei,[76] figs. 180, 195.
[127] Grabar, Oprescu, *Bemalte Kirchen*,[76] fig. on p. 10 and
pl. XX (not *links vom Thron der Ethymasia* (as on p. 16);
ein Heiliger, der das Kreuz trägt, is not *vielleicht Johannes
der Täufer*, but the good thief.
[128] Musicescu, Ulea, *Voroneţ*,[76] fig. 55; Drăguţ, Lupan,
Wandmalerei,[76] fig. 189.
[129] Grabar, Oprescu, *Bemalte Kirchen*,[76] pl. XVI.
[130] Grabar, Oprescu, *Bemalte Kirchen*,[76] pl. XXI;
Garidis, *La représentation*,[1] fig. 8; Garidis, *Études*,[1] fig. 96.
[131] Papadopoulo-Kérameus, p. 140; Didron, *Manuel*, p.
263; Schäfer, *Handbuch*, p. 263; Hetherington, *Manual*, p.
49; Erminia, p. 214.
[132] Rothemund, *Handbuch*,[94] p. 207, figs. on pp. 209,
211; Onasch,[15] p. 72.
[133] Underwood, *The Kariye Djami*,[14] vol. 1, pp. 200, 203-
204, pls. 368-370, 384, 385.

[134] Underwood, *The Kariye Djami*,[14] vol. 1, p. 199, vol. 3., pls. 368, 369, 373, 374, 381, 386, 390.

[135] K. Papadopoulos, *Die Wandmalereien des XI. Jahrhunderts in der Kirche Παναγία τῶν Χαλκέων in Thessaloniki* [Byzantina Vindobonensia, 2], Graz, Köln 1966, p. 62.

[136] D. Z. Sofianos, *Meteora Wegweiser*,[14] fig. on p. 32.

[137] Drăguţ, Lupan, *Wandmalerei*,[76] figs. 192, 193; legend: *Die Gerechten auf dem Weg ins Paradies*.

[138] Musicescu, Ulea, *Voroneţ*,[76] figs. 47-49, 51; Drăguţ, Lupan, *Wandmalerei*,[76] fig. 180.

[139] In Voroneţ: Drăguţ, Lupan, *Wandmalerei*,[76] figs. 182, 183; in Dragalevci (1476): A. Boschkov, *Die bulgarische Malerei. Von den Anfängen bis zum 19. Jahrhundert*, Recklinghausen 1969, fig. 98.

[140] Misunderstood by Schäfer, *Handbuch*, p. 271 (*Ein großer Engel entfaltet den Himmel wie ein Blatt*), by Rice, *A concise history*,[86] legend of fig. 54 (*angels at the top of the painting unfurl a scroll*), and by Garidis, *Études*,[1] p. 26 (Torcello: *un ange développe le firmament sous forme d'un rouleau*).

[141] Numbering of the chapters and verses as in NETS.[8]

[142] A. Deissler, A. Vögtle with J. M. Nützel (eds.), *Neue Jerusalemer Bibel*, Freiburg, Basel, Wien, [2]1985, p. 1305: *Joschafat "Jahwe richtet", symbolischer Name, an der Jahwe mit den Völkern ins Gericht geht... dürfte es in der Nähe von Jerusalem zu suchen sein, ohne daß man es mit dem späteren "Tal Joschafat" (Kidrontal, südöstlich vom Tempel) gleichsetzen müßte.*

[143] *Cf.* Ps 44, 2: ἡ γλῶσσα μου κάλαμος γραμματέως ὀξγράφου. Neither a scroll nor the name of the man in the otherwise identical scene in the monastery of the princess (княгинин монастырь) in Vladimir (1647-1648): Danilowa, Mnewa, *Malerei*,[82] p. 257, fig. 186 (among the people *on the left hand* there are *westeuropäische Ausländer* in contemporary costume).

[144] Garidis, *La représentation*,[1] pp. 94, 95; Garidis, *Études*,[1] pp. 100, 101, figs. 36, 38 (Johannes; *cf.* H. Skrobucha, *Meisterwerke der Ikonenmalerei*, Recklinghausen 1961, pl. L; *The George R. Hann Collection* (auction, catalogue), vol. 1, New York 1980, No. 90; Grabar, *La représentation*,[2] fig. 4), pp. 92, 110, figs. 11, 12, 52 (Aaron, as the leader of the 12 tribes of Israel: Garidis, *Études*,[1] p. 85), pp. 103, 111, figs. 39, 59 (Moses; *cf.* Rice, *A Concise History*,[86] fig. 119). Without alien peoples: Garidis, *Études*,[1] figs. 52, 54, 66.

[145] Grabar, *La représentation*,[2] p. 191.

[146] Grabar, *La représentation*,[2] p. 193.

[147] Papadopoulo-Kérameus, p. 141; Didron, *Manuel*, p. 269; Schäfer, *Handbuch*, p. 267; Hetherington, *Manual*, p. 49; Erminia, p. 217.

[148] Schäfer, *Handbuch*, p. 268.

[149] Papadopoulo-Kérameus, p. 141.

[150] Hetherington, *Manual*, p. 105 for p. 49.

[151] In Dt *18*, κατὰ πάντα belongs to verse 16 and is the beginning of a new sentence.

[152] Proastio: προφήτην ὑμῖν ἀναστήσει ΚС ὁ ΘС ἐκ τῶν ἀδελ[φῶν]; Kastanea: only until ἀναστήσει ΚС (both inscriptions orthographically emended).

[153] Sch-22, p. 511.

[154] In Levkothea without ὡς ἐμε.

[155] Didron, *Manuel*, pp. 137-138; Schäfer, *Handbuch*, p. 155, note 1.

[156] Καπεσοβίτες Ζωγράφοι. Ἡμερολόγιο,[77] fig. illustrating the week 25th to 31st of August; Sch-22, figs. 6, 7.

[157] Sch-22, p. 514.

[158] Didron, *Manuel*, p. 271; Schäfer, *Handbuch*, p. 271.

[159] P. Hunt, "Confronting the end. The interpretation of the Last Judgment in a Novogorod Wisdom icon", *Byzantinoslavica 65* (2007) 275-325, p. 295.

[160] D. M. Goldfrank, "Who put the snake on the icon and the tollbooths on the snake? A problem of Last Judgment

iconography", *Harvard Ukrainian Studies 19* (1995) 180-199, p. 184, note 15.

[161] Garidis, *La représentation*,[1] fig. 9; Danilowa, Mnewa, *Malerei*,[82] p. 308, figs. 247, 248; F. Kudrjawzew,, *Der goldene Ring*, Leningrad 1976/1988, fig. 24; Garidis, *Études*,[1] fig. 101.

[162] N. Ζιάς, Σ. Καδᾶς, *Ἱερά Μονή Ὁσίου Γρηγορίου Ἁγίου Ὄρους. Οἱ τοιχογραφίες τοῦ καθολικοῦ*, Ἅγιον Ὄρος 1998, figs. 265, 266.

[163] Skrobucha, *Meisterwerke*;[144] Onasch, *Ikonen*;[79] Rice, *Ikonen*;[85] H. P. Gerhard [Skrobucha], *Welt der Ikonen*, Recklinghausen ²1963; Антонова, Мнева, *Каталог*;[88] S. Radojčić, *The Icons of Serbia and Macedonia*, New York 1963; Catalogue *Kunstschätze in Bulgarischen Museen*;[45] Weitzmann, Chatzidakis, Miatev, Radojčić, *Frühe Ikonen*;[101] В. Н. Лазарев / V. N. Lazarev, *Новгородская Иконопись / Novgorodian Icon-Painting*, Москва 1969; A. Papageorgiou, *Ikonen aus Zypern*, Genf 1969; Boschkov, *Die bulgarische Malerei*;[139] Smirnowa, *Moskauer Ikonen*;[69] I. J. Danilowa, *Dionissi*, Wien, München 1970; С. И. Масленицын / S. I. Maslenitsyn, *Яарославская Iконопись / Jaroslavian Icon-Painting*, Москва / Moscow 1973; Alpatov, *Early Russian Icon Painting*;[78] Lasarew, *Ikonen*;[82] A. Tschilingirov, *Die Kunst des christlichen Mittelalters in Bulgarien. 4. bis 18. Jahrhundert*, Berlin, München 1979; *Hann Collection*;[144] Lichatschow, Laurina, Puschkarjow, *Nowgoroder Ikonen*;[88] Weitzmann, Chatzidakis, Radojčić, *Le grand livre*;[101] K. Boyadjiévski (ed.), *Le trésor artistique de la Macédoine*, Skopje 1984; K. Weitzmann, G. Alibegašvili, A. Volskaja, M. Chatzidakis, G. Babić, M. Alpatov, T. Voinescu, *The Icon*, New York 1987; Grierson, *Gates of Mystery*;[82] Catalogue *1000-Летие*;[32] Алпатов, Родникова, *Псковская Икона*;[94] G. Popow, *Twerer Ikonen, 13. bis 17. Jahrhundert*, St. Petersburg 1993 ; V. N. Lazarev (G. I. Vzdornov, ed.), *Die russische Ikone*, Darmstadt, Zürich, Düsseldorf 1997, and others.

[164] Papageorgiou, *Ikonen aus Zypern*,[163] fig on p. 93
(A.D. 1545). - John *8*, 12 on the book of Christ is old:
Constantinople, Hagia Sophia, mosaic above the door of
entrance: Weitzmann, Alibegašvili, Volskaja, Chatzidakis,
Babić, Alpatov, Voinescu, *The Icon*,[163] p. 25.
[165] Tschilingirov, *Kunst des christlichen Mittelalters*,[163]
fig. 193.
[166] *Cf.* H. Sachs, E. Badstübner, H. Neumann,
Christliche Ikonographie in Stichworten, Leipzig [3]1988, pp.
240-241: *Lichtsymbolik.*
[167] Also in Greek: Papageorgiou, *Ikonen aus Zypern*,[163]
fig on p. 96 (A.D. 1554).
[168] Rice, *Ikonen*,[78] pl. 12; Lazarev, *Novgorodian Icon
Painting*,[163] pl. 45; Maslenitsyn, *Jaroslavian Icon-Painting*,[163] pl. 22; Alpatov, *Early Russian Icon Painting*,[78] fig.
97; Smirnowa, *Moskauer Ikonen*,[69] pl. 128; Popow, *Twerer
Ikonen*,[163] pl. 123. Also in Greek: Wall painting in the
Protaton (Mount Athos): P. Huber, *Heilige Berge. Sinai
Athos Golgota – Ikonen Fresken Miniaturen*, Zürich,
Einsiedeln, Köln [2]1982, fig. 109.
[169] Papadopoulo-Kérameus, p. 140; *cf.* Didron, *Manuel*,
p. 268; Schäfer, *Handbuch*, p. 267; Hetherington, *Manual*,
p. 49; Erminia, p. 215. *Cf.* 2Tim *4*, 8. On icons: catalogue
Kunstschätze in Bulgarischen Museen,[45] No. 324, pl. XII (O

ΔΙΚΕΟC ΚΡΙΤΗC Ο ΕΛΕΜΩΝ, not φοβερὸς κριτής!);
Papageorgiou, *Ikonen aus Zypern*,[163] fig. on p. 96; as wall
painting in the Toplitchki monastery, Djvan near Demir
Hissar, Makedonija: Boyadjiévski, *Le trésor artistique*,[163] p.
225.
[170] In Greek: catalogue *Kunstschätze in Bulgarischen
Museen*,[45] No. 262 (with fig.); Weitzmann, Chatzidakis, Miatev, Radojčić, *Frühe Ikonen*,[101] fig. on p. 111 (Sofia, Art
Gallery, 16th cent.) ; Papageorgiou, *Ikonen aus Zypern*,[163]
fig. on p. 79 (icon in the monastery of Saint Neophytos, 16th
cent.), the beginning also in Elmalı kilise, Göreme: G. de
Jerphanion, *Une nouvelle province de l'art byzantin. Les*

églises rupestres de Cappadoce [Bibliothèque archéologique et historique, 5], *1* (1925), p. 433.

[171] Catalogue *Kunstschätze in Bulgarischen Museen*,[45] No. 360 (Slavonic).

[172] Gerhard, *Welt der Ikonen*,[163] fig. 19 (in Greek, 1653).

[173] Catalogue *Kunstschätze in Bulgarischen Museen*,[45] No. 324, pl. XII (in Greek).

[174] Gerhard, *Welt der Ikonen*,[163] fig. XXII; Danilowa, *Dionissi*,[163] fig. 79; Lasarew, *Ikonen*,[82] fig. 27; Weitzmann, Alibegašvili, Volskaja, Chatzidakis, Babić, Alpatov, Voinescu, *The Icon*,[163] fig. on p. 289; Grierson, *Gates of Mystery*,[82] No. 10; Smirnowa, *Moskauer Ikonen,*[69] pl. 55; Lazarev (Vzdornov), *Die russische Ikone*,[163] fig. 127; Popow, *Twerer Ikonen*,[163] pl. 97.

[175] D. C. W[infield], *Asinou. A Guide*, Nicosia 1969, fig. A; Stylianou, *The Painted Churches* (1985),[66] p. 114; A. Papageorgiou, 'The Architecture of the Church of the Panagia Phorbiotissa', in: *Asinou Across Time*,[32] 39-66, p. 55, fig. 2.1.

[176] A. Stylianou, J. A. Stylianou, *The Painted Churches of Cyprus*, Stourbridge 1964, fig. 22; *Asinou Across Time*,[32] figs. 5.11, 5.28, 5.29.

[177] Winfield, *Asinou*,[175] pp. 16, 17 (No. 103); S. Kalopissi-Verti, "The Murals of the Narthex: The Paintings of the Late Thirteenth and Fourteenth Centuries", in: *Asinou Across Time,*[32] 115-208, pp. 152-153, figs. 5.11, 5.28, 5.29.

[178] Winfield, *Asinou*,[175] pp. 14, 15; Stylianou, *The Painted Churches* (1985),[66] pp. 137-140; Kalopissi-Verti, *Murals*,[177] p. 131. The painters of the *Last Judgment* respected the somewhat older paintings (*Asinou Across Time*,[32] pp. 92, 114, 312, figs. 4.1-4.4, 5.1, 5.2, 5.4-5.8, 5.10, 5.11, 7.2, 7.7, 7.26-7.29) (*cf.* Kalopissi-Verti, *Murals*,[177] pp. 131, 207, A. W. Carr, "Conclusion", *Asinou Across Time*,[32] 361-370, p. 366).

[179] The word has not been used; *cf.* Th. v. Bogyay, "Hetoimasia", *RBK 2* (1971) 1189-1202, col. 1190.

[180] Tzioras,[74] fig. on p. 55; *Ζίας, Καδᾶς, Ἱερά Μονή*,[162] figs. 214, 215.

[181] Papadopoulo-Kérameus, p. 141; Didron, *Manuel*, p. 271; Schäfer, *Handbuch*, p. 268; Hetherington, *Manual*, p. 49; Erminia, p. 215.

[182] Καπεσοβίτες Ζωγράφοι,[77] fig. illustrating the week 25th to 31st of August.

[183] Onasch, *Liturgie*,[15] p. 329. *Cf.* A. Schott, *Das vollständige Römische Meßbuch*, Freiburg 1956, pp. 444ff. (*Ordo Missae*), 460 (*Sanctus*).

[184] Elias, *Divine Liturgy*,[107] pp. 160-161.

[185] *Cf.* Mk *11*, 9, Lk *19*, John *12*, 12.

[186] Erminia, p. 214 (referring only to Is *6*, 3, not to Mt *21*, 9).

[187] Figs.: I. Grabar, V. Lasareff, O. Demus, *UdSSR. Frühe russische Ikonen* [UNESCO-Sammlung der Weltkunst], Paris 1958, pl. IX (quoted by Garidis, *La représentation*,[1] p. 95 note 1, as the *Last Judgment* icon in Stockholm); Антонова, Мнева, *Каталог*,[88] *1*, fig. 72; Alpatov, *Early Russian Icon Painting*,[78] pl. 113; Felicetti-Liebenfels, *Geschichte* (1972),[87] fig. 353; Onasch, *Liturgie*,[15] fig. 44; Lichatschow, Laurina, Puschkarjow, *Nowgoroder Ikonen*,[88] pl. 72; Garidis, *Études*,[1] fig. 36; M. Alpatov, *The Icons of Russia*, in: Weitzmann, Alibegašvili, Volskaja, Chatzidakis, Babić, Alpatov, Voinescu, *The Icon*,[163] fig. on p. 281; Hunt, Confronting the end,[159] pl. 1; Lazarev (Vzdornov), *Die russische Ikone*,[163] fig. 48.

[188] Grabar, *La représentation*,[2] fig. 4.

[189] Skrobucha, *Meisterwerke*,[144] p. 250, pl. L; *Hann Collection*,[144] No. 90, p. 189.

[190] Catalogue *1000-Летие*,[32] No. 124 (16th cent.).

[191] Garidis, *Études*,[1] p. 42; Goldfrank, Who put the snake?[153] *Cf.* Kalopissi-Verti, Murals,[177] p. 146.

[192] GRABAR[3] insists that in St it winds around the *peoples* (pp. 191, 194, 196); *cf.*, however, fig. 4.

[193] The *hetoimasia* with the cross between two angels also in the *Last Judgment* in the cathedral of the Archangels

in the Kremlin of Moscow (though without scrolls or incense burners); adjacent to the right angel is Moses who points with his right arm to Christ, the central figure of the *deesis*. Immediately to the right of Moses people with white headgears (= the doctors of the law and Pharisees; *cf.* Garidis, *Études*,[1] pp. 83-85): H. Faensen, *Siehe die Stadt, die leuchtet*, Leipzig 1989, fig. 187 (17th cent.).

[194] Hunt, Confronting the end,[159] p. 295.

[195] Hunt, Confronting the end,[159] p. 295: *the saints and the sinners are on one continuous path*; the sinners, too, are *invitees into the kingdom*.

[196] Hunt, Confronting the end,[159] p. 295: *while he drops the arm holding his scroll, presumably with his traditional words of excoriation.*

[197] Skrobucha, *Meisterwerke*,[144] pl. L; *Hann Collection*,[144] No. 90; Grabar, *La représentation*,[2] fig. 4. GRABAR misunderstood Moses in St. as John the Theologian and postulated Mt *25*, 41 as the text on his scroll. A statement of Jesus recorded by Matthew in John's mouth is impossible.

[198] Lichatschow, Laurina, Puschkarjow, *Nowgoroder Ikonen*,[88] pl. 71.

[199] Didron, La dalmatique,[73] p. 163; Papadopoulo-Kérameus, p. 128 (Τὸ πᾶσα πνοή); Didron, *Manuel*, p. 235 (*La réunion de tous les esprits*); Schäfer, *Handbuch*, p. 237 (*Die ganze Geisterwelt*); Hetherington, *Manual*, p. 45 (*The "Let everything that has breath [praise the Lord]"*); Erminia, p. 214 (*Toată suflarea să laude pe Domnul*), identified as *All Saints*: Sch-22.

[200] Garidis, *Études*,[1] pp. 42, 97-98, 101, fig. 76; Skrobucha, *Meisterwerke*,[144] p. 250; Weitzmann, Chatzidakis, Miatev, Radojčić, *Frühe Ikonen*,[101] p. XIII-XIV, fig. on p. 19; I. Shalina, "The Vision of the Heavenly Ladder and the Vision of Evlogii", in: Grierson, *Gates of Mystery*,[82] 198-203; Weitzmann, Chatzidakis, Radojčić, *Le grand livre*,[101] p. 23, fig. on p. 41.

[201] Grabar, *La représentation*,[2] fig. 4; Catalogue *1000-Летие*,[32] No. 124.

[202] Hetherington, *Manual*, p. 49. *Cf.* Papadopoulo-Kérameus, p. 141; Didron, *Manuel*, p. 268; Schäfer, *Handbuch*, p. 267.

[203] von Bogyay, Hetoimasia,[175] cols. 1189-1202; Onasch, *Liturgie*,[15] pp. 156-157.

[204] Millet, *Dalmatique,*[89] p. 28; ДавидовТемерински, Циклус,[13] fig. 1, Todić, Čanak Medić, *The Dečani Monastery*,[13] fig. 368.

[205] Garidis, *Études*,[1] pp. 83-85.

[206] Until ἀκούσεσθε (not Dt *18*, 15).

[207] Sch-22, fig. 4 (in Slavonic; until **послȣшаите по всемȣ**).

[208] Grabar, Oprescu, *Bemalte Kirchen*,[76] p. 16, pl. XIX.

[209] Musicescu, Ulea, *Voroneţ*,[76] fig. 56; Drăguţ, Lupan, *Wandmalerei*,[76] figs. 180, 195.

[210] Lazarev, *Old Russian Murals*,[91] p. 186; Rice, *Byzantinische Malerei*,[14] fig. 135; Лазарев, *Древнерусские Мозаики и Фрески*,[74] p. 73, fig. 412; Kudrjawzew, *Der goldene Ring*,[161] fig. 89; G. K. Wagner, *Alte russische Städte [Kunstdenkmäler in der Sowjetunion* ((ed. R. Hootz)], Darmstadt 1980, p. 390, fig. 319; Г. К. Вагнер, *Старые русские города*, Москва 1980, p. 356, fig. 11.

[211] **МИНIА**, мѣсацъ Iȣнïй, Кıевъ 1893, fol. 214r: Паѵле, оуста Господна, ѡснованïе оученïй, иногда оубѡ гонитель Iисоуса спаса, нынѣ же и первопрестольникъ апостолѡвъ бывъ, блаженне. Тѣмже неизглагѡланнаѧ видѣлъ еси моудре, даже до третïагѡ небесе возшедъ и взывалъ еси: Прïидите со мною, и благихъ не лишимсѧ. Dr. Marina A. Bobrik, Moscow, kindly deciphered and identified the text.

[212] The sticheron refers to 2Cor *12*, 2-4.

[213] I am indebted to Professor Dr. K. C. Felmy, Erlangen, for a translation of the Slavonic text.

[214] Winfield, *Asinou*,[175] pp. 16, 17; Kalopissi-Verti, *Murals*,[177] figs. 5.28, 5.29.

The Role of the Inscription Bands in Wall
Paintings of the *Laud Psalms*

[1] Lesnovo and Chrelju's tower in the Rila monastery, perhaps Kučevište. It has often been taken for granted that Ps 150 has been illustrated, too, but this assumption has not been corroborated. *Cf.* Sch-24, pp. 351-352; Sch-26, p. 143; Sch-28, p. 155.
[2] Sch-2, pp. 26-28; Sch-3, pp. 182, 188, 226, 232; Sch-4, p. 231; Sch-8, p. 151; Sch-10, p. 289; Sch-11, pp. 142, 154; Sch-12, p. 53; Sch-15, p. 203; Sch-16, p. 184; Sch-19, p. 145; Sch-20, pp. 89-90; Sch-21, p. 194; Sch-24, p. 352; Sch-26, pp. 143-145; Sch-29, p. 186; Sch-28, p. 155 (later paintings at Korona (Thessaly), Redina (Agrapha), in the church of the Three Hierarchs at Filipeştii de Pădure (Rumania; 1692)).
[3] Sch-25, p. 302; Sch-26, p. 153; Sch-27, p. 3 (only at Vilitza and Melissourgoi, both in Epirus). At Ano Doloi (Mani), the circular inscription consists of the verses Ps 150, 1-2. In Iviron (Athos), beside King David there is an altar with a book on it which shows verse 1 and the beginning of verse 2: Θ. Μ. Προβατάκης, *Τὸ Ἅγιον Ὄρος, Ἰσττορία – Τέχνη – Παράδοση*, Ἀθῆνα *s. a.*, fig. on p. 108.
[4] Sch-13, p. 183; Sch-15, p. 221; Sch-22, p. 496; Sch-30, p. 3.
[5] Strzygowski, pp. 67-68, pl. XLV and facsimile in colours; Belting, b) fol. 185.
[6] In Hagios Nikolaos Vathias, at Galataki (both on Euboea), in the Philanthropinon monastery and presumably at Tsepelovo (both in Epirus): Sch-13, p. 194; Sch-15, p. 221; Sch-22, note 83.
[7] F.-L. Hossfeld, E. Zenger, *Psalmen 101-150* [Herders Theologischer Kommentar zum Alten Testament], Freiburg, Basel, Wien 2008, p. 883.
[8] Sch-10, p. 277; Sch-22, p. 496; Sch-25, p. 285.

[9] Millet, *Monuments,* pp. 55, 58, 65, legends of pls. 244-1 and 263-1, 2; F. Fichtner, *Wandmalereien der Athos-Klöster. Grundsätzliches zu den Planungen der Bildfolgen des 14.-17. Jahrhundert. Welt- und Lebensanschauung, Ritus, Architektur, Malerei*, Berlin 1931, p. 36; C. Christov, G. Stojkov, K. Mijatev, *Das Rila-Kloster* [Aus dem Erbgut der bulgarischen Baukunst, 6], Sofia 1957, pp. 50, 275, 315, 316; W. Felicetti-Liebenfels, *Geschichte der russischen Ikonenmalerei in den Grundzügen dargestellt* [Forschungen und Berichte des Kunsthistorischen Institutes der Universität Graz, 3], Graz 1972, p. 160, legend of fig. 329; Κ. Δ. Καλοκύρης, *Βυζαντιναὶ ἐκκλησίαι τῆς Ἱερας Μητροπόλεως Μεσσηνίας*, Θεσσαλονίκη 1973, pp. 190-192, 218, legends of figs. 162, 166, 167β (here legible inscription Ps *148*, 9a), 168α (here legible inscription Ps *149*, 1b-2a), 202α,β (scenes of Ps *148*, 10), 204α, 205α, p. 218, *cf.* p. 190 (there is nowhere a relation with Ps *150*, 6); H. Deliyanni-Doris, *Die Wandmalereien der Lite der Klosterkirche von Hosios* Meletios [Miscellanea Byzantina Monacensia, 18], München 1975, p. 10; Л. Прашков, *Църквата Рождество Христово в Арбанаси*, София 1979, p. 138 and legend of fig. 120; P. Huber, *Athos. Leben Glaube Kunst*, Zürich, Freiburg ³1982, pp. 329, 332, 334; Κ. Μ. Φούσκας, *Ἱερά Μονή Ἁγίου Νικολάου Ἄνω Βαθείας Εὔβοιας. 500 Χρόνια ζωῆς καὶ μαρτυρίας* , Ἄνω Βαθείας 1988, p. 151; V. Mamukelashvili, *Svetitskhoveli*, Мцхета 2004, p. 43.
[10] Sch-15, p. 217; Stichel, *Beiträge*, pp. 252-256.
[11] H. Brockhaus, *Die Kunst in den Athos-Klöstern*, Leipzig 1891, ²1924, p. 80; Stichel, *Beiträge*, pp. 252-255. *Cf.* Sch-8, pp. 156, 174, 181; Sch-10.
[12] Brockhaus, *Die Kunst*,[11] pp. 68-69; Sch-15, p. 218.
[13] *E. g.*: A. Grabar, *Les grands siècles de la peinture: La peinture byzantine*, Genève 1953, fig. on p. 114; A. Papageorghiou, *Masterpieces of the Byzantine Art of Cyprus*, Nicosia 1965, pl. XXIII-1; A. Stylianou, J. A. Stylianou, *The Painted Churches of Cyprus. Treasures of*

Byzantine Art, London 1985, frontispiece, figs. 247, 294, 300; W. F. Volbach, J. Lafontaine-Dosogne, *Byzanz und der christliche Osten* [Propyläen Kunstgeschichte, 3], Berlin 1968, fig. 23b; A. Nicolaïdès, "L'église de la Panagia Arakiotissa à Lagoudéra, Chypre: Etude iconographique des fresques de 1192", *Dumbarton Oaks Papers 50* (1996) 1-137, figs. 35, 36; D. Winfield, J. Winfield, *The Church of the Panaghia tou Arakos at Lagoudhera, Cyprus: The Paintings and Their Painterly Significance* [Dumbarton Oaks Studies, 37], Washington D. C. 2003, pl. 1, fig. 42; Sch-14, figs. 1, 9; Sch-15, p. 207; likewise the iconographically identical IC XC ὁ ἐλεήμων: D. Z. Sofianos, *Meteora. Wegweiser*, Kloster Megalou Meteorou s. a., fig. on p. 65; Erminia, 1ˢᵗ (unnumb.) pl.

[14] Sch-15, p. 219; Sch-20, p. 94 (note 78), 103; Sch-25, p. 285. – English translations of OT texts are quotations of *A New English Translation of the Septuagint* (NETS), Oxford University Press, 2009 (electronic edition with corrections and emendations, 2014), occasionally slightly adapted to the *Christian view*.

[15] Bust of the *Kyrios* in Hagios Nikolaos Vathias (Euboia), in the Colţea church in Bucarest and in the monasteries Grigoriou, Xeropotamou and Philotheou on Mount Athos (Ν. Ζιάς, Σ. Καδᾶς, *Ἱερά Μονή Ὁσίου Γρηγορίου Ἁγίου Ὄρους. Οἱ τοιχογραφίες τοῦ καθολικοῦ*, Ἅγιον Ὄρος 1998, fig. 220; Sch-5, p. 116, pl. 3/2; Sch-6, p. 42, fig. 1; Sch-10, figs. 6, 7).

[16] Its central scene, the Deesis, as an Icon: W. Felicetti-Liebenfels, *Geschichte der byzantinischen Ikonenmalerei*, Olten, Lausanne 1956, pl. 120; K. Weitzmann, M. Chatzidakis, K. Miatev, S. Radojčić, *Frühe Ikonen. Sinai Griechenland Bulgarien Jugoslawien*, Wien, München 1965, fig. on p. 113; A. Tschilingirov, *Die Kunst des christlichen Mittelalters in Bulgarien. 4. bis 18. Jahrhundert*, Berlin, München 1979, fig. 172. Other icons of the Pantokrator of the Deesis type: P. Huber, *Heilige*

Berge. Sinai Athos Golgota – Ikonen Fresken Miniaturen, Zürich, Einsiedeln, Köln ²1982, figs. 100, 101.

[17] An open book in Megali Panagia (Samos), Timios Ioannes near Serres, Vathia (Euboia), Kozani (Macedonia), Vilitza (Epirus), on Mount Athos in the monasteries Grigoriou (katholikon and cemetery chapel), Xeropotamou, Koutloumousiou and Dochiariou II; a closed book in Kleidonia (Epirus): Huber, *Athos*,⁹ fig. 180; Προβατάκης,³ fig. on p. 108; Th. Provatakis, *Berg Athos* [Griechische Landschaften, 13], Thessaloniki s.a., fig. on p. 34 (not Megisti Lavra, Koukouzelissa chapel); Ζιάς, Καδᾶς, *Γρηγορίου*,¹⁵ fig. 220; Sch-1, fig. 23; Sch-4,17.2; Sch-6, pp. 42-43, fig. 1; Sch-10, figs. 6, 11; Sch-28, fig. 18.

[18] As a matter of course, the *Kyrios* of all *laud psalms* paintings is Jesus Christ (*cf.* Sch-29, p. 2). This is, however, Christian interpretation; *Kyrios* of the LXX text is the equivalent of Masoretic JHWH (E. Hatch, H. A. Redpath, *A Concordance To the Septuagint and the other Greek Versions of the Old Testament (Including the Apocryphal Books)*, 2, Oxford 1897, pp. 800-839). To be strictly descriptive, for the Ps *148*, 1 illustration the designation *Kyrios* is always used. For the identification of the Κύριος of Ps *148*, 1 with Jesus Christ see (*e. g.*) K. Barth, *Erklärung des Philipperbriefes*, München 1928, pp. 58-62; J. Gnilka, *Paulus von Tarsus. Apostel und Zeuge* [Herders Theologischer Kommentar zum Neuen Testament, suppl. vol. 6], Freiburg, Basel, Wien 1996 [reprint: *Wie das Christentum entstand*, 2, 1997, 2004], pp. 199, 232; Woo-Jin Shim, *Kyrios im Johannesevangelium. Eine exegetische Untersuchung zum Kyrios-Titel im Johannesevangelium*, diss. (theol.), University of Heidelberg 2003, pp. 7-10.

[19] Sch-15, p. 222; Sch-20, p. 103. *Cf.* Ἀ. Γ. Τούρτα, *Οἱ ναοί τοῦ Ἁγίου Νικολάου στή Βίτσα καὶ τοῦ Ἁγίου Μηνᾶ στό Μονοδένδρι. Προσέγγιση στό ἔργο τῶν ζωγράφων ἀπό τό λινοτόπι* [Ὑπουργεῖο Πολιτισμοῦ, Δημοσιεύματα τοῦ Ἀρχαιολόγικοῦ Δελτίου, 44], Ἀθήνα 1991, pl. 114β; Δ.

Καμαρουλίας, *Τὰ Μοναστήρια τῆς Ἤπειρου*, vol. 1, Ἀθῆνα 1996, fig. 203.

[20] Millet, *Monuments*, pl. 244-1; G. Tzioras (ed.), *Meteora. Die heiligen Felsen und ihre Geschichte*, Kalabaka *s. a.*, fig. on p. 54; Γ. Ν. Οἰκονόμου, *Ἡ Ρεντίνα τῶν Ἀγράφων καὶ τά μεταβυζαντινά τῆς μνημεῖα*, Ρεντίνα τῶν Ἀγράφων *s. a. (ca.* 2000), p. 124, fig. 57; Χ. Γ. Χοτζάκογλου, *Σκιάποδες, στερνόφθαλμοι, κυνοκέφαλοι. Προέλεση καὶ πρόσληψη τριῶν ἀρχαιοελληνικῶν τεράτων στὴ βυζαντινὴ τέχνη καὶ ἡ «Σχολὴ τῶν Θήβῶν»* [Βραχέα Μελετήματα Ἀρχαιολογίας καὶ Ἱστορίας τῆς Τέχνης, 1], Λευκωσία 2003, fig. 53; Sch-1, p. 170, figs. 10, 13-15; Sch-2, pp. 11-12, fig. on p. 10; Sch-4, pp. 226, 228, 236, figs. 17.1, 17.2; Sch-6, p. 43; Sch-8, p. 156; Sch-9, p. 181; Sch-10, pp. 284-285; Sch-12, pp. 49, 59; Sch-15, p. 216; Sch-16, pp. 190-198; ; Sch-22, p. 493; Sch-23, p. 75; Sch-26, p. 166; Sch-27, pp. 193-195.

[21] Okunev, p. 240, pls. XXXVI, XXXVII; Belting, a) pl. XXIX.1; R. Hootz (ed.), L. Trifunović, *Kunstdenkmäler in Jugoslawien. Ein Bildhandbuch*, vol. 1, Darmstadt 1981, fig. on p. 226 (erroneous legend: *Kuppelfresko, Christus Pantokrator*); C. Ђурић, "Христ Космократор у Леснову", *Зограф 13* (1982) 65-72, fig. 1; Gabelić, p. 184, fig. 87; I. Jevtić, "Le nouvel ordre du monde ou l'image du cosmos à Lesnovo", in: A. Cutler, A. Papaconstantinou (eds.), *The Material and the Ideal. Essays in Medieval Art and Archaeology in Honour of Jean-Michel Spieser* [The Medieval Mediterranean, 70], Leiden 2007, 129-148, figs. 2, 3; Sch-24, fig. 3; Sch-27, p. 196.

[22] For the terms *Dochiariou I* and *II* see Sch-12, p. 53, note 3; Sch-15, notes 15 and 20. Datings *ad annum* are based on dedicatory inscriptions. However, the relation between the *laud psalms* paintings and the respective inscription is often debatable (*cf.* Sch-13, p. 191; Sch-27, pp. 187-189; Sch-27).

[23] Millet, *Monuments*, pl. 244-1; Sch-1, p. 171, figs. 10, 14; Sch-27, pp. 198-199.

[24] Millet, *Monuments*, pl. 244-1; Tzioras, *Meteora*,[20] fig. on p. 54; Sch-1, fig. 10.

[25] Okunev, pls. XXXVI, XXXVII; G. Millet, T. Velmans, *La peinture du moyen âge en Yougoslavie (Serbie, Macédoine et Monténégro)*, IV, Paris 1969, figs. 46, 47; Belting, a) pl. XXIX.1; Hootz, Trifunović, *Kunstdenkmäler*,[21] vol. 1, fig. on p. 226; Ђурић, Христ Космократор,[21] fig. 1; Gabelić, fig. 87; Jevtić, Le nouvel ordre,[21] figs. 2, 3; Sch-1, fig. 20; Sch-24, fig. 3; Sch-27, pp. 196-197.

[26] H. G. Gundel, *Zodiakos. Tierkreisbilder im Altertum. Kosmische Bezüge und Jenseitsvorstellungen im antiken Alltagsleben* [Kulturgeschichte der antiken Welt, 54], Mainz 1992. V. MAMUKELASHVILI, *Svetitskhoveli*,[9] viewed the circular zodiac in Mcxeta as a representation of a calendar. Because of its role in the measurement of time, it certainly may have such meaning in an appropriate context. In a *laud psalms* composition, however, it serves to illustrate Ps *148*, 6 and is devoid of details which would justify a broader interpretation (*cf. Ockham's razor*: *non sunt multiplicanda entia praeter necessitatem*). *Cf.* Sch-12, pp. 60-61.

[27] Sch-27, p. 197. *Cf.* Sch-1, p. 175; Sch-7, pp. 76, 77. Having neither a beginning nor an end, the circle is a symbol of eternity: E. Droulers, *Dictionnaire des attributs, allégories, emblèmes et symboles*, Turnhout *s. a.* [*ca.* 1949], p. 37.

[28] Okunev, pls. XXXVI, XXXVII; Belting, a) pl. XXIX.1; Hootz, Trifunović, *Kunstdenkmäler*,[21] vol. 1, fig. on p. 226; Ђурић, Христ Космократор,[21] fig. 1; Gabelić, fig. 87; Jevtić, Le nouvel ordre,[21] figs. 2, 3; Sch-24, fig. 3; Sch-27, p. 200.

[29] Sch-2, p. 12.

[30] S. Kadas, *Der Berg Athos. Illustrierter Führer der Klöster: Geschichte und Schätze*, Athen 1986, fig. 88; K. Τσεκούρα, "Ο χορός στο Βυζάντιο", *Ἀρχαιολογία & Τέχνες 91* (2004) 6-7, fig. 1; M. Παρχαρίδου-Ἀναγνώστου, "Ο

χορός στή μεταβυζαντινή μνημειακή ἐκκλησιαστική ζωγραφική (15ος -19ος αι.)", Ἀρχαιολογία & Τέχνες 91 (2004) 50-58, fig. 6.

[31] Okunev, pl. XXXVI; Belting, a) pl. XXIX.1; Hootz, Trifunović, *Kunstdenkmäler*,[21] vol. 1, fig. on p. 226; Ђурић, Христ Космократор,[21] fig. 1; Gabelić, fig. 87; Jevtić, Le nouvel ordre,[21] figs. 2, 3; Sch-24, fig. 3.

[32] Ђурић, Христ Космократор,[21] fig. 1; Gabelić, pp. 184, 280, fig. 87; Jevtić, Le nouvel ordre ,[21] figs. 2, 3; Sch-24, fig. 3; Sch-27, pp. 196-197.

[33] Mcxeta (Georgia), Cetăţuia (Rumania, 1671/72), Nigrita, Redina (W. Beridse, E. Neubauer, *Die Baukunst des Mittelalters in Georgien vom 4. bis zum 18. Jahrhundert*, Berlin 1980, fig. 97; Οἰκονόμου, *Ρεντίνα*,[20] fig. 57; Sch-1, p. 167, fig. 6; Sch-17, p. 97; Sch-19, p. 146) (not in Nicosia (Cyprus)).

[34] Millet, *Monuments*, pl. 244-1; Tzioras, *Meteora*,[20] fig. on p. 54; Sch-1, p. 170, fig. 10.

[35] Sch-4, fig. 17.6; Sch-7, p. 67, fig. 2; Sch-10, fig. 9.

[36] Sch-2, p. 11, fig. on p. 10; Sch-4, fig. 17.1; Sch-10, fig. 10, col. fig. 27.

[37] Sch-18, pp. 81-95; Sch-19, p. 156 (Corrigendum: one year *after* the treaty of Georgievsk (1783)); Sch-27, pp. 205, 206.

[38] Okunev, p. 240; Gabelić, p. 184.

[39] Sch-3, pp. 171, 212.

[40] Sch-2, p. 12; Sch-10, col. fig. 27 (above the head of the *Kyrios*).

[41] Прашков, *Арбанаси*,[9] fig. 108; Sch-8, p. 153, figs. 2-4.

[42] Deliyanni-Doris, *Wandmalereien*,[9] p. 11.

[43] Τούρτα, *Οἱ ναοί*,[19] pls. 18, 74α,β; ; Μ. Γαρίδης, Ἀ. Παλιούρας, *Μοναστήρια νήσου Ἰωαννίνων. Ζωγραφική*, Ἰωάννινα 1993, figs. 190-194; Ἀ. Ρουμπή, "Χεῖρ' ἐπί καρπῷ ἤ Τό ταξίδι ἑνός εἰκονογραφικοῦ μοτίβου στό χρόνο", Ἀρχαιολογία & Τέχνες 91 (2004) 37-42, figs. 1, 5; Παρχαρίδου-Ἀναγνώστου, Ὁ χορός,[30] fig. 5; Β. Ν.

Papadopoulou, *The Monasteries of the Island of Ioannina. History – Architecture – Painting*, Ioannina 2004, fig.on p. 85; Χ. Πέννας, *Ή Βυζαντινή Αΐγινα*, Ἀθήνα 2004, fig. 65.

[44] Καλοκύρης, *Βυζαντιναὶ ἐκκλησίαι*,[9] pl. 204β; Χοτζάκογλου, *Σκιάποδες*,[20] fig. 83; Sch-13, pp. 174-175, 188.; Sch-23, pp. 78-79; Sch-26, pp. 167-168; Sch-27, p. 201.

[45] Sch-15, pp. 205-206; Sch-19, p. 157; Sch-21, p. 198; Sch-26, pp. 153-158.

[46] Παρχαρίδου-Ἀναγνώστου, Ὁ χορός,[30] fig. 7; Sch-10, fig. 8; Sch-19, pp. 146-148, 151, figs. 3, 4, 8, 12; Sch-26, pp. 155, 157.

[47] Sch-19, figs. 8-10.

[48] *Cf.* Οἰκονόμου, *Ρεντίνα*,[20] p. 124.

[49] E. Hein, A. Jakovljević, B. Kleidt, *Zypern – byzantinische Kirchen und Klöster. Mosaiken und Fresken*, Ratingen 1996, fig. 142; Παρχαρίδου-Ἀναγνώστου, Ὁ χορός,[30] fig. 4; Sch-19, figs. 1, 2, 4, 8, 11-14, 16-18; Sch-26, fig. 3.

[50] Hein, Jakovljević, Kleidt, *Zypern*,[49] fig. 142; Παρχαρίδου-Ἀναγνώστου, Ὁ χορός,[30] fig. 4; Sch-3, figs. 3, 4, 11, 12; Sch-11, fig. 1a; Sch-19, fig. 2; Sch-28, fig. 11.

[51] Sch-3, fig. 11; Sch-19, fig. 2.

[52] Hein, Jakovljević, Kleidt, *Zypern*,[49] fig. 142; Παρχαρίδου-Ἀναγνώστου, Ὁ χορός,[30] fig. 4; Sch-3, figs. 4, 5, 12; Sch-19, fig. 2.

[53] Hein, Jakovljević, Kleidt, *Zypern*,[49] fig. 142; Παρχαρίδου-Ἀναγνώστου, Ὁ χορός,[30] fig. 4; Sch-3, figs. 6-8, 11-13; Sch-11, fig. 1b; Sch-15, fig. 1; Sch-19, fig. 2; Sch-20, fig. 1; Sch-26, fig. 7; Schi-28, figs. 1, 2.

[54] Sch-25, p. 301; Sch-26, p. 153.

[55] Sch-28, fig. 7.

[56] English translation of Phil *2*, 8-11 by P. T. O'Brien, *The Epistle to the Philippians. A Commentary on the Greek Text*, Grand Rapids MI, Carlisle 1991, p. 203.

[57] Γαρίδης, Παλιούρας, *Μοναστήρια*,[43] fig. 209; Sch-15, pp. 212, 213, 217, figs. 13, 14. With reference to dated

dedicatory inscriptions, the *laud psalms* paintings in Makryalexi and in the Philanthropinon monastery have been dated to 1599 and 1560, respectively. *Cf.*, however, Sch-13, p. 191; Sch-27, pp. 187-189.

[58] Sch-15, p. 212, fig. 10.

[59] Sch-13, p. 180; Sch-15, p. 213, fig. 16; Sch-20, p. 104.

[60] Sch-15, pp. 208, 212, fig. 9.

[61] Sch-28, fig. 19.

[62] *Cf.* at Mcxeta the scroll of the first king of Ps *148*, 11 pointing not to the *Kyrios*, but to the great sea at the left: Sch-13, p. 182.

[63] Καλοκύρης, *Βυζαντιναὶ ἐκκλησίαι,*[9] pl. 205α;; Sch-15, p. 209, fig. 11.

[64] A. Boschkov, *Die bulgarische Malerei. Von den Anfängen bis zum 19. Jahrhundert*, Recklinghausen 1969, fig. 171; Sch-8, p. 168; Sch-15, p. 214, fig. 3; Sch-21, p. 198.

[65] Sch-20, p. 102, fig. 5.

[66] *Cf.* David at Lagoudera: Nicolaïdès, Panagia Arakiotissa,[13] pp. 44-45, pl. 42; Winfield, Winfield, *Lagoudhera,*[13] pp. 140-141, fig. 69; Sch-15, p. 208, fig. 8.

[67] *E. g.*, Sch-15, p. 206, fig. 5.

[68] Sch-20, p. 102, fig. 13.

[69] Sch-3, figs. 7, 8, 12; Sch-15, fig. 1; Sch-19, fig. 1.

[70] Hein, Jakovljević, Kleidt, *Zypern,*[49] fig. 142; Παρχαρίδου-Ἀναγνώστου, Ὁ χορός,[30] fig. 4; Sch-3, pp. 183-184, 227, figs. 7, 11, 12; Sch-15, fig. 1; Sch-19, figs. 1, 2, Sch-20, fig. 1.

[71] Sch-15, p. 206; Sch-20, p. 102.

[72] Sch-15, fig. 4.

[73] Sch-15, fig. 6.

[74] Sch-15, fig. 5.

[75] Sch-20, p. 102, fig. 8.

[76] Sch-15, p. 212, fig. 13.

[77] At first sight intriguing, this inscription establishes a relation with the kings of Ps *148*, 11a whose protagonist holds likewise a scroll with a well preserved text.

Regrettably, I have no photograph of this scroll. However, Makryalexi and the katholikon of the Pateron monastery have been painted within a few years by the same cohort of painters so that presumably the relation is the same in both churches.

[78] Sch-1, p. 177; Sch-12, p. 70; Sch-13, pp. 177-178; Sch-15, p. 213, fig. 15; Sch-20, p. 104.

[79] Sch-20, p. 104; Sch-13, p. 180; Sch-15, fig. 16; Sch-25, p. 301.

[80] Ἀ. Σ. Ἰωάννου, «Ἡ ἐκκλησία τοῦ ἅη-Γιώργη τοῦ Ἄρμα στὴν Εὔβοια», Ζυγός # 21 (July 1957) 6-7, 31, 32, p. 6; Παρχαρίδου-Ἀναγνώστου, Ὁ χορός,[30] p. 54, 56; Sch-19, p. 146 (note 38).

[81] Sch-15, pp. 210-211. *Cf.* Sch-10, fig. 3; N. M. Elias, *The Divine Liturgy Explained*, Athens 1984[4], pp. 160-161.

[82] Millet, *Monuments*, pl. 244-1; Brockhaus, *Die Kunst*,[11] p. 65; Sch-1, p. 171, figs. 10, 14, 15.

[83] Sch-10, fig. 5; Sch-12, p. 58, figs. 1-3.

[84] Καμαρουλίας, *Μοναστήρια*,[19] fig. 629.

[85] Huber, *Athos*,[9] fig. 180; Sch-1, fig. 23.

[86] Sch-10, fig. 11.

[87] Ἰωάννου, Ἡ ἐκκλησία,[80] pp. 6-7; Sch-10, fig. 8.

[88] Sch-10, fig. 4.

[89] Sofianos, *Meteora*,[13] fig. 28; Tzioras, *Meteora*,[20] fig. on pp. 64-65; Sch-16, p. 189, fig. on p. 187.

[90] Sch-13, p. 179; Sch-15, p. 212, fig. 12; Sch-20, p. 103.

[91] Τούρτα, *Οἱ ναοί*,[19] pls. 17, 73α.

[92] Πέννας, *Ἡ Βυζαντινή Αἴγινα*,[43] fig. 65.

[93] Sch-15, pp. 212, 217, fig. 10; Sch-26, p. 166.

[94] Προβατάκης,[3] fig. on p. 108; Provatakis, *Berg Athos*,[17] fig. on p. 34.

[95] Ζιάς, Καδᾶς, *Γρηγορίου*,[15] fig. 220.

[96] Sch-25, p. 300 (in part visible on figs. 4-6, 8).

[97] Sch-10, fig. 3.

[98] Sch-23.

[99] Sch-23, p. 77; Sch-26, p. 169.

[100] Прашков, *Арбанаси*,[9] fig. 120; Sch-8, pp. 154-156, fig. 1; Sch-10, fig. 12; Sch-15, p. 214.
[101] Sch-15, fig. 6.
[102] Sch-15, p. 208; Sch-20, p. 107.
[103] Sch-20, p. 103; Sch-25, pp. 301-302; Sch-26, p. 166.
[104] G. Spitzing, *Lexikon byzantinisch-christlicher Symbole. Die Bilderwelt Griechenlands und Kleinasiens*, München 1989, p. 81. *Cf.* Sch-20, p. 103; Sch-25, pp. 301-302
[105] Sch-20, p. 103; Sch-26, p. 167.
[106] Gabelić, p. 161, pl. XXXVII; Sch-13, p. 180; Sch-15, p. 208; Sch-20, p. 103. In the *Hermeneia*, this is King David's text in the illustration of the Sunday after Christmas: Didron, *Manuel*, p. 137; Schäfer, p. 154; Papadopoulo-Kérameus, p. 77; Hetherington, *Manual*, p. 28; Erminia, p. 91.
[107] Not on my photograph; space for *ca.* 1½ verses.
[108] Sch-5, pp. 117-118; Sch-10, fig. 7.
[109] Sch-6, pp. 42, 44.
[110] Brockhaus, *Die Kunst*,[11] pp. 80, 155; most recently Stichel, *Beiträge*, pp. 255-256. *Cf.* Sch-10, pp. 289-290: Sch-22, p. 490; Sch-26, p. 137.
[111] Sch-13, pp. 183, 194; Sch-22, p. 496. In the monastery Hlincea near Iaşi (Rumania), the illustrations and the text of the circular inscription are even restricted to Ps *148*, 1-3.
[112] Прашков, *Арбанаси*,[9] fig. 120; Sch-2, p. 29; Sch-8, pp. 154-155; Sch-10, p. 290.
[113] Ὡρολόγιον τὸ μέγα, Ἀθῆναι 1988, p. 41.
[114] Ὡρολόγιον,[113] p. 99.
[115] Sch-13, p. 182; Sch-15, pp. 213-214; Sch-20, p. 104.
[116] Ὡρολόγιον,[113] pp. 169-171.
[117] Millet, *Monuments*, pl. 244-1; Tzioras, *Meteora*,[20] fig. on p. 54; Sch-1, p. 170, fig. 10; Sch-28, p. 161, fig. 5.
[118] *Cf.* N. Thierry, M. Thierry, *Nouvelles églises rupestres de Cappadoce, région du Hasan Daǧı*, Paris 1963, p. 109 (*Jésus... bénit, la main en dehors*), pl. 56a.

[119] Phil. *2*, 6-11. *Cf.* Gnilka, *Paulus von Tarsus*,[18] p. 199.
[120] Sch-13, pp. 178, 180; Sch-14, pp. 203, 230; Sch-15, pp. 206, 208, 209, 213, 217; Sch-22, pp. 508, 509; Sch-23, p. 77; Sch-25, p. 286; Sch-28, p. 158. *Cf.* Didron, *Manuel*, pp. 137-138; Schäfer, *Handbuch*, p. 155.
[121] Sch-4, fig. 17.6; Sch-7, fig..2; Sch-10, fig. 9.
[122] Sch-11, pl. 8a,b; Sch-22, pp. 507-515; figs. 2, 3, 6-8, 11, 12.
[123] Sch-22, pp. 507-508.
[124] Didron, *Manuel*, pp. 423-424; Schäfer, *Handbuch*, p. 393; Papadopoulo-Kérameus, p. 215; Hetherington, *Manual*, p. 84; Erminia, p. 233.
[125] Sch-15, p. 219; Sch-20, p. 94. The half verse 13a also on the scroll of a standing angel in the *Last Judgment* in the church of St. Nicholas of the Probota monastery (Moldavia): V. Drăguţ, P. Lupan, *Die Wandmalerei in der Moldau im 15. und 16. Jahrhundert*, Bukarest 1983, fig. 70.
[126] In Dousiko ἀποκτενω, in Roussanou und Dochiariou I ἀπεκτενω: Millet, *Monuments*, pl. 244-1; Sch-1, figs. 10-12; Sch-28, figs. 3, 5.
[127] Sch-28, p. 159, fig. 4.
[128] At Kampos the final part is not preserved; in Hagios Ioannes Chrysostomos at Skoutari only ἴδετε ἴδετε is still legible.
[129] Sch-3, pp. 170, 211.
[130] Beridse, Neubauer, *Baukunst*,[33] legend of fig. 97; P. Hetherington, *Byzantine and Medieval Greece. Churches, castles, and art of the mainland and the Peloponnese*, London 1991, p. 147; Sch-1, pp. 167, 178-179.
[131] Dionyssios de Trikala, *Qu'est Varlaam?*, Athènes 1962, p. 18; S. Papadopoulos, *Meteora (West-Thessalien)*, Athen *s. a.*, p. 11, fig. 66; Sister Theotekni (Mitsikosta), *Meteora, the Rocky Forest of Greece*, Meteora 1986, p. 127, fig. on p.. 132; Tzioras, *Meteora*,[20] figs. on pp. 54, 55, 64-65; Sofianos, *Meteora*,[13] pp. 27, 31, 32; Hetherington, *Byzantine and Medieval Greece*,[130] p. 146; Sch-2, p. 28; Sch-13, p. 177; Sch-16, p. 210.

[132] Καλοκύρης, *Βυζαντιναὶ ἐκκλησίαι*,[9] pl. 162.

[133] Sch-12, pp. 71-72.

[134] As the *Kyrios* of Ps *148*, 1 IC XC is *standing*. This is also the case in the Ps *148*, 1 illustrations of Philanthropinon (Sch-10, fig. 1), Hosios Meletios (Deliyanni-Doris, *Wandmalereien*,[9] figs. 8, 9), Vanista (Sch-28, fig. 6) and Tsepelovo – presumably borrowed from the iconography of the Metamorphosis: Sch-15, p. 207, Sch-27, p. 207. NOTA: The essence of Phil *2*, 8-11 is the exaltation of the Saviour to the dignity of *Kyrios*. The Metamorphosis is an exaltation of the human Jesus.

[135] At Dekoulou and Kastanea, the *Crucifixion* in this position is also motivated as the main picture of the Passion scenes painted in the western part of the northern and southern walls below the *laud psalms*.

[136] The exaltation to the dignity of *king* consisted of the anointment (LXX 2 Kings *2*, 4; *5*, 3, 17). Therefore the text on the scroll of the *Kyrios* at Tsepelovo and Levkothea, the first sentence of Is *61*, 1 / Lk *4*, 18, is virtually synonymous with Phil *2*, 9-11.

[137] *Cf.* Καμαρουλίας, *Μοναστήρια*,[19] fig. 505; Sch-28, fig. 18. This is another detail which the *laud psalms* have in common with the *Last Judgment*: *Hermeneia* (Didron, *Manuel*, p. 268; Schäfer, *Handbuch*, p. 267; Papadopoulo-Kérameus, p. 141; Hetherington, *Manual*, p. 49; Erminia, p. 215). In the *Last Judgment* in the narthex of the katholikon of Dochiariou, the marks of the wounds at both hands and both feet are clearly visible (Millet, *Monuments*, pl. 245-1).

[138] Καμαρουλίας, *Μοναστήρια*,[19] fig. 589.

[139] Καμαρουλίας, *Μοναστήρια*,[19] fig. 629.

[140] On the other hand, the gesture of speaking does not exclude the meaning of benediction. Both the *Hermeneia* (Didron, *Manuel*, pp. 455-456; Schäfer, *Handbuch*, p. 418; Papadopoulo-Kérameus, pp. 226-227; Hetherington, *Manual*, p. 87; Erminia, pp. 228-229) and Elias, *Divine Liturgy*,[81] p. 86, describe for the benediction a crossing of the ring finger and the thumb so that the letter X of IC XC

results. In fact, this prescription is seldom followed; in the
Zoodochos Piyi Zarnatas, the *Kyrios* of Ps *148*, 1 does
comply, though the text on his scroll – Dt *32*, 39 – is not a
formula of benediction. It is not possible to discriminate
between the gestures of speaking and of benediction,
because the latter is likewise a spoken text (*cf.* K. Wessel,
"Gesten", *RBK 2* (1971) 766-783, col. 779). (By the way,
WESSEL's attempt to iconographically discriminate between
the general gesture of speaking and a specific gesture of
benediction (*loc. cit.* and "Christusbild", *RBK 1* (1966) 966-
1047, section II) was doomed to failure, because the
adduced examples do not show Christ blessing:
Throughout, the Pantokrator holds a book in his left hand.
If this is opened, the text is never a formula of benediction.
Hence, his right hand performs a gesture of *speaking*. When
the book is closed, no different meaning can be inferred.)
Cf. P. Hauptmann, "Das russische Alrgläubigentum und die
Ikonenmalerei", in: *Erste Studien-Sammlung* [Beiträge zur
Kunst des christlichen Ostens, 3], Recklinghausen 1965, 5-
36, pp. 9-11, 19-20. In Sch-5, p. 117, line 6, delete the word
seg*nend*; in Sch-23, p. 75, lines 10-11, delete the words *in a
gesture of benediction.*
[141] Wessel, Christusbild,[140] col. 1031; Sch-22, p. 511.
Lesnovo: Okunev, p. 243, pl. XL-2; Gabelić, p. 199, fig.
101.
[142] Sch-22, pp. 507-515.
[143] Millet, *Monuments*, pls. 210-2, 245-1; M. A.
Musicescu, S. Ulea, Voroneţ, Bucarest [2]1971, fig. 46;
Drăguţ, Lupan, *Wandmalerei*,[125] figs. 96, 201; Tzioras,
Meteora,[20] fig. on p. 64; Sofianos, *Meteora*,[13] fig. on p. 32.
[144] Sch-12, p. 72.
[145] Sch-28, fig. 19.
[146] Sch-3, fig. 1; Sch-12, p. 69; Sch-28, fig. 8.
[147] Sch-19, p. 142; Sch-27, p. 204.
[148] Sch-17, p. 92; Sch-19, pp. 154-156, 161, figs. 17, 18;
Sch-20, p. 113, fig. 19; Sch-26, pp. 157-158.

[149] Sch-4, p. 236; Sch-8, p. 182; Sch-11, pp. 145-146, 152, 158, 165; Sch-12, pp. 67-68, 72; Sch-13, pp. 183, 184; Sch-19, p. 161; Sch-21, p. 200; Sch-26, p. 149.
[150] Sch-3, fig. 6; Sch-11, pl. 1b; Sch-19, pp. 157, 160; Sch-26, pp. 161, 163-164, fig. 7; Sch-27, p. 205.
[151] Inconclusively dated to ca. 1585: Sch-27, pp. 187-188.
[152] In the literature concerning Phil *2*, 8-11, the *Kyrios* has also been termed *Kosmokrator*, virtually synonymous with *Pantokrator*. Occasionally, the zodiac instigated assignment of this epithet to the *Kyrios* of Ps *148*, 1, here with the connotation of the Lord of the extraterrestrial cosmos (Huber, *Athos*,[9] p. 329: *Dem kosmischen Christus dient das ganze Firmament; daher die Darstellung der 14 Tierkreiszeichen*; Ђурић; Христ Космократор,[21] Jevtić, Le nouvel ordre,[21]). The hypothesis is not supported by factual evidence; *cf.* note 26.

»Omnis spiritus laudet dominum«.
Psalm *150*, 6 and the Realm of Spirits in the
Illustration of the *Laud Psalms*

[1] According to F.-L. Hossfeld, E. Zenger, *Psalmen 101-150* [Herders Theologischer Kommentar zum Alten Testament], Freiburg, Basel, Wien 2008, p. 807, the term *laud psalms* applies to Ps 146-150, the *little hallel*. However, the restriction to Ps 148-150 is common.
[2] Okunev, pp. 239-242; A. Nikolovski, D. Ćornakov, K. Balabanov, *The Cultural Monuments of the People's Republic of Macedonia* [The Historical and Cultural Heritage of the People's Republic of Macedonia, 8], Skopje 1961, p. 27; L. Prachkov, "Peintures murales récemment découvertes dans la chapelle de la tour de Hrélio au monastère de Rila en Bulgarie", *Actes XIVe Congr. Int. Ét. Byz., Bucarest, 6-12 Sept. 1971*, III, Bucarest 1976, 415-418, p. 417; Đurić, p. 79; Belting, Text, figs. XIX.1-3; A. Tschilingirov, *Die*

Kunst des christlichen Mittelalters in Bulgarien. 4. bis 18. Jahrhundert, Berlin, München 1979, fig. 136; R. Hootz (ed.), L. Trifunović, *Kunstdenkmäler in Jugoslawien. Ein Bildhandbuch*, vol. 1, Darmstadt 1981, p. 383; D. Piguet-Panayotova, *Recherches sur la peinture en Bulgarie du bas moyen âge*, Paris 1987, pp. 259-269, figs. 118-120; И. М. Ђорђевић, *Зидно сликарство српске властеле у доба Немањића*, Београд 1994, pp. 136-137, 160-162; Gabelić, pp. 183-189, 280-281; Sch-12, pp. 50-52.

[3] Sch-2, pp. 27-28; Sch-7, pp. 74-76; Sch-3, pp. 188, 232; Sch-4, p. 231; Sch-8, pp. 151, 182; Sch-10, p. 289; Sch-11, pp. 142, 154; Sch-16, p. 184; Sch-19, p. 145; Sch-20, p. 90; Sch-21, p. 194; Sch-25, p. 296; Sch-26, pp. 143-144.

[4] S. Dufrenne, *Tableaux synoptiques de 15 psautiers médiévaux à illustrations intégrales issus du texte*, Paris 1978.

[5] J. J. Tikkanen, *Die Psalterillustration im Mittelalter*, Helsingfors 1895, reprint Soest/NL 1975, p. 89.

[6] Sch-2, p. 28; Sch-7, pp. 72, 75; Sch-19, pp. 145, 147.

[7] Sch-12, pp. 51-52; Sch-24, pp. 351-352; Sch-26, p. 143.

[8] Đurić, p. 79; N. K. Moran, *Singers in Late Byzantine and Slavonic Painting* [Byzantina Neerlandica, 9], Leiden 1986, pp. 89-91; Ђорђевић, *Зидно сликарство*,[2] p. 136.

[9] Moran, *Singers*,[8] fig. 56. *Cf.* Rila monastery, Chrelju's tower: A. Boschkov, *Die bulgarische Malerei. Von den Anfängen bis zum 19. Jahrhundert*, Recklinghausen 1969, fig. 61; Tschilingirov, *Bulgarien*,[2] fig. 137; R. Hootz (ed.), P. Berbenliev, *Kunstdenkmäler in Bulgarien. Ein Bildhandbuch*, Darmstadt 1983, fig. on p. 209; Piguet-Panayotova, *Recherches*,[2] figs. 118, 120. The instrumentalists of Ps *149*, 3 / *150*, 3-5 should accompany people performing a round dance. In Chrelju's tower and in Lesnovo, they do; in Kučevište, they do not.

[10] Okunev, pp. 241-242, pl. XL-2; D. T. Rice, *Byzantinische Kunst*, München 1964, fig. 258; П. Мијовић, "Царска иконографија у српској средњовековној уметности", *Старинар*, нова серија *18* (1967) 103-118, fig. 14; D. T. Rice, *Byzantinische Malerei. Die letzte Phase*,

Frankfurt/Main 1968, pp. 114-115 and legend of fig. 97, with quotation of Ps *150*, 3; G. Millet, T. Velmans, *La peinture du moyen âge en Yougoslavie (Serbie, Macédoine et Monténégro)*, IV, Paris 1969, fig. 35; Đurić, fig. 64; Belting, Text, fig. XIX.3 (*Darstellung von Ps 150!*); Hootz, Trifunović,[3] fig. on p. 227; Gabelić, pp. 187, 281, fig. LVII (colour).

[11] B. Vidoeska, / Б. Видоеска, The Church of the Presentation of the Holly Virgin Kucheviste. Drawings of the Frescoes / Воведение на Богородица Кучевиште. Скопје, Н. У. Конзерваторски Центар, 2008. The singers and the musicians have been assigned to Ps *150*, 3-5.

[12] Didron, *Manuel*.

[13] Schäfer, *Handbuch*, p. 237; ΕΡΜΗΝΕΙΑ ΤΩΝ ΖΩΓΡΑΦΩΝ, ΩΣ ΠΡΟΣ ΤΗΝ ΕΚΚΛΗΣΙΑΣΤΙΚΗΝ ΖΩΓΡΑΦΙΑΝ, ΥΠΟ ΔΙΟΝΥΣΙΟΥ ΤΟΥ ΙΕΡΟΜΟΝΑΧΟΥ ΚΑΙ ΖΩΓΡΑΦΟΥ, τοῦ ἐκ Φουρνᾶ τῶν Ἀγράφων, ΑΘΗΝΗΣΙ 1853, p. 159; Papadopoulo-Kérameus, p. 128.

[14] Sch-22.

[15] Sch-8, p. 155; Sch-13, p. 182; Sch-15, pp. 222-223; Sch-20, p. 115; Sch-23, p. 74.

[16] *Sic* Hossfeld, Zenger, *Psalmen*,[1] p. 855, for Ps 149; Gunkel, p. 619: *der Frommen*.

[17] ΕΡΜΗΝΕΙΑ (1853),[13] p. 160; Papadopoulo-Kérameus, p. 128.

[18] Sch-3, p. 175; Sch-6, p. 46; Sch-7, p. 76; Sch-8, p. 157; Sch-13, p. 176; Sch-16, p. 182; Sch-20, pp. 86, 99, 115; Sch-24, p. 354; Sch-25, p. 300. Quite different in the Carolingian Utrecht-Psalter: E. T. De Wald, *The Illustrations of the Utrecht Psalter* [Illuminated Manuscripts of the Middle Ages], Princeton, London, Leipzig [1932], p. 65; K. van der Horst, J. H. A. Engelbregt, *Utrecht-Psalter, Kommentar* [Codices Selecti, Commentarium vol. LXXV*], Graz 1984, p. 92.]

[19] Sch-15, p. 221; Sch-22, p. 496; *cf.* Sch-13, p. 183; Sch-16, p. 184; Sch-25, p. 294; Sch-26, pp. 142, 146.

[20] Didron, *Manuel*, p. 235; Schäfer, *Handbuch*, p. 237;
EPMHNEIA (1853),[13] p. 160; Papadopoulo-Kérameus, p.
128; Hetherington, *Manual*, p. 45.
[21] B. Rothemund, *Handbuch der Ikonenkunst*, München
[2]1966, p. 333; T. Velmans, "Le dimanche de tous les saints
et l'icône exposée à Charleroi (cat. no. 32)", *Byzantion* 53
(1983) 17-35, p. 17; Sch-22, p. 498; Sch-25, pp. 278, 284,
311; Erminia, p. 231; Ἡμεροδείκτης, Ἱερᾶς Μονῆς
Παναγουλακη, Καλαμάτα, 2003-2012. A different date in
The Book of Ceremonies: Constantine Porphyrogennetos,
The Book of Ceremonies (A. Moffatt, M. Tall, translators)
[Byzantina Australiensia, 18], Canberra 2012, pp. 535-538.
[22] Didron, *Manuel*, p. 467; Schäfer, *Handbuch*, p. 428;
EPMHNEIA (1853),[13] p. 266; Papadopoulo-Kérameus, p.
230; Hetherington, *Manual*, p. 89; Erminia, p. 228.
[23] Sch-4, p. 224; Sch-10, pp. 288-289; Sch-15, pp. 222-
223; Sch-20, p. 115; Sch-23, p. 74; Sch-22, pp. 491, 501;
Sch-25, pp. 286, 292.
[24] R. H. Randall, Jr., *Masterpieces of Ivory from the Wal-
ters Art Gallery*, New York 1985, no. 216; A. Effenberger,
*Goethe und die »Russischen Heiligenbilder«. Anfänge by-
zantinischer Kunstgeschichte in Deutschland* [Beiträge der
Winckelmann-Gesellschaft, 18], Mainz 1990, figs. 4, 6; I.
Pleshanova, "Praise the Lord", in: R. Grierson (ed.), *Gates
of Mystery. The Art of Holy Russia*, Fort Worth TX s. a., p.
271; Sch-9, pp. 170-178, figs. 1, 2. The length of the
quotation is conditioned by the available space; the abrupt
ends indicate that the reader is supposed to add what not
has been written (*cf.* [A. N.] Didron, "La dalmatique
impériale", *Ann. Archéol. 1* (1844) 152-167, p. 155; Didron, *Manuel*, pp. 137-138; Schäfer, *Handbuch*, p. 155;
Sch-3, pp. 198, 243-244; ; Sch-14, pp. 203, 230; Sch-13, pp.
178-180, 191-192; Sch-15, pp. 209, 210, 213; Sch-19, p.
154; Sch-22, p. 509; Sch-23, p. 77; Sch-25, p 286; Sch-28,
p. 158). The four inscriptions, then, are virtually identical
and feature the characteristics of hymn texts. A late (18-
19th c.?) *Chvalite gospoda* icon (Sch-22, fig.10) is headed

by the complete text of Ps 148 (*cf.* Sch-9, pp. 199-200).
Obviously, the long inscription qualifies neither as the title
nor as the explanatory legend of the composition below
while it may well be the text of the chant sung in praise of
the **ГОСПОДЬ**.

[25] H. Brockhaus, *Die Kunst in den Athos-Klöstern*, Leipzig 1891, Leipzig [2]1924, p. 80; *Ὡρολόγιον τὸ μέγα*, Ἀθῆναι 1988, p. 99.

[26] *Ὡρολόγιον*,[25] pp. 99-101; Moran, *Singers*,[8] p. 89; Sch-4, p. 224. *Cf.* Stichel, *Beiträge*, pp. 252-253.

[27] Millet, *Monuments*, pl. 244-1; Sch-1, fig. 10; Sch-2, fig. on p. 10; Sch-7, p. 69, fig. 2; Sch-4, pp. 226, 231, 233, figs. 17.1, 17.6; Sch-10, p. 289, figs. 9, 10, colour fig. 27.

[28] Sch-10, p. 285; Sch-6, p. 43.

[29] G. Heil, A. M. Ritter (eds.), *Corpus Dionysiacum II, Pseudo-Dionysius Areopagita, De coelesti hierarchia, De ecclesiastica hierarchia, De mystica theologiae epistulae* [Patristische Texte und Studien, 67], Berlin, Boston [2]2012, pp. 27, 33; [A. N.] Didron, "Iconographie des anges", *Annales archéologiques 18* (1858) 33-48; Didron, *Manuel*, pp. 71-74; Schäfer, *Handbuch*, pp. 99-104; Papadopoulo-Kérameus, pp. 45-46; Hetherington, *Manual,* p. 18; Erminia, p. 67.

[30] Sch-8, pp. 154-155; Sch-4, p. 236; Sch-10, pp. 289, 290; Sch-16, p. 185; Sch-23, p. 77; Sch-26, pp. 165, 169; Θ. Μ. Προβατάκης, *Τὸ Ἅγιον Ὅρος, Ἱσττορία – Τέχνη – Παράδοση*, Ἀθῆνα s. a., fig. on p. 108; Th. Provatakis, *Berg Athos* [Griechische Landschaften, 13], Thessaloniki s. a., fig. on p. 34 (not *Große Lavra, Koukouzelissa-Kapelle*); in Redina Ps *148*, 1a, *64*, 2, *148*, 1a,b, *64*, 2 + αἰνεῖτε αὐτὸν.

[31] Stichel, *Beiträge*, p. 252. *Cf.* Sch-15, p. 217; Sch-26, p. 165.

[32] Sch-13, pp. 178-180; Sch-16, p. 208; Sch-15, pp. 209-214; Sch-20, p. 104; Sch-26, p. 166.

[33] Sch-3, fig. 7; Sch-13, pp. 177, 190; Sch-15, pp. 205-206, 208-209, fig. 1, 4-6, 9, 10; Sch-26, p. 166.

[34] Sch-1, p. 177; Sch-13, pp. 177-178; Sch-15, pp. 212, 213, figs. 12, 15, 16; Sch-18; Sch-20, p. 103; Sch-24, p. 375; Sch-25, p. 301; Sch-26, p. 153.

[35] Sch-8, p. 155;[3] p. 90; Sch-10, p. 290; Sch-16, p. 189. *Cf.* Sch-26, p. 167.

[36] Sch-7, p. 81; Sch-8, pp. 174-175, 181; Sch-10, p. 277; Sch-19, pp. 148-149; Sch-22, pp. 490-492; Sch-24, p. 347; Sch-25, pp. 295-296.]

[37] Didron, *Manuel*, p. 236.

[38] Didron, *Manuel*, pp. 238-239; Sch-22, p. 498.

[39] P. K. Enepekides, "Josef Strzygowski's ungedrucktes Ms. aus dem Jahre 1888 über den Heiligen Berg Athos", *Balkan Studies* 27 (1986) 105-127, p. 107; R. Billetta, *Der Heilige Berg Athos in Zeugnissen aus sieben Jahrhunderten, 1* (Wien, New York, Dublin 1992), p. 296. *Cf.* Sch-4, p. 232.

[40] Strzygowski, p. 62.

[41] Strzygowski, p. 63.

[42] Billetta, *Berg Athos*,[39] p. 296.

[43] Brockhaus, *Die Kunst*,[25] p. 80.

[44] Sch-2, pp. 27-28; Sch-3, pp. 188, 232; Sch-4, p. 231; Sch-7, pp. 74-76; Sch-8, pp. 151, 182; Sch-10, p. 289; Sch-19, p. 145.

[45] F. Wickhoff, "Das Speisezimmer des Bischofs Neon von Ravenna", *Repertorium für Kunstwissenschaft 17* (1894) 10-17, p. 15. WICKHOFF refers to BROCKHAUS' remark concerning the ὄρθρος chants, though without new aspects.

[46] Billetta, *Berg Athos*,[39] p. 228.

[47] Strzygowski, p. 65; Sch-4, p. 233.

[48] Billetta, *Berg Athos*,[39] p. 295.

[49] This assignment already by Didron, *Manuel*, p. 238; Schäfer, *Handbuch*, p. 240, as well as by Strzygowski, p. 65.

[50] Strzygowski, p. 67.

[51] Sch-4, p. 233; Sch-16, p. 207; Προβατάκης, *Τὸ Ἅγιον Ὄρος*,[30] figs. on pp. 71, 108. *Cf.* Sch-3, pp. 186, 230.

[52] Didron, *Manuel*, p. 237; Schäfer, *Handbuch*, p. 239; Strzygowski, p. 67. STRZYGOWSKI states expressly that in Iviron the *Spukgestalten*, (*spooky figures*), *i. e.* the fabulous creatures of Aulus Gellius, Plinius and Augustinus, are absent. DIDRON does not mention them either, but since his description is not comprehensive, STRZYGOWSKI's statement cannot exclusively be based on it. On the other hand, the new paintings of 1888 (Billetta, *Berg Athos*,[39] p. 295) do include these fabulous creatures (Sch-4, p. 233). Unless his notes were erroneous, STRZYGOWSKI therefore must have seen the old paintings, though he visited Mount Athos only during the *autumn* of 1888. The fires of 1845, 1860 and 1865 (Billetta, *Berg Athos*,[39] pp. 259, 271, 275) seem to have spared the katholikon and its porch; the repaintings of 1842 und 1846 (Billetta, *Berg Athos*,[39] pp. 255, 260) presumably took place in the naos, not in the porch. Some details of DIDRON's description cannot be corroborated, *e. g. La mer gronde* in the illustration of the natural phenomena (Ps *148*, 8), the scene of the three Hebrews in the fiery furnace inserted between Ps 148 and 150, the organ (Ps *150*, 4), and David shouting *Que tout esprit loue le Seigneur* (*cf.* Sch-15, p. 211). According to STRZYGOWSKI, the *prophetanax* Salomon holds a scroll; in the present paintings, it is a tablet (possibly a codex) with inscription, in compliance with DIDRON's decription *Salomon, qui chante sur un cahier de musique,* (*Manuel*,[12] p. 238; Schäfer, *Handbuch*, pp. 239-240: *Salomon aus einem Notenhefte singend*). STRZYGOWSKI's statements concerning the localization (pp. 63-65, 67) do not agree with the arrangement of the present paintings.
[53] Strzygowski, p. 67.
[54] *Cf.* Chrelju's tower (Sch-12, p. 52; figures: Belting, *Text*, fig. XIX.2 (*Darstellung von Ps 150!*); Tschilingirov,[2] fig. 136 (*Der 150. Psalm!*); Piguet-Panayotova, *Recherches*,[2] fig. 118) and Lesnovo (figures: above, note 10; *cf.* Sch-24, p. 351, note 15).

[55] Didron, *Manuel*, p. 237. It is conceivable that DIDRON did not read the complete text and added an erroneous extrapolation to the correctly identified verses Ps *148*, 1, 2.

[56] Sch-10, p. 290, fig. 3.

[57] Е. Рѣдинъ, "Триклиній базилики Урса въ Равеннѣ", *Византійскій Временникъ 2* (1895) 512-520.

[58] Millet, *Monuments*, pl. 263-1; Sch-2, pp. 21-23, figs. on pp. 18-19, 24-25.

[59] Millet, *Monuments*, pp. 55, 58, legends of pls. 244-1 and 263-1, 2.

[60] F. Fichtner, *Wandmalereien der Athos-Klöster. Grundsätzliches zu den Planungen der Bildfolgen des 14.-17. Jahrhundert. Welt- und Lebensanschauung, Ritus, Architektur, Malerei*, Berlin 1931, p. 36.

[61] Sch-7, p. 72.

[62] Κ. Δ. Καλοκύρης, *Βυζαντιναὶ ἐκκλησίαι τῆς Ἱερας Μητροπόλεως Μεσσηνίας*, Θεσσαλονίκη 1973, legends of figs. 162, 166, 167β (with legible inscription Ps *148*, 9a), 168α (with legible inscription Ps *149*, 1b-2a), 202α,β (scenes of Ps *148*, 10), 204α, 205α, p. 218, *Cf.* p. 190. Ps *150*, 6 is nowhere referred to.

[63] P. Huber, *Athos. Leben Glaube Kunst*, Zürich, Freiburg [3]1982, pp. 327, 329, 332, 334, 350.

[64] Moran, *Singers*,[8] legend of fig. 56.

[65] Sch-9, p. 206, pl. 15; Sch-25, p. 287.

[66] Didron, *Manuel*, p. 435; Schäfer, *Handbuch*, p. 402; Hetherington, *Manual*, p. 85; Erminia, p. 237.

[67] Sch-9, pp. 202-203, fig. on p. 202.

[68] W. Felicetti-Liebenfels, *Geschichte der russischen Ikonenmalerei in den Grundzügen dargestellt* [Forschungen und Berichte des Kunsthistorischen Institutes der Universität Graz, 3], Graz 1972, p. 160, legend of fig. 329.

[69] Рѣдинъ, Триклиній базилики Урса;[57] Effenberger, *Goethe*,[24] legends of figs. 4, 6: *Darstellung des 148. Psalms »Lobpreiset den Herrn«*; Sch-9, legends of pls. 13, 15, figs. 1-8 and fig. on p. 202; passim.

[70] Effenberger, *Goethe*,[24] pp. 36-37.

[71] Stichel, *Beiträge*, pp. 253, 255.
[72] Effenberger, *Goethe*,[24] p. 37, figs. 4, 6.
[73] I. Pleshanova,[24] pp. 270-271 (in the sentence *The com-position PRAISE THE LORD illustrates the text of psalm 149* replace *149* by *148*. In the sentence ... *the celestial scroll studded with stars and with lamps at its side*, the *lamps* can be identified as the sun and the moon); Sch-9, p. 171, fig. 1. - Similar in a painted *Chvalite gospoda* icon: H. Кондаков, *Лицевой Иконописный Подлинникъ, I, Иконографія Господа Бога и Спаса Нашего Іисуса Христа*, 1905, pl. E.
[74] *E. g.*, H. Skrobucha, *Meisterwerke der Ikonenmalerei*, Recklinghausen 1961, pl. L; *The George R. Hann Collection* (auction catalogue), *1*, New York 1980, # 90, p. 189; M. K. Garidis, *Études sur le Jugement Dernier post-byzantin du XVe à la fin du XIXe siècle. Iconographie – Esthétique* [Ἑταιρία Μακεδονικῶν Σπουδῶν, σειρά φιλ. καὶ θεολ., 16], Θεσσαλονίκη 1985, fig. 38; E. Smirnowa, *Moskauer Ikonen des 14. bis 17. Jahrhunderts*, Leningrad 1989, pl. 113. According to K. Onasch, *Liturgie und Kunst der Ostkirche in Stichworten unter Berücksichtigung der Alten Kirche*, Leipzig 1981, p. 134, the sun, the moon and the zodiac (as, *e. g.*, in Voroneţ and Dragalevci) in the *Last Judgment* are symbols of the universal salvation by Christ. However, the colour of the celestial bodies (the red moon, the dark sun) refer unambiguously to Apc *6*, 12 (and eventually to Joel *3*, 4); the movements of the stars, represented by the zodiac, serve to measure *time* which comes to an end at the Day of Judgment. The sky in shape of a scroll, hence, is an adequate illustration of Apc *6*, 12-14 in which no symbolic meaning is indicated.
[75] Effenberger, *Goethe*,[24] p. 37.
[76] I. Grabar, V. Lasareff, O. Demus, *UdSSR. Frühe russische Ikonen* [UNESCO-Sammlung der Weltkunst], Paris 1958, pl. IX ; В. И. Антонова, Н. Е. Мнева, *Государственная Третьяковская Галлерея, Каталог Древнерусской Живописи XI-начала XVIII в. в.*, vol. 1,

Москва 1963, fig.72; Felicetti-Liebenfels, *Geschichte*,[68] fig. 353; М. В. Алпатов / M.V. Alpatov, *Древнерусская Иконопись, Early Russian Icon Painting*, Москва / Moscow 1974, pl. 113; Skrobucha, *Meisterwerke*,[74] pl. L; Catalogue *Hann Collection*,[74] no. 90, fig. on p. 189; D. S. Lichatschow, V. K. Laurina, W.A. Puschkarjow, *Nowgoroder Ikonen des 12. bis 17. Jahrhundert*, Leningrad 1981, pl. 72; Onasch, *Liturgie und Kunst*,[74] fig. 44; Garidis, *Études*,[74] figs. 36, 38, 40, 42; M. Alpatov, "The Icons of Russia", in: K. Weitzmann, G. Alibegašvili, A. Volskaja, M. Chatzidakis, G. Babić, M. Alpatov, T. Voinescu, *The Icon*, New York 1987, fig. on p. 281; catalogue *1000-Летие Русской Художественной Культуры, 1000 Jahre russische Kunst – Zur Erinnerung an die Taufe der Rus im Jahr 988*, Москва, Schleswig, Wiesbaden, 1988/89, # 124 (p. 102); V. N. Lazarev (G. I. Vzdornov, ed.), *Die russische Ikone*, Darmstadt, Zürich, Düsseldorf 1997, fig. 48; P. Hunt, "Confronting the end. The interpretation of the Last Judgment in a Novgorod Wisdom icon", *Byzantinoslavica* 65 (2007) 275-325, pl. 1.

[77] *Sic*; according to the Hebrew Bible, קיטור (*kitor*, 'Dampf'); *ice*, κρύσταλλος in the Septuagint, голоть in its Russian translation.

[78] Effenberger, *Goethe*,[24] p. 37.

[79] Sch-9, pp. 203, 206. This paper requires major revision.

[80] Stichel, *Beiträge*, pp. 255-256 (note 677).

[81] Rothemund, *Handbuch*,[21] pp. 333, 332 (*cf.* Sch-22, p. 498; Sch-25, p. 285, note 61).

[82] Randall, *Masterpieces*,[24] p. 134, # 216 with fig. (*cf.* Sch-9, p. 178).

[83] Stichel, *Beiträge*, p. 252.

[84] Stichel, *Beiträge*, p. 252.

[85] Stichel, *Beiträge*, p. 253.

[86] Stichel, *Beiträge*, p. 252-253 (implicit).

[87] Stichel, *Beiträge*, p. 255-256 (note 677).

[88] Stichel, *Beiträge*, p. 253, 255.

[89] Stichel, *Beiträge*, p. 227.

[90] Hossfeld, Zenger, *Psalmen*,[1] p. 807.

[91] Or 151.

[92] Stichel, *Beiträge*, p. 160.

[93] Stichel, *Beiträge*, p. 253.

[94] Sch-8, p. 155; Sch-10, p. 284; Sch-12, p. 50; Sch-26, p. 138.

[95] *Cf.* Sch-16, p. 181.

[96] Didron, *Manuel*, p. 238; Schäfer, *Handbuch*, pp. 239-240. Similarly, the zodiac of the *laud psalms* composition in Sveti Cxoveli, Mcxeta, Georgia, has been believed to represent a calendar: V. Mamukelashvili, *Svetitskhoveli*, Tbilisi 2004, p. 43.

[97] Strzygowski, p. 68.

[98] Didron, *Manuel*, p. 238 (Schäfer, *Handbuch*, p. 240); correctly assigned by Strzygowski, p. 65.

[99] С. Ђурић, "Христ Космократор у Леснову", *Зограф* *13* (1982) 65-72, fig. 5.

[100] H. Holländer, *Kunst des frühen Mittelalters* [Belser Stilgeschichte, 5], Stuttgart 1969, p. 60 (legend of fig. 49; *cf.* H. Holländer, „Die Entstehung Europas", in: C. Wetzel (ed.), *Mittelalter* [Belser Stilgeschichte, Studienausgabe, 2-1], Stuttgart 1999, 151-384, p. 271). Pertinent figures: *Jupiter Cosmocrator*: Holländer (1969), fig. 51; E. G. Grimme, *Das Evangeliar Kaiser Ottos III. im Domschatz zu Aachen*, Freiburg, Basel, Wien 1984, fig. 6; C. Wetzel, "Das frühe Mittelalter", in: Wetzel, *Mittelalter*, 9-78, fig. 28; *Maiestas Domini*: H. Schrade, *Vor- und Frühromanische Malerei. Die karolingische, ottonische und frühsalische Zeit,* Köln 1958, fig. 70; W. Braunfels, *Die Welt der Karolinger und ihre Kunst*, München 1968, fig. XIX; Holländer (1969), fig. 49; Wetzel, l. c., fig. 27. Note, however, that in this *Maiestas Domini* Christ is *not* surrounded by the zodiac, and that the *Jupiter Cosmocrator* sculpture was pieced together from an ancient Atlas holding two *zodia* and a modern Jupiter enthroned between 10 more *zodia*: H. G. Gundel, *Zodiakos. Tierkreisbilder im Altertum. Kosmische Bezüge und*

Jenseitsvorstellungen im antiken Alltagsleben [Kulturge-
schichte der antiken Welt, 54], Mainz 1992, pp. 105-106,
219, fig. on p. 220. For Christ Cosmocrator, *cf.* Onasch,
Liturgie und Kunst,[74] p. 134.
[101] Ђурић, Христ Космократор.[99] Virtuoso variations of
the theme by Ivana Jevtić, "Le nouvel ordre du monde ou
l'image du cosmos à Lesnovo", in: A. Cutler, A. Papaconstantinou (eds.), *The Material and the Ideal. Essays in
Medieval Art and Archaeology in Honour of Jean-Michel
Spieser* [The Medieval Mediterranean, 70], Leiden 2007,
129-148.
[102] *Cf. The New Encyclopedia Britannica*, *8*, Chicago
etc. [15]2005, pp. 867-868.
[103] Millet, *Monuments*, p. 58, legends of pl. 263-1,2;
Sch-2, pp. 4, 5, 9, 21; Sch-16, p. 183; reproduced also by K.
Τσεκούρα, "Ο χορός στο Βυζάντιο", *Ἀρχαιολογία & Τέχνες
91* (2004) 6-7, fig. 1; Μ. Παρχαρίδου-Ἀναγνώστου, "Ο
χορός στή μεταβυζαντινή μνημειακή ἐκκλησιαστική
ζωγραφική (15ος -19ος αι.)", *Ἀρχαιολογία & Τέχνες 91*
(2004) 50-58, fig. 6..
[104] Stichel, *Beiträge,*[26] p. 227.
[105] Strzygowski, p. 63; Sch-1, pp. 180-181; Sch-2, pp.
14-16; Sch-3, pp. 173, 215; Sch-4, pp. 226, 231, 233; Sch-
6, pp. 54-55; Sch-7, pp. 76-77; Sch-8, p. 173; Sch-10, p.
291; Sch-12, p. 63; Sch-16, pp. 201-202; Sch-25, p. 307;
Huber, *Athos,*[63] figs. 183-185; P. Huber, *Heilige Berge. Sinai Athos Golgota – Ikonen Fresken Miniaturen*, Zürich,
Einsiedeln, Köln [2]1982, fig. 151 (*Die Erschaffung der
Welt!*); Χ. Γ. Χοτζάκογλου, *Σκιάποδες, στερνόφθαλμοι,
κυνοκέφαλοι. Προέλεση καὶ πρόσληψη τριῶν
ἀρχαιοελληνικῶν τεράτων στὴ βυζαντινὴ τέχνη καὶ ἡ «Σχολὴ
τῶν Θηβῶν»* [Βραχέα Μελετήματα Ἀρχαιολογίας καὶ
Ἱστορίας τῆς Τέχνης, 1], Λευκωσία 2003.
[106] Sch-13, p. 192; Sch-15, pp. 208, 213; Sch-18, pp. 87,
94; Sch-20, pp. 97, 104.
[107] According to Stichel, *Beiträge*, pp. 227, 705, 750, *Alles, was Odem hat, lobe den Herrn*. In fact, Ps *150*, 6 has

not been illustrated (the text on David's sroll is not a legend of the picture, but the beginning of the chant which he and his companions sing in praise of the Lord: Sch-15, p. 209).
[108] Stichel, *Beiträge*, pp. 227--229.
[109] Further cases of the joint illustration of several psalm verses in one composition: Sch-25, pp. 293-294; Sch-26, p. 153.
[110] Hossfeld, Zenger, *Psalmen*,[1] p. 855.
[111] Stichel, *Beiträge*, pp. 227-228. In Lesnovo, an individual picture has been devoted to Ps *149*, 5 (Gabelić, pp. 187, 281, fig. 94; Sch-24, fig. 5), but in the illustration of Ps *149*, 6, the character of the sword-bearers as ὅσιοι is expressed in their representation as nimbed militäry saints (*cf.* Sch-24, fig. 6; Sch-26, pp. 138, 163, fig. 4).
[112] New English translation of the Septuagint (http://ccat.sas.upenn.edu/nets/edition); ὅσιοι, *the devout,* replaced by *The Faithful* (*cf.* Gunkel, p. 619). *Cf.* Sch-21, p. 197. For the importance to read the whole psalms in context, *i. e.* across the boundaries between the verses, *cf.* Sch-19, esp. p. 156.
[113] Stichel, *Beiträge*, pp. 705, 748.
[114] Stichel, *Beiträge,* pp. 255-256.
[115] Fol. 82v, 83r; De Wald, *Utrecht Psalter*,[18], pls. CXXIX, CXXX, pp. 64-65; van der Horst, Engelbregt, *Utrecht-Psalter*,[18] facsimile and pp. 39, 92; Ps 148: Sch-1, fig. 1.
[116] J. H. A. Engelbregt, *Het Utrechts Psalterium. Een Eeuw Wetenschappelijke Bestudering (1860-1960) The Utrecht Psalter. A century of critical investigation (1860-1960)*, Utrecht 1965, pp. 163-164, 168-169, legends of figs. 102, 121.
[117] J. Eschweiler, B. Fischer, H. J. Frede und F. Mütherich (henceforth: EFFM), "Der Inhalt der Bilder", in: *Der Stuttgarter Bilderpsalter Bibl. Fol. 23 Württembergische Landesbibliothek Stuttgart, 2, Untersuchungen*, Stuttgart 1968, 55-150, p. 149; P. Burkhart, "Kunsthistorische Einführung", in: V. Trost, A. Pataki-Hundt, E. Huhsmann

(eds.), *Kupfergrün, Zinnober & Co. Der Stuttgarter Psalter*, Stuttgart 2011, 19-77, p. 35.

[118] E. T. DE Wald, *Vaticanus Graecus 1927* [The Illustrations in the Manuscripts of the Septuagint, 3, Psalms and Odes, Part 1], Princeton, London, The Hague 1941.

[119] Fol. 162r, 163r; E. T. DE Wald, *The Stuttgart Psalter Biblia folio 23 Wuerttembergische Landesbibliothek, Stuttgart* [Illuminated Manuscripts of the Middle Ages], Princeton 1930, facsimile and pp. 110-111; *Der Stuttgarter Bilderpsalter Bibl. Fol. 23 Württembergische Landesbibliothek Stuttgart, 1, Faksimile,* Stuttgart 1965; EFFM, Der Inhalt der Bilder,[117] pp. 148, 149; Sch-1, fig. 3; E. Huhsmann, "Der Umgang mit Handschriften", in: *Kupfergrün, Zinnober,*[117] fig. on p. 159.

[120] Folio 163v; DE Wald, *Stuttgart Psalter,*[119] facsimile; *Bilderpsalter, Faksimile;*[119] R. McKitterick, "The Historical Context: Carolingian Wealth, Faith and Culture", in: K. van der Horst, W. Noel, W. C. M. Wüstefeld (eds.), *The Utrecht Psalter in Medieval Art. Picturing the Psalms of David,* Utrecht 1996, 1-21, fig. 6; Burkhart, Kunsthistorische Einführung,[117] fig. on p. 34.

[121] DE Wald, *Stuttgart Psalter,*[119] p. 111.

[122] EFFM, Der Inhalt der Bilder,[117] p. 149.

[123] *recte: Cimbeln-Spielerin* (verse 5). *tympanum* (verse 4, LXX: τύμπανον) is a big drum, as in the illustration of Ps *149*, 3 at Lesnovo (*cf.* note 10).

[124] Burkhart, Kunsthistorische Einführung,[117] p. 35, in his interpretation of EFFM's description of the miniature (Der Inhalt der Bilder,[117] p. 149).

[125] Burkhart, Kunsthistorische Einführung,[117] p. 35: *„auf einem Berg steht an der höchsten Stelle des Bildes die Bundeslade."*

[126] DE Wald, *Utrecht Psalter,*[18], pls. CIV, CXV, pp. 51, 58; van der Horst, Engelbregt, *Utrecht-Psalter,*[18] facsimile and pp. 39, 92 (Ps *113*, 3, *131*, 7-8).

[127] A. Grabar, "Mosaiken und Wandmalereien", in: A. Grabar, C. Nordenfalk, *Die grossen Jahrhunderte der Ma-*

lerei. Das frühe Mittelalter vom vierten bis zum elften Jahrhundert, Genève 1957, fig. on p. 69; Schrade, *Vor- und Frühromanische Malerei*,[100] fig. 32; Holländer, *Kunst des frühen Mittelalters*,[100] fig. 75; H. Holländer, *Die Entstehung Europas* [Belser Stilgeschichte, Studienausgabe, 2], Stuttgart 2004, 151-384, fig. 200; J.-P. Caillet, *L'Art Carolingien*, Paris 2005, fig. 12.

[128] Grabar, Nordenfalk, *Die grossen Jahrhunderte*,[127] fig. on p. 153; C. Nordenfalk, *Die Buchmalerei im Mittelalter*, Genf 1988, fig. on p. 71. Similar in a Bible belonging to the realm of the Emperor Charles the Bald in Rome, San Paolo fuori le mure, fol. 40v: C. Eggenberger, *Psalterium aureum Sancti Galli. Mittelalterliche Psalterillustration im Kloster St. Gallen*, Sigmaringen 1987, fig. 113.

[129] EFFM, Der Inhalt der Bilder,[117] p. 149.

[130] De Wald, *Utrecht Psalter*,[18] pp. 5, 7-44, 46-50, 52-64 (but not in the miniature of Ps 150: p. 65); van der Horst, Engelbregt, *Utrecht-Psalter*,[18] pp. 63ff.

[131] Burkhart, Kunsthistorische Einführung,[117] p. 35.

[132] EFFM, Der Inhalt der Bilder,[117] p. 149; Burkhart, Kunsthistorische Einführung,[117] p. 35.

[133] Vilitza (1737), Tsepelovo (1786): *Καπεσοβίτες Ζωγράφοι. Ἡμερολόγιο 2003*, picture for week 4; Ἐ. Ἄντζακα-Βέη, "«Ὁ χορός παρά Βυζαντινοίς» τοῦ Φ. Κουκουλέ. Κριτικές παρατηρήσεις", *Ἀρχαιολογία & Τέχνες* 91 (2004) 72-77, fig. 5.

[134] Eggenberger, *Psalterium aureum Sancti Galli*,[128] pp. 47, 94-96, figs. 22, 107, 108, 110.

[135] Great Lavra (Millet, *Monuments*, pl. 118-3), Dionysiou (Millet, *Monuments*, pl. 201-2), Barlaam (M. Chatzidakis, "Contribution à l'étude de la peinture postbyzantine", in: *1453 – 1953. Le cinq-centième anniversaire de la prise de Constantinople* [L'Hellénisme Contemporain, 2ème série, 7ème année, fascicule hors série], Athènes 1953, 193-216, fig. 21 (reprinted in *Etudes sur la peinture postbyzantine*, Variorum, London 1976, ch. 1, fig. 21); monastery of Dryovouno.

[136] A dancer whirling a veil in the psalter of Charles the Bald,, Paris B. N. lat. 1152, fol. 1V (middle of 9th c.): J. Hubert, J. Porcher, W. F. Volbach, *Die Kunst der Karolinger von Karl dem Grossen bis zum Ausgang des 9. Jahrhunderts* [Universum der Kunst], München 1969, fig. 134; Holländer, *Kunst des frühen Mittelalters*,[100] fig. 70; R. Kahsnitz, *Der Werdener Psalter in Berlin Ms. theol. lat. fol. 358. Eine Untersuchung zu Problemen mittelalterlicher Psalterillustration* [Beiträge zu den Bau- und Kunstdenkmälern im Rheinland, 24], Düsseldorf 1979, fig. 236; Eggenberger, *Psalterium aureum*,[128] fig. 49; K. Corrigan, "Early Medieval Psalter Illustration in Byzantium and the West", in: van der Horst, Noel, Wüstefeld, *The Utrecht Psalter*,[120] 85-103, fig. 5; Holländer, *Die Entstehung Europas*,[127] fig.133; *ca.* 900 two similar dancers in the *Psalterium aureum*, St. Gallen, Stiftsbibliothek, cod. 22, 1, frontispiece (Kahsnitz, *l. c.*, fig. 140; Eggenberger, *Psalterium aureum*,[128] figs. 1, 39, 40); Caillet, *L'Art Carolingien*,[127] fig. 114.

[137] K. Weitzmann, *Geistige Grundlagen und Wesen der Makedonischen Renaissance* [Arbeitsgemeinschaft für Forschung des Landes Nordrhein-Westfalen, Geisteswissenschaften, 107], Köln, Opladen 1963, pp. 8, 39, figs. 1, 36; H. Sichtermann, *Späte Endymion-Sarkophage. Methodisches zur Interpretation* [Deutsche Beiträge zur Altertumswissenschaft, 19], Baden-Baden 1966, figs. 2, 8, 50, 52; Holländer, *Kunst des frühen Mittelalters*,[100] fig. 66; K. Weitzmann, *Studies in Classical and Byzantine Manuscript Illumination*, Chicago, London 1971, figs. 159, 193; E. Kitzinger, *Byzantinische Kunst im Werden. Stilentwicklungen in der Mittelmeerkunst vom 3. bis zum 7. Jahrhundert*, Köln 1984, fig. 53; Wetzel, *Das frühe Mittelalter*,[100] fig. 34.

[138] Fol. 54r; De Wald, *Stuttgart Psalter*,[119] facsimile and p. 43; *Bilderpsalter*, *Faksimile*;[119] EFFM, Der Inhalt der Bilder,[117] p. 89.

[139] Sichtermann, *Endymion-Sarkophage*,[137] fig. 23. The motif is also common in Byzantine art; here it suffices to refer to objects of Carolingian art.

[140] EFFM, Der Inhalt der Bilder,[117] p. 149; Burkhart, Kunsthistorische Einführung,[117] p. 35.

[141] C. Sachs, *Handbuch der Musikinstrumentenkunde*, Leipzig 1920, reprint Wiesbaden 1976, p. 13, fig. 3; W. Stauder, *Alte Musikinstrumente in ihrer vieltausendjährigen Entwicklung und Geschichte*, Braunschweig 1973, pp. 53, 166-167, fig. 247 (*cf.* pp. 42-43); *Musical Instruments of the World. An Illustrated Encyclopedia by the Diagram Group, s. l.* 1976, p. 124. *Cf.* G. Bruns, *Der Obelisk und seine Basis auf dem Hippodrom zu Konstantinopel* [Istanbuler Forschungen, 7], Istanbul 1935, p. 67: *Krotalen*.

[142] In the LXX text of the psalms, ὄργανον has the general meaning of *instrument*; but in the Utrecht-Psalter, the word *organum* of the Vulgate means an *organ*: De Wald, *Utrecht Psalter*,[18] p. 65, pl. CXXX; Engelbregt, *Het Utrechts Psalterium*,[116] pp. 162, 167, fig. 68; van der Horst, Engelbregt, *Utrecht-Psalter*,[18] facsimile and p. 92; K. van der Horst, "The Utrecht Psalter: Picturing the Psalms of David", in: van der Horst, Noel, Wüstefeld, *The Utrecht Psalter*,[120] 23-84, pp. 72-73.

[143] *Cf.* L. Arlt, E. Huhsmann, "Die Digitalisierung", in: *Kupfergrün, Zinnober*,[117] pp. 147-152.

[144] *Cf.* Sch-13, pp. 178, 180, 192; Sch-15, pp. 209, 212, 213, 217; Sch-18, p. 81; Sch-19, p. 154; Sch-20, pp. 102, 108; Sch-23, p. 77; Sch-22, pp. 508-510; Sch-24, p. 354. *Cf.* Sch-3, pp. 198, 243-244; Sch-4, p. 232; Sch-20, p. 108; Sch-25, p. 286; Sch-26, pp. 169, 170.

[145] Fol. 160v; De Wald, *Stuttgart Psalter*,[119] facsimile and p. 110; *Bilderpsalter, Faksimile*;[119] EFFM, Der Inhalt der Bilder,[117] p. 148.

[146] B. Fischer, "Die Texte", in: *Stuttgarter Bilderpsalter, 2*,[117] 223-288, p. 283.

[147] Fischer, Die Texte,[146] p. 223.

[148] E. Hatch, H. A. Redpath, *A Concordance To the Septuagint and the other Greek Versions of the Old Testament (Including the Apocryphal Books)*, 2, Oxford 1897, p. 1153.

[149] Fol. 55r; De Wald, *Stuttgart Psalter*,[119] facsimile and p. 44; *Bilderpsalter, Faksimile*;[119] EFFM, Der Inhalt der Bilder,[117] p. 90; Burkhart, Kunsthistorische Einführung,[117] fig. on p. 32 (text p. 33).

[150] In Byzantine art, too, the souls were depicted as naked children: J. J. Tikkanen, "Die Genesismosaiken von S. Marco in Venedig und ihr Verhältniss zu den Miniaturen der Cottonbibel nebst einer Untersuchung über den Ursprung der mittelalterlichen Genesisdarstellung besonders in der byzantinischen und italienischen Kunst", *Acta Societatis Scientiarium Fennicae 17* (1891) 205-357, p. 236, note 1.

[151] Fol. 160v; De Wald, *Stuttgart Psalter*,[119] facsimile and p. 110; *Bilderpsalter, Faksimile*;[119] EFFM, Der Inhalt der Bilder,[117] p. 148.

[152] De Wald, *Stuttgart Psalter*,[119] p. 33.

[153] Vulgate, gallicanic; De Wald, *Stuttgart Psalter*,[119] facsimile and p. 44; *Bilderpsalter, Faksimile*;[119] EFFM, Der Inhalt der Bilder,[117] p. 90.

[154] Fol. 25r; De Wald, *Stuttgart Psalter*,[119] facsimile and p. 23; *Bilderpsalter, Faksimile*;[119] EFFM, Der Inhalt der Bilder,[117] p. 73.

[155] Fol. 126r,v; De Wald, *Stuttgart Psalter*,[119] facsimile and pp. 89, 90; *Bilderpsalter, Faksimile*;[119] EFFM, Der Inhalt der Bilder,[117] p. 130.

[156] Fol. 30r; De Wald, *Stuttgart Psalter,*[119] facsimile; *Bilderpsalter, Faksimile*.[119]

[157] Fol. 122r; De Wald, *Stuttgart Psalter*,[119] facsimile and p. 88; *Bilderpsalter, Faksimile*;[119] EFFM, Der Inhalt der Bilder,[117] pp. 128-129.

[158] Miniature: fol. 146v, text of the psalm: fol. 147r; De Wald, *Stuttgart Psalter*,[119] facsimile and p. 101; *Bilderpsalter, Faksimile*;[119] EFFM, Der Inhalt der Bilder,[117] p. 140.

[159] Wickhoff, Speisezimmer,[45] p. 14; Tikkanen, Genesismosaiken,[150] pp. 303-323; K. Weitzmann, "The Genesis Mosaics of San Marco and the Cotton Genesis Miniatures", in: O. Demus, *The Mosaics of San Marco in*

Venice, 2, The Thirteenth Century, vol. 1, *Text*, Chicago, London 1984, 105-142.

[160] Tikkanen, Genesismosaiken,[150] pp. 235-236, pl. I-3; K. Weitzmann, "Die Illustration der Septuaginta", *Münchner Jahrbuch der bildenden Kunst*, 3. Folge, *3-4* (1952-53) 96-120, fig. 20 (*Beseelung des Adam*; p. 115: *seine* [= Adams] *Beseelung durch Einführen einer kleinen geflügelten Psyche.* ψυχή is the word used in L*X*X at the end of the verse Gen *2, 7*); K. Weitzmann, *Illustrations in Roll and Codex. A Study of the Origin and Method of Text Illustration* [Studies in Manuscript Illumination, 2], Princeton 1970, fig. 179; Weitzmann, *Studies in Manuscript Illumination*,[137] fig. 47; K. Weitzmann, "The Study of Byzantine Book Illumination. Past, Present, and Future", in: K. Weitzmann, W. C. Loerke, E. Kitzinger, H. Buchthal, *The Place of Book Illumination in Byzantine* Art, Princeton 1975, 1-60, fig. 49; Demus, *The Mosaics of San Marco*,[159] vol. 2, *Plates*, fig. 118 (the complete cupola: vol. 1, *Text*, frontispiece (colour)); H. N. Loose, G. Hellenkemper Salies, *Im Anfang schuf Gott Himmel und Erde. Die Mosaiken in der Vorhalle des Markusdoms in Venedig*, Freiburg, Basel, Wien 1986, fig.on p. 32 (colour); O. Demus, W. Dorigo, A. Niero, G. Perocco, E. Vio, *San Marco. Die Mosaiken. Das Licht. Die Geschichte*, München 1993, fig. (colour) of the complete cupola on p. 197.

[161] The noun *spiritus* is also contained in the verb of the sentence *Dominus Deus... inspiravit in faciem eius spiraculum vitae* (Vulgate, Gen *2, 7*).

[162] Hossfeld, Zenger, *Psalmen*,[1] p. 883.

[163] According to Weitzmann, The Genesis Mosaics,[159] p. 112, *in faciem eius spiraculum vitae* means that the *soul* (Psyche) enters through Adam's *mouth. omnis spiritus* praises the Lord through his mouth.

[164] Lc *16*, 19-31.

[165] *ca.* 1045; A. Grebe, *Codex Aureus. Das Goldene Evangelienbuch von Echternach*, Darmstadt 2007, fol. 78r, fig. 65.

[166] Lc *16*, 23-24.

[167] H. O[mont], *Bibliothèque Nationale, Département des Manuscrits, Psautier illustré (XIIIe siècle). Reproduction des 107 miniatures du manuscrit latin 8846 de la Bibliothèque Nationale*, Paris *s. a.*, pl. 70 (fol. 106).

[168] K. Koshi, *Die frühmittelalterlichen Wandmalereien der St. Georgskirche zu Oberzell auf der Bodenseeinsel Reichenau*, Textband, Berlin 1999, fig. 336; H. F[illitz], "Die Gruppe der Magdeburger Elfenbeintafeln", in: M. Puhle (ed.), *Otto der Große, Magdeburg und Europa, 2*, Katalog [of the exhibition in Magdeburg, 2001], Mainz 2001, 363-380, fig. on p. 370 (p. 377 ... *nach Mt 8, 28-34, recte nach Mk 5, 2, 8, Lc 8, 29*); H. Fillitz, *Die Gruppe der Magdeburger Elfenbeintafeln. Eine Stiftung Kaiser Ottos des Großen für den Magdeburger Dom* [Schriften des Dom-Museums Hildesheim, 1], Mainz 2001, # 5, p. 39.

[169] Schrade, *Vor- und Frühromanische Malerei*,[100] p. 208, pl. 10 (colour), drawing 11; O. Demus, *Romanesque Mural Painting*, New York 1970, pl. 240 (bl.-w.); K. Martin, *Die ottonischen Wandbilder der St. Georgskirche Reichenau-Oberzell*, Sigmaringen [2]1975, fig. on p. 37 (colour); W. Erdmann, *Die acht ottonischen Wandbilder der Wunder Jesu in St.Georg zu Reichenau-Oberzell,* Sigmaringen [2]1986, pl. 1 (colour; p. 10: *Die bösen Geister* [*sic*, plural] *verlassen als kleine geflügelte Wesen den Besessenen durch seinen Mund* (*recte* singular); Koshi, *Wandmalereien der St. Georgskirche*,[168] Textband, Berlin 1999 (pp. 111-112 a very detailed description of the *spiritus* which is hardly recognizable on the figures); K. G. Beuckers, J. Cramer, M. Imhof (eds.), *Die Ottonen. Kunst – Architektur – Geschichte*, Petersberg, Darmstadt 2002, fig. on p. 198.

[170] The gospel of the Emperor Otto III in Munich: Schrade, *Vor- und Frühromanische Malerei*,[100] fig. 78 (bl.-w.); *Das Evangeliar Ottos III. CLM 4453 der Bayerischen Staatsbibliothek München*, Faksimile, Frankfurt/Main, München, Stuttgart 1978, fol. 103v (F. Mütherich in *Begleitband*, p. 101: *Ein Teufel fährt aus seinem Munde aus*);

Grimme, *Das Evangeliar Kaiser Ottos III.*,[100] fig. 17; H. Mayr-Harting, *Ottonian Book Illumination. An Historical Study, Part One: Themes*, London, New York 1991, fig. 72; F. Mütherich, K. Dachs, *Das Evangeliar Ottos III. Clm 4453 der Bayerischen Staatsbibliothek München*, München, London, New York 2001, pl. 34; Koshi, *Wandmalereien der St. Georgskirche*,[168] fig. 331; Codex of Egbert: H. Schiel (ed.), *Codex Egberti der Stadtbibliothek Trier*, Basel 1960, fol. 26v; Grimme, *Das Evangeliar Kaiser Ottos III.*,[100] fig. 16; G. Franz (ed.), *Das Leben Jesu. Der Egbert Codex. Ein Höhepunkt der Buchmalerei vor 1000 Jahren. Handschrift 24 der Stadtbibliothek Trier*, Darmstadt 2005, pp. 125-127, fig. on p. 126 (colour); Koshi,[168] fig. 333; the gospel of Ottos III in Aachen: G. Schiller, *Ikonographie der christlichen Kunst*, vol. 1, Gütersloh 1966, fig. 526 (bl.-w.); Grimme, *Das Evangeliar Kaiser Ottos III.*,[100] p. 45, pl. on p. 46 (colour); Koshi,[168] fig. 334; evangelistary of Bernulphus in Utrecht: Koshi,[168] fig. 332.

[171] P. Bloch, H. Schnitzler, *Die Ottonische Kölner Malerschule*, vol. 1, *Katalog und Tafeln*, Düsseldorf 1967, pl. 139, vol. 2, *Textband*, fig. 366; C. Winterer, *Das Evangeliar der Äbtissin Hitda. Eine ottonische Prachthandschrift aus Köln*, Darmstadt 2010, fig. on p. 91 (colour) (fol. 76r).

[172] Grebe, *Codex Aureus*,[165] fol. 53r, figs. 52, 54 (also dark, though not anthropomorphous at the right maniac; according to Schiller, *Ikonographie*,[170] (for fig. 487) *geht* [out of his mouth] *Feuer oder Qualm hervor, was der Höllenvorstellung ebenso entspricht wie der personifizierte Teufel*; *cf.* Koshi, *Wandmalereien der St. Georgskirche*,[168] fig. 335).

[173] Grimme, *Das Evangeliar Kaiser Ottos III.*,[100] fig. 18; Mütherich, Dachs, *Das Evangeliar Ottos III.*,[170] pl. 44.

[174] Grimme, *Das Evangeliar Kaiser Ottos III.*,[100] p. 49, pl. on p. 50 (colour).

[175] Millet, Velmans, *La peinture du moyen âge*,[10] figs. 36, 37; Gabelić, fig. XXIII (colour).

[176] Sch-24, p. 352 (note 17); Gabelić, fig. 88 (according to OKUNEV, p. 240, and GABELIĆ, *l. c.*, pp. 184, 280, the *zodion* Capricorn, according to DJURIĆ, Христ Космократор,[99] pp. 66, 72, and JEVTIĆ, Nouvel ordre du monde,[101] pp. 131, 132, 133, the z*odion* Sagittarius, but unambiguous because of the legend доухь [боуренъ].

[177] Dochiariou, Roussanou, Dousiko, Koukouzelissa, Redina: Millet, *Monuments*, pl. 244-1; Sch-1, pp. 171, 188, fig. 10; Sch-2, pp. 13-14; Sch-3, pp. 176, 218; Sch-4, p. 226, fig. 17.1; Sch-6, p. 53; Sch-7, p. 70; Sch-8, pp. 151-152, 160; Sch-10, fig. 10, fig. 27 (colour); Sch-16, p. 199; Γ. Ν. Οἰκονόμου, *Ἡ Ρεντίνα τῶν Ἀγράφων καὶ τά μεταβυζαντινά τῆς μνημεῖα*, Ρεντίνα τῶν Ἀγράφωνs, *s. a.* (*ca.* 2000), fig. 57. For the half-naked man in a cave, *vide supra.*

[178] DE Wald, *Stuttgart Psalter*,[119] facsimile and p. 88; *Bilderpsalter, Faksimile*;[119] EFFM, Der Inhalt der Bilder,[117] p. 129; F. Mütherich, "Die Stellung der Bilder in der frühmittelalterlichen Psalterillustration", in: *Stuttgarter Bilderpsalter, 2,*[117] 151-222, p. 180; K. Koshi, *Wandmalereien der St. Georgskirche*,[168] Textband, Berlin 1999, fig. 356; Burkhart, Kunsthistorische Einführung,[117] p. 75, fig. on p. 74.

[179] *E. g.*, two heads in Ottonian miniatures: A. Boeckler; P. Bloch, H. Schnitzler, *Die Ottonische Kölner Malerschule*, vol. 2, *Textband*, Düsseldorf 1967, fig. 381; Grimme, *Das Evangeliar Kaiser Ottos III.*,[100] pl. on p. 31 (colour), fig. 17; Mayr-Harting, *Ottonian Book Illumination*,[170] *Part One: Themes*, fig. 72, *Part Two: Book*, fig. 75; Koshi, *Wandmalereien der St. Georgskirche*,[168] Tafelband, pls. 42a, 79-82, 89, 99a, Textband, p. 127 (*Windgeister*, extensively described), figs. 151, 152, 154, 155, 347, 349- 351, 353; Mütherich, Dachs, *Das Evangeliar Ottos III.*,[170] pl. 34; Grebe, *Codex Aureus*,[165] fig. 56.

[180] Sch-10, p. 276.

[181] Hossfeld, Zenger, *Psalmen*,[1] p. 883.

[182] Les pseaumes de David traduits en françois avec une explication Tirée des Saints Peres, & des Auteurs Ecclesias-

tiques. Par le Sieur Le Maistre de Sacy, Prêtre &c. Tome troisieme, Bruxelles 1710; La Sainte Bible contenant l'ancien et le nouveau testament, traduit sur la Vulgate par Mr. Le Maistre de Saci, St. Petersbourg 1817.

[183] Le Maistre de Sacy,[182] Bruxelles 1710, pp. 566-568 (p. 561 note to Ps 149: *Dieu est un pur esprit*).

[184] Didron, *Manuel*, p. 234.

[185] Didron, *Manuel*, p. 235.

[186] Schäfer, *Handbuch*, p. 237 (p. 402 *Geisterschaar*, ad-opted by FICHTNER, *Wandmalereien*,[60] p. 22; p. 424 *Schaar der Geister*).

[187] *Cf.* Sch-25, pp. 284-285.

[188] G. Millet, *La Dalmatique du Vatican. Les Élus, Images et Croyances*, Paris 1945, pl. I-2; Skrobucha, *Meis-terwerke*,[74] pl. XXXI; Rothemund, *Handbuch*,[21] fig. on p. 333; M. Chatzidakis, *Etudes sur la peinture postbyzantine*, London 1976, chapter IV, pl. IΓ'; E. Piltz, *Trois sakkoi byzantins. Analyse iconographique* [Acta Universitatis Upsaliensis. Figura. N.S. 17], Stockholm 1976, fig. 13; Hu-ber, *Athos*,[63] fig. 157; Velmans, Le dimanche,[21] figs. 5-7; Θησαυροὶ τοῦ Ἁγίου Ὄρους, Thessaloniki ²1997, p. 189, object 2.126.

[189] *E. g.*, E. Swedenborg, *Vom Himmel und von den wunderbaren Dingen desselben; wie auch von der Geisterwelt und von dem Zustand des Menschen nach dem Tod; und von der Hölle; So, wie es gehöret und gesehen worden*, 2nd German edition s. 1.1775.

[190] Faust, in his soliloquy: *Jetzt erst erkenn' ich, was der Weise* [= *the magician Nostradamus*] *spricht: »Die Geisterwelt ist nicht verschlossen«* (… when he said, »The world of spirits is not closed« in the translation of S. T. Coleridge (London 1821): F. Burwick, J. C. McKusick (eds.), *Faustus. From the German of Goethe. Translated by Samuel Taylor Coleridge*, Oxford 2007, p. 11).

[191] Sch-13, p. 180; Sch-15, p. 213, figs. 15, 16; Sch-20, p. 103; Sch-24, p. 375; Sch-26, p. 166.

[192] Sch-13, p. 192; Sch-15, p. 213, fig. 9; Sch-18, pp. 87, 94; Sch-20, pp. 97, 104; Sch-26, p. 157.

[193] Sch-3, fig. 7; Sch-13, pp. 177, 190; Sch-15, pp. 205-206, 208-209, 212, figs. 1, 4-6, 9, 10; E. Hein, A. Jakovlje-vić, B. Kleidt, *Zypern – byzantinische Kirchen und Klöster. Mosaiken und Fresken*, Ratingen 1996, fig. 142; Παρχαρίδου-Ἀναγνώστου, Ὁ χορός,[103] fig. 4.

[194] Tikkanen,[4] pp. 143-147; Stichel, *Beiträge*, pp. 253-255. B. Bischoff, "Die Handschrift", in: *Stuttgarter Bilderpsalter, 2,*[117] 15-30, p. 25, pointed out that the Stuttgart Psalter and the Simon Psalter have significant common traits.

[195] Okunev, p. 241, pl. XXXVII; Мијовић, Царска иконографија,[10] fig. 13; Габелић, *Манастир Лесново,*[2] pp. 186, 281, fig. 92; Moran, *Singers,*[8] fig. 55; Sch-26 pp. 145, 172.

[196] Hossfeld, Zenger, *Psalmen,*[1] p. 854.

[197] Sch-19,

[198] Sch-19, pp. 154-156; Sch-20, pp. 112-113; Sch-26 pp. 157-158.

[199] Hossfeld, Zenger, *Psalmen,*[1] pp. 857, 859.

[200] Gunkel, p. 621.

[201] Sch-18, p. 86; Sch-21, p. 194; Sch-22, Sch-24, p. 355.

[202] Sch-3, pp. 193-201, 238-247; Sch-4, pp. 225-226; Sch-8, pp. 170, 182; Sch-11, pp. 152, 165; Sch-12, pp. 67-68; Sch-19, p. 161; Sch-20, p. 114; Sch-21, espec. p. 200. Stichel, *Beiträge*, pp. 227-229, preferred another interpretation.

[203] Hossfeld, Zenger, *Psalmen,*[1] p. 854 (Gunkel, p. 619: *Gemeinde der Frommen*).

[204] Sch-18, p. 88.

[205] Sch-3, fig. 1. For more examples of the Κύριος of Ps *148,* 1 with empty hands see Sch-5, fig. 2; Sch-15, p. 209; Sch-22, p. 512.

Abbreviations

Belting: H. Belting (ed.) with S. Dufrenne, S. Radojčić, R. Stichel, I. Ševčenko, *Der serbische Psalter. Faksimile-Ausgabe des Cod. Slav. 4 der Bayerischen Staatsbibliothek München*, a) Text, Wiesbaden 1978; b) Facsimile, Wiesbaden, 1983.
Didron, *Manuel*: [A. N.] Didron, *Manuel d'iconographie chrétienne grecque et latine* (Paris 1845) (reprint New York 1964, [Burt Franklin Research & Source Works Series, 45]).
Đurić: V. J. Đurić, *Byzantinische Fresken in Jugoslawien*, München 1976.
Erminia: *Dionisie din Furna, Erminia picturii bizantine*, Bucureşti 2000.
Gabelić: С. Габелић, *Манастир Лесново. Историја и сликартво*, Београд 1998.
Gunkel: H. Gunkel, *Die Psalmen*, Göttingen 1968.
Hetherington, *Manual*: P. Hetherington, *The 'Painter's Manual' of Dionysius of Fourna*, London 1974.
Millet, *Monuments*: G. Millet, *Monuments de l'Athos, 1, Les peintures*, Paris 1927.
Okunev: N. L. Okunev, "Lesnovo", in: *L'art Byzantin chez les Slaves, Les Balkans*, 1 [Orient et Byzance, IV], Paris 1930.
Papadopoulo-Kérameus: A. Papadopoulo-Kérameus, Denys de Fourna, *Manuel d'iconographie chrétienne*, Ἑρμηνεία τῆς ζωγραφικῆς τέχνης, St-Pétersbourg 1909.
Schäfer, *Handbuch*: G. Schäfer, ἑρμηνεία τῆς ζωγραφικῆς. *Das Handbuch der Malerei vom Berge Athos*, Trier 1855.
Sch-1: G. P. Schiemenz, "Die Sintflut, das Jüngste Gericht und der 148. Psalm. Zur Ikonographie eines seltenen Bildes in der ravennatischen, byzantinischen und georgischen Kunst", *Cahiers archéologiques 33* (1990) 159-194.

Sch-2: G. P. Schiemenz, "Gabriel Millet's Ark of the Covenant in the Great Lavra at the Holy Mountain", *Macedonian Studies 12*, N. S. *1* (1995), 3-42.
Sch-3: G. P. Schiemenz, "Der 148. Psalm in der Johannes-Kathedrale von Nicosia", *Ἐπετηρίδα Κέντρου Μελετῶν Ἱερᾶς Μονῆς Κύκκου 3* (1996) 163-256.
Sch-4: G. P. Schiemenz, "The painted psalms of Athos", in: A. Bryer, M. Cunningham (eds.), *Mount Athos and Byzantine Monasticism*, Aldershot 1996, 223-236.
Sch-5: G. P. Schiemenz, "Der 148. Psalm im Athos-Kloster Philotheou", *Georgica 20* (1997) 111-127.
Sch-6: G. P. Schiemenz, "The Last Psalms in the Monastery Xeropotamou on Mount Athos", *Cahiers Balkaniques 27* (1997) 39-56.
Sch-7: G. P. Schiemenz, "The 148th Psalm in the Monastery Karakallou on Mount Athos", *Cahiers Balkaniques 27* (1997) 59-81.
Sch-8: G. P. Schiemenz, "Die letzten Psalmen in der Christi-Geburt-Kirche in Arbanasi", *Ἐπετηρὶς Ἑταιρ. Βυζ. Σπουδῶν 49* (1994-1998) [1999] 151-184.
Sch-9: G. P. Schiemenz, "»Lobet den Herrn vom Himmel her, lobet ihn in der Höhe«. Russische Ikonen zu den Lobpsalmen", in: K. C. Felmy, E. Haustein-Bartsch, *»Die Weisheit baute ihr Haus«. Untersuchungen zu Hymnischen und Didaktischen Ikonen*, München 1999, 167-212.
Sch-10: G. P. Schiemenz, "Die Hermeneia und die letzten Psalmen. Gibt es eine spezifische Athos-Kunst?", in: G. Koch (ed.) *Byzantinische Malerei. Bildprogramme – Ikonographie – Stil. Symposium in Marburg vom 25. – 29. 6. 1997* [Spätantike – Frühes Christentum – Byzanz. Kunst im ersten Jahrtausend, Reihe B: Studien und Perspektiven, 7], (Wiesbaden 2000) 275-292.
Sch-11: G. P. Schiemenz, "Who are the Kings of Psalms 148, 11 and 149, 8 in St. John's Cathedral in Nicosia? Iconographical and Iconological Relations between the Revelation of St. John and the Last Psalms", *Ἐπετηρίδα Κέντρου Μελετῶν Ἱερᾶς Μονῆς Κύκκου 5* (2001) 141-173.

Sch-12: G. P. Schiemenz, "Paintings of the Laud Psalms in Roumania", Ἐπετηρὶς Ἑταιρ. Βυζ. Σπουδῶν 51 (2003) 49-84.

Sch-13: G. P. Schiemenz, "Herr, wie zahlreich sind deine Werke! Eine verborgene Psalm-Illustration in Mcxeta", *Georgica 27* (2004) 173-194.

Sch-14: G. P. Schiemenz, "The Significance of the Prophet Gideon in Lagoudera", Ἐπετηρίδα Κέντρου Μελετῶν Ἱερας Μονῆς Κύκκου 6 (2004) 193-254.

Sch-15: G. P. Schiemenz, "King David's Chant in St. John's Cathedral in Nicosia and its Place in the Iconography of the Last Psalms", Ἐπετηρίδα Κέντρου Μελετῶν Ἱερᾶς Μονῆς Κύκκου 7 (2006) 199-232.

Sch-16: G. P. Schiemenz, "The Ainoi Psalms in the Barlaam Monastery (Meteora)", *Cahiers Balkaniques 34, Autour de l'icône*, (2006) 179-214.

Sch-17: G. P. Schiemenz, "«In der Kirche der Heiligen freue sich Israel», 1. Die Umdeutung eines Psalm-Zitats in Sveţicxoveli im Context der georgischen Geschichte", *Georgica 29* (2006) 89-105.

Sch-18: G. P. Schiemenz, "«In der Kirche der Heiligen freue sich Israel», 2. Ein Psalm-Zitat in Sveţicxoveli, Kaiser Erekle (Herakleios) und der Heilige Evsţati Mcxeteli (Eustathios von Mcxeta)", *Georgica 30* (2007) 81-95 (replace *Erekle (Herakleios)* by *Herakleios*; correct in the submitted manuscript).

Sch-19: G. P. Schiemenz, "The Role of the Church in the Laud Psalms Paintings in St. John's Cathedral in Nicosia", Ἐπετηρίδα Κέντρου Μελετῶν Ἱερᾶς Μονῆς Κύκκου 8 (2008) 141-170.

Sch-20: G. P. Schiemenz, "The Seven Councils in St. John's Cathedral in Nicosia and their Relation to the Laud Psalms", Ἐπετηρίδα Κέντρου Μελετῶν Ἱερᾶς Μονῆς Κύκκου 9 (2010) 81-128.

Sch-21: G. P. Schiemenz, "IC XC ὁ βασιλεὺς τῶν βασιλευόντων und die Könige der Erde: Zur Bedeutung des Christus-Epithets eines postbyzantinischen Ikonentyps", in:

E. Gerousis, G. Koch with A. Fehrmann, *Griechische Ikonen, Byzantinische und Nachbyzantinische Zeit. Symposium in Marburg vom 26. - 29. 6. 2000*, (Athen 2010) 191-201.

Sch-22: G. P. Schiemenz, "The Hermeneia and the Convocation of the Chosen People", *Études Byzantines et Post-Byzantines 6* (2011) 487-515. (Corrigenda: In note 83, lines 7 and 8, replace *und* by *and*. In note 83, pp. 496 and 497, replace *Hagios Meletios* by *Hosios Meletios*.)

Sch-23: G. P. Schiemenz, "The Paintings of the Last Psalms in the Church of Hagios Achilleios at Pentalopho and the Hermeneia", *Revue des Études Sud-Est Européennes 49* (2011) 73-84. (Corrigendum: On page 75, line 2, replace *The figures* by *Three figures*.)

Sch-24: G. P. Schiemenz, "A New Look at the Narthex Paintings at Lesnovo", *Byzantion 82* (2012) 347-396.

Sch-25: G. P. Schiemenz, "*All Saints* in Post-Byzantine Wall Painting", *Byzantinoslavica 71* (2013) 278-312.

Sch-26: G. P. Schiemenz, "*The Faithful with Two-Edged Swords in Their Hands.* The Illustration of Psalm 149, 6 in St. John's Cathedral in Nicosia", *Ἐπετηρίδα Κέντρου Μελετῶν Ἱερᾶς Μονῆς Κύκκου 10* (2013) 137-182.

Sch-27: G. P. Schiemenz, "Laud Psalms Paintings in the Palaiologan Realm? The Case of Hagios Nikolaos Zarnatas", *Revue des Études Sud-Est Européennes 51* (2013) 185-210.

Sch-28: G. P. Schiemenz, "*Behold, Behold that I Am the Lord.* The Theological Message of the Laud Psalms Paintings in St. John's Cathedral in Nicosia", *Ἐπετηρίδα Κέντρου Μελετῶν Ἱερᾶς Μονῆς Κύκκου 11* (2016) 153-180.

Sch-29: G. P. Schiemenz, ""Laudate Dominum de caelis..." Die Lobpsalmen-Darstellung im Triclinium des Erzbischofs Neon in Ravenna", *Zeitschrift für Kirchengeschichte 127* (2016) 1-18.

Sch-30: G. P. Schiemenz,, "The Gothic Psalter in Munich – A Witness in the Case of the Orthodox *ainoi* Wall

Paintings", *Проблеми на Изкуството* (Sofia) *50* (2017) 1-
6.
Stichel, *Beiträge*: R. Stichel, *Beiträge zur frühen
Geschichte des Psalters und zur frühen Wirkungsgeschichte
der Psalmen* [Abhandlungen der Nordrhein-Westfälischen
Akademie der Wissenschaften, 116], Paderborn 2007.
Strzygowski: J. Strzygowski, *Die Miniaturen des
serbischen Psalters der königl. Hof- und Staatsbibliothek in
München. Nach einer Belgrader Kopie ergänzt und im
Zusammenhange mit der syrischen Bilderredaktion des
Psalters untersucht* [Denkschriften der kaiserlichen
Akademie der Wissenschaften, Phil.-hist. Kl. 52-II], Wien
1906.

List of Illustrations

The *Last Judgment* icon in the Uspenskij cathedral in
the Kremlin of Moscow // p. 52
The Novgorodian *Last Judgment* icon in the Tretya-
kov Gallery // p. 53
Monastery Voroneţ, *Last Judgment*: The *Ancient of
Days* // p. 54
Monastery Voroneţ, *Last Judgment*: The scroll of St.
Paul // p. 55
The Stuttgart Psalter, Ps 150 // p. 140

The technical assistance of R. M. Engel,
schrift-bilder (Berlin)
(Handschriften- und Bildforschung)
in the production of this book
is greatly appreciated